BATTLE CRIES ON THE
HOME FRONT

ABOUT THE EDITORS

Judith D. Mercier, a former social worker, received a B.A. in communications from the University of New Haven, a M.A. in English from Old Dominion University in Norfolk, Virginia, and is currently completing her M.F.A. in creative writing at Old Dominion University. In addition to having taught writing and literature courses at Christopher Newport University, Old Dominion University, and St. Leo College, she has been the nonfiction and managing editor for the *Dominion Review*, Old Dominion University's national literary journal. Her articles, profiles, and reviews have appeared in *Tidewater Directions, Virginia Woman*, and *Nova*. At present, she is working on a collection of nonfiction stories about Duck, North Carolina, and a book-length critical study of contemporary literary nonfiction.

Peter J. Mercier, a special agent with the Naval Criminal Investigative Service, has a B.S. in criminal justice administration from the University of New Haven, a M.A. in applied sociology from Old Dominion University, and 16 years of law enforcement experience. A former adjunct instructor at Old Dominion University, St. Leo College, and City Colleges of Chicago, he is working on research in domestic violence and computer deviance. He recently wrote a chapter entitled "On-line Crime: In Pursuit of Cyber Thieves," which appears in *Criminal Justice Technology in the 21st Century*, edited by Laura Moriarty and David Carter (1998, Charles C Thomas).

BATTLE CRIES ON THE HOME FRONT
Violence In The Military Family

Edited by

Peter J. Mercier, M.A.

Naval Criminal Investigative Service

and

Judith D. Mercier, M.A., M.F.A.

Old Dominion University

Charles C Thomas

PUBLISHER • LTD.

SPRINGFIELD • ILLINOIS • U.S.A.

Published and Distributed Throughout the World by

CHARLES C THOMAS • PUBLISHER, LTD.
2600 South First Street
Springfield, Illinois 62794-9265

.

ISBN 0-398-07034-2 (cloth)
ISBN 0-398-07035-0 (paper)

Library of Congress Catalog Card Number: 99-050281

With THOMAS BOOKS *careful attention is given to all details of manufacturing
and design. It is the Publisher's desire to present books that are satisfactory as to their
physical qualities and artistic possibilities and appropriate for their particular use.*
THOMAS BOOKS *will be true to those laws of quality that assure a good name
and good will.*

Printed in the United States of America
CR-R-3

Library of Congress Cataloging-in-Publication Data

Battle cries on the home front : violence in the military family / edited by
Peter J. Mercier and Judith D. Mercier.
    p. cm.
  Includes bibliographical references and index.
  ISBN 0-398-07034-2 -- ISBN 0-398-07035-0 (paper)
    1. Family violence--United States. 2. Families of military personnel--
United States. 3. Military spouses--Abuse of--United States. 4. Children
of military personnel--Abuse of--United States. I. Mercier, Peter J. II.
Mercier, Judith D.

HV6626.2 .B28 2000
362.82'92'088355--dc21
                                                  99-050281

Dedicated to the Memory of Peter Neidig,
Whose Research on Domestic Violence in
the Military Community Paved the Way for Others

DISCLAIMER

The views, opinions, and findings contained throughout this book are those of the authors and editors and should not be construed as official Department of Defense positions, policies, or decisions, unless so designated by other official documentation.

CONTRIBUTORS

Leana C. Allen is a graduate student in the Department of Criminology and Criminal Justice at the University of Maryland. Her research interests include domestic violence, criminological theory, and sentencing. She is currently collaborating with Sally Simpson and Joel Garner on an evaluation of the Maryland preferred arrest policy for domestic violence cases.

Leasley K. Besetsney is the research and data program manager for the U. S. Air Force Family Advocacy Program at Brooks Air Force Base, Texas. He is responsible for child and spouse abuse treatment and prevention program evaluation projects.

Albert L. Brewster was formerly the director of Family Advocacy Research at Brooks Air Force Base, Texas.

Raymond V. Burke is the director of parent training programs at the National Resource and Training Center, Father Flanagan's Boys Home, Boys Town, Nebraska. He and his staff have trained more than 1600 parent trainers throughout the United States and Europe. He is also on the faculty at the University of Nebraska at Omaha.

Dianne Cyr Carmody, Ph.D., is an assistant professor in the Department of Sociology and Criminal Justice at Old Dominion University. Her research interests include police response to domestic violence, media depictions of violence against women, and campus crime. Dr. Carmody's work has appeared in the *Journal of Family Violence*, the *Journal of Marriage and the Family*, and *Violence and Victims*.

Loretta Cepis, a major in the U.S. Air Force, is a clinical nurse specialist. She received her M.S. in nursing from the University of Maryland. Her research interests include domestic violence and perinatal health outcomes. She has been in the Air Force for 16 years and is currently stationed in San Antonio, Texas.

Beth Gering, a lieutenant commander in the U.S. Navy, is a perinatal clinical nurse specialist. She received her B.S. in nursing from Clemson University and a M.S. in nursing from the University of Maryland. Her research interests are domestic violence and perinatal health outcomes. She has been in the Navy for 13 years and is currently stationed in Roosevelt Roads, Puerto Rico.

E. Heath Graves received his M.A. in criminal justice from Virginia Commonwealth University. He has served as a pilot and as a security officer in the U.S. Air Force for six years, serving in Texas, North Carolina, Cuba, and South Korea. Presently, he is a captain at Andrews Air Force Base, California.

Marilyn D. McShane, Ph.D., is professor and chair of the Criminal Justice Department at Northern Arizona University. Her research interests include corrections and criminal justice management. She has co-authored several books in criminological theory, community corrections, and correctional management, as well as co-edited *The Encyclopedia of American Prisons.* Dr. McShane has also participated in a number of federal-and state-funded research projects with the National Institute for Corrections, San Bernardino County Probation Department, and the California Department of Corrections, Parole Division.

David Marshall obtained his Masters in criminal justice from California State University, San Bernardino. He served as a lieutenant in the U.S. Marine Corps, where he worked in training and the development of domestic violence policy. He is currently employed in local law enforcement in Michigan.

Joel S. Milner, Ph.D., is Professor of Psychology, Distinguished Research Professor, and Director of the Center for the Study of Family Violence and Sexual Assault at Northern Illinois University. He has received research funding from federal agencies such as the National Institute of Mental Health, National Center on Child Abuse and Neglect, and the Department of Defense. He is the author or co-author of more than 140 book chapters and articles; his recent programmatic research has focused on the description and assessment of child physical and sexual abusers and on the testing of a social information processing model of child physical abuse.

Willard W. Mollerstrom, Ph.D., is director of the Clinical Investigation Facility and Senior Biomedical Science Corps Advisor to the Commander, David Grant Medical Center, Travis Air Force Base, CA. He oversees 250 research protocols, a staff of 28 personnel, and coordinates career progression for 77 biomedical officers assigned to the center. He has numerous publications in the family violence arena and has taught graduate research courses as an adjunct clinical research professor. His experience includes private practice in clinical social work and state and federal level program and policy administrative positions.

Laura J. Moriarty, Ph.D., is an associate professor in the Department of Criminal Justice and Assistant Dean, College of Humanities and Sciences, Virginia Commonwealth University in Richmond. She has a Ph.D. in criminal justice from Sam Houston State University. Dr. Moriarty is the co-author (with R. A. Jerin) of the textbook *Victims of Crime* (Nelson-Hall, 1998). Her research interests include violent crime, victimology, and domestic violence. Her published work has appeared in the *American Journal of Criminal Justice, Journal of Criminal Justice Education, Criminal Justice Policy Review, Criminal Justice Review, Journal of Contemporary Criminal Justice,* among others. She is also the co-editor (with R. A. Jerin) of *Current Issues in Victimology Research* (forthcoming, Carolina Academic Press) and (with David Carter) of *Criminal Justice Technology in the 21st Century* (1998, Charles C Thomas).

Michael A. Patchner, Ph.D., is Professor and Associate Dean at the School of Social Work, University of Pittsburgh. For the past 20 years, he has served as a faculty member or administrator at three universities where he engaged in social work teaching, research, and administration. He has numerous publications and is the co-author of two research methods texts, *Planning for Research* and *Implementing the Research Plan.* He has administered a number of publicly funded research projects and has served as a consultant to various human service organizations, including the U.S. Air Force Family Advocacy Program.

Nancy Raiha, a colonel in the U.S. Army, is currently chief of social work service and director of the Behavioral Science Service Line at Madigan Army Medical Center, Tacoma, Washington. She has previously served as chief, Social Work Service, Fort Campbell, Kentucky. Colonel Raiha received both her M.S.W. and Ph.D. in social welfare from the University of Washington in Seattle.

Penney R. Ruma is a senior data analyst for youth information services at Father Flanagan's Boys Home in Boys Town, Nebraska. She has been instrumental in the research and evaluation activities for the Common Sense Parenting program.

Phyllis Sharps, Ph.D., a retired colonel from the U.S. Army Reserve Nurse Corps, is an associate professor and associate director of the maternal and child health concentration of the Master's in public health program at the School of Public Health and Health Services, George Washington University, Washington, DC. Her research interests include women's health and violence, specifically lethality assessment in violent intimate relationships.

David J. Soma, Ph.D., a retired colonel from the U.S. Army Medical Corps, is presently the chief deputy assessor-treasurer for Pierce County, Washington. He has 26 years experience in all aspects of governmental, community, and hospital-based program development, organization, and management. Dr. Soma is a certified social worker and mediator, and he has extensive experience as an individual and group therapist. He has also taught for several colleges and universities and has presented numerous classes and training sessions in stress management, conflict resolution in the workplace, mediation, stress related to downsizing, suicide prevention, positive parenting, expert witness testimony, and family violence.

Ronald W. Thompson, Ph.D., is the director of research at Father Flanagan's Boys Home in Boys Town, Nebraska. He is also associate professor of human communication at Creighton University School of Medicine in Omaha and adjunct assistant professor of human development and family life at the University of Kansas.

Mallary Tytel, Ph.D., is the president and chief executive officer of Education and Training Programs (ETP), Inc., an international health and human resource development corporation headquartered in East Hartford, CT. Prior to joining ETP, Dr. Tytel was the project director for prevention, education, and program development working under contract for the U.S. Army Center for Substance Abuse Programs. She has over 15 years experience in health and human services, education and training, leadership, and organization development, as well as solid expertise in the integration of theory and practice. She has worked with federal, state, and local organizations in public health promotion, risk management and risk reduction, injury prevention and control, HIV/education, substance abuse, and youth and family services. Her special interests include community capacity building, qualitative research methodologies, and health communication. Dr. Tytel received her Ph.D. in Public Health Promotion from the Union Institute.

FOREWORD

Recent decades have produced substantial evidence that violence in the American family is both widespread and damaging. Following Kempe's initial studies of child abuse in the 1960s and Straus' national surveys of family violence in the 1970s and 1980s, more focused research has examined the impact of violence on the victims, offenders, and society at large. More recent research has evaluated a variety of interventions aimed at the reduction of violence and the treatment of both victims and offenders. In response to the women's movement and increased societal awareness of these issues, services for victims of family violence have been established and expanded nationwide.

With the increased attention accorded family violence by the research community and mass media, it is surprising that violence in military families has received so little attention. Given the demographic composition of the military, the unique stresses experienced by its members, and the value and emphasis placed on aggression in military training, one might expect violence rates among military families to be exceptionally high. In spite of this, military families have been largely ignored by family violence researchers. With few exceptions, spousal-violence and child-abuse research in military families has been limited in its scope and focus.

Peter and Judy Mercier's unique collection addresses this gap in the literature. This book brings together current research on violence in military families, making an important contribution to the literature on family violence. It contains research from all major branches of the military and confirms the fears many researchers have long shared–that those entrusted with our national defense are also engaged in a critical battle at home.

The research included in this book offers more than documentation of the problem; it summarizes what we know about effective family violence intervention and prevention among military families. It illuminates a once hidden problem and takes the first critical steps toward a solution. In doing so, it offers us hope that all military families may one day enjoy peace at home.

Dianne Cyr Carmody, Ph.D.
Old Dominion University

PREFACE

Battle Cries on the Home Front: Violence in the Military Family is a collection of social science research on domestic violence in the military. This collection attempts to define, both theoretically and conceptually, and explore issues of domestic violence as they specifically pertain to the military family. The studies contained herein use contemporary qualitative and quantitative research and may focus on the occurrence, prevalence, or risk factors for domestic violence found in four military branches—Air Force, Army, Marine Corps, and Navy.

This project begins to fill the void of published research on domestic violence in the military. Though researchers have actively been engaged in studying domestic violence for the past 25 years, little of it has been specifically targeted on the military population. What research has focused on the military is scant and only sporadically published in professional journals. Thus unlike research on domestic violence in the general population that has been widely anthologized (e.g., *Physical Violence in American Families: Risk Factors and Adaptations to Violence in 8,145 Families* edited by M. A. Straus, R. J. Gelles, and C. Smith; *The Social Causes of Husband-Wife Violence* edited by M. A. Straus and G. T. Hotaling; *Intimate Violence: Interdisciplinary Perspectives* edited by E. C. Viano; *Battered Women: A Psychological Study of Domestic Violence* edited by M. Roy), this collection is *unique* as it is the *first compilation* of research on domestic violence as it affects the military population.

OVERVIEW OF CONTENT

Battle Cries on the Homefront is divided into three sections with an introductory chapter intended to provide a brief explanatory survey of domestic violence in the military family. Each chapter in the collection reports findings from empirical research or posits new theoretical explanations for violence in the military family. Section One deals with issues related to wife battering in the military. All of the research in this section is recently completed, never before published, and diverse in approach. Section Two includes readings pertaining to child abuse in the military. Of the three chapters in this section, two are reprints. Section Three addresses prevention and treatment issues regarding domestic violence in the military. One of the three chapters in this section is a reprint.

Due to a lack of previously published research on domestic violence in the military, contributors frequently cite the same sources and studies. Our hope is that this collection not only contributes to an understanding of domestic violence in the military but also precipitates interest in the field and future studies on family violence.

PROJECTED AUDIENCE

This collection is likely to interest researchers, students, and professionals in the fields of social work, health, family counseling, criminal justice, sociology, human services, and psychology. Though domestic violence has become an issue of national attention, its causes, effects, and occurrence in the military community has been neglected. Therefore, these studies may enhance both professionals' and students' understanding of the issues and dynamics particular to domestic violence in military families and offer them the most current literature for future research in this area.

This book could also serve as a resource for those working with military families, especially those in family advocacy programs, or civilian social workers with military clients. Likewise, medical practitioners and other health professionals may also find research on domestic violence important in their work.

Battle Cries on the Home Front: Violence in the Military Family could easily be adopted as a textbook or supplementary reader for graduate-level work in violence against women, marriage and family, military sociology, social theory, contemporary social problems, social psychology, family therapy and counseling, women's studies, victimology, criminal behavior, and social work. Finally, this text seems a suitable resource book for all college and university libraries with programs in criminal justice, sociology, and psychology.

P.J.M.
J.D.M.

ACKNOWLEDGMENTS

We would like to thank all of the contributors for their research and articles, their efforts in transforming the concept of this collection into a reality. Our gratitude goes to Dr. Laura Moriarty, Virginia Commonwealth University, for her constant wellspring of ideas and encouragement.

Likewise, we appreciate the support this project received from faculty in the sociology and criminal justice department of Old Dominion University. We offer a special thanks to Charles C Thomas Publisher, particularly to our editor, Michael Payne Thomas, for believing in this project and following it through to completion.

Finally, we say, "Thanks, Petey." Your love, patience, and understanding allowed us to devote hours of family time to this project without parental guilt.

CONTENTS

Section II: Child Abuse in the Military Family

Section III: Prevention and Treatment of Domestic Violence in the Military

BATTLE CRIES ON THE HOME FRONT

Chapter 1

INTRODUCTION: VIOLENCE IN THE MILITARY FAMILY

PETER J. MERCIER

Over the past twenty-five years, domestic violence has come out of hiding. Americans have come to see that wife battering and child abuse are more extensive than previously realized. Few of us can ignore the media's regular coverage of high-profile cases of domestic violence, particularly when either the victim or the perpetrator is a sports or Hollywood celebrity. As such high-profile cases surface, the general public might agree wholeheartedly with Daniel Saunders' (1992, p. 208) assertion that "the view of the family as a haven in a heartless world has been tempered in recent years by the knowledge that it is often a place of great cruelty."

Although accurate data have been somewhat obscure and difficult to obtain, researchers estimate that over one-half of the couples in relationships–whether marital or cohabitive–in the United States will engage in some type of physical violence during their lifetime (Langley & Levy, 1977). In any given year, over two million wives will be physically battered by their husbands (Straus, Gelles, & Steinmetz, 1980; Saunders, 1992); similarly, nearly three million children will be reported to social service agencies as victims of abuse and other forms of maltreatment (McCurdy & Daro, 1993). Consequently, social scientists have been gathering information on the incidence of wife battering and child abuse in attempts to develop prevention and treatment programs.

Research has identified specific subpopulations within the larger society that have differing needs and require specialized attention in dealing with the social problem of domestic violence. One such subpopulation is the United States armed forces. Although domestic violence statistics comparing civilian and military families are limited, relevant literature suggests that military

---

Note: The views, opinions, and findings contained in this chapter are those of the author and should not be construed as official Department of Defense positions, policies, or decisions, unless so designated by other official documentation.

families are at a particularly high risk for family violence because of assorted demographic variables and various stressors affecting the family unit (Montalvo, 1976; West, Turner, & Dunwoody, 1981; Neidig & Friedman, 1984; Schwabe & Kaslow, 1984; Neidig, 1985; Sonkin, Martin, & Walker, 1985; Waldo, 1986; Cantos, Neidig, & O'Leary, 1993, 1994; Pan, Neidig, & O'Leary, 1994a, 1994b; Mercier, 1996).

Because of the self-policing nature of the military and its desire not to let outsiders in, the real problem of domestic violence in the military has been difficult to assess. On January 17, 1999, however, the television news magazine "60 Minutes" may have opened the proverbial Pandora's box when it suggested that the rate of spousal assault in the miliary is significantly higher than the national average. Moreover, its report alleged that the military routinely fails to punish service members who are perpetrators of extreme cases of domestic violence. In support of its assertions, "60 Minutes" reviewed Pentagon records from 1992 through 1996 and found that 50,000 military spouses were victims of domestic violence, a rate five times higher than the civilian population when compared to Justice Department records for the same five years. The report further indicated that less than 5 percent of military batterers are ever court-martialed.

The "60 Minutes" segment created a tempest of debate during that following week–a congresswoman from New York, Carolyn Maloney, announced plans to introduce legislation mandating harsher punishment for military personnel convicted of domestic violence. The commander of the U.S. Army Community and Family Support Center in Alexandria, Virginia, strongly disagreed with the coverage presented by "60 Minutes," claiming that substantiated cases of spouse abuse in the Army have declined 15 percent in the past five years (Rice, 1999). Although this telecast contributed to an increase in dialogue among those who believe there may be a problem and those who do not, it neither addressed factors associated with domestic violence nor discussed preventative methods.

While research suggests that the occurrence of domestic violence spans age, income, and educational boundaries, these and other factors, such as work-related stressors, appear to affect the frequency of abuse (Straus et al., 1980; West et al., 1981). Age may be a contributing factor in occurrences of domestic violence. Generally, the younger the spouses, the greater the chance of aggression: the rate of violence for a couple who are 30-years-old or younger is more than twice that of the 31 to 50-year-old group. In the military, over 55 percent of active duty males are 30-years-old or younger as compared to 25.1 percent of the males in the civilian population (West et al., 1981; Elder, 1988).

Evidence also suggests that families living at lower socioeconomic levels experience higher levels of domestic violence (West et al., 1981; Elder, 1988).

According to Straus et al. (1980) and Gelles and Cornell (1990), low family income, in addition to age, characterizes wife abuse. More than one-third, 37 percent, of the lowest pay grades of E-1 to E-4 are composed of soldiers 30-years-old and younger who are married (West et al., 1981; Elder, 1988). Therefore, because of age and economic status, the military may be a sub- population with a higher risk for domestic violence (West et al., 1981).

Studies indicate that in addition to age and socio-economic risk factors, military families are at a particularly high risk for family violence as a result of additional demographic variables and family stressors (e.g., dissatisfaction with one's employment status, responsibility for raising a family) which are habitually associated with wife abuse in the general population (Montalvo, 1976; Neidig & Friedman, 1984; Schwabe & Kaslow, 1984; Neidig, 1985; Sonkin et al., 1985; Schumm & Hammond, 1986; Waldo, 1986; Cantos et al., 1993, 1994; Pan et al., 1994a, 1994b). Moreover, military members may experience other tensions, such as long deployments and family separations, as well as the stress associated with financial and work-related pressures (West et al., 1981; Neidig & Friedman, 1984; Sonkin et al., 1985; Waldo, 1986; Eastman, 1988; Griffin & Morgan, 1988; Mercier, 1996).

West et al. (1981) note the prevalence of work-related and financial pressures in military members within the pay grades of E-1 to E-4. Typically, service members in low pay grades hold subordinate positions. They have limited control in work settings and are generally subjected to orders from other higher-ranking service members. Rarely asked to make suggestions for improvements in their work place, they are continually subjected to conditions that they may find undesirable yet are incapable of changing (Neidig & Friedman, 1984; Sonkin et al., 1985). Recent pay scales for the ranks of E-1 to E-4 reveal low annual incomes: from $11,113.20 for an E-1 with less than two years of service to $17,204.40 for an E-4 with more than six years of service (Mace & Yoder, 1998). These figures indicate not only low starting pays, but also limited potential for salary increases. Though this income range only reflects base-pay (military members may receive other financial allowances such as sea pay, submarine pay, basic allowance for quarters, basic allowance for subsistence, or variable housing allowance), military families headed by an E-1 to E-4 member may suffer financial hardships.

Though it is likely that no one single factor causes domestic violence, multiple risk factors may increase the risk of abuse in the military family (West et al., 1981). Most military families, at one time or another, experience family separations, serious financial pressures, isolation from family and peer support systems, and frequent moves. Moreover, the demographic makeup (young adults, with low status, who are on the lower end of the socioeconomic scale) of military families closely parallels that of violent families in the general population; thus, military families may be particularly vulnerable to incidences of domestic violence (West et al., 1981).

Current research suggests that stress, although strongly related to marital violence (Farrington, 1986; Neidig, Friedman, & Collins, 1986; Julian & McKenry, 1993), does not cause spouse or child abuse (Straus, 1992). Other research (West et al., 1981; Neidig & Friedman, 1984; Sonkin et al., 1985; Mercier, 1996) implies that family separations as a result of temporary duty assignments or deployments and financial and work-related pressures associated with low pay grades are stressors which may encourage violence in men who are already at risk of physically expressing anger. Arguing that the military ethic has always emphasized mission accomplishment over individual needs, Neidig and Friedman (1984) advance the notion of the military as a group of individuals who are prepared to fight during war. This is the military's primary concern; family welfare is secondary. The term "dependent," which refers to wives and children of active duty servicemen, tends to reinforce a pejorative image of military family members not actively engaged in the mission. Borrowing a Navy adage, Neidig and Friedman (1984, p. 114) remind us that "if the [Navy]...had wanted [a sailor] to have a wife, they would have issued [him] one."

MILITARY FAMILY ADVOCACY PROGRAMS

The establishment of family advocacy programs in the U.S. military are designed to respond to family violence. An increase in family advocacy programs has paralleled the public's growing concern with child abuse and wife battering, coupled with doubts that strategies and resources for coping with these problems were adequate. For the military community, family abuse not only poses a serious threat to family life but also compromises preparedness by reducing the readiness and performance of individual military members.

When media attention focused on the increased number of children who were being abused by their caretakers, Congress passed the Child Abuse Prevention and Treatment Act of 1974. This legislation established national programs to protect children. In 1981, the Department of Defense (DOD) designed directives in accordance with congressional mandates. These required that military services establish and operate programs that addressed child and spouse abuse. The DOD directives defined specific categories and types of child and spouse abuse, mandated that each military service establish a central registry, and required the reporting of all such incidents to the respective service's central registry (Department of Defense, 1987; McNelis, 1988).

The Air Force Program

In response to Congressional passage of the Child Abuse Prevention and Treatment Act of 1974, the U.S. Air Force predated DOD directives by organizing the first official Child Advocacy Program Regulation in 1975, with the medical service given the primary responsibility to administer the program. As the title suggests, the program was initially designed to address issues of child abuse. However by 1985, the Air Force had expanded the Family Advocacy Program, broadening its scope to the prevention of family maltreatment, which included wife battering. With Congressionally designated funding, the Air Force hired outreach workers to implement prevention and education services. In the course of doing their jobs, outreach workers identified family problems and made referrals to Air Force treatment staff (Mollerstrom, Patchner, & Milner, 1992).

The overall goal of the Family Advocacy Program is to enhance the health and well-being of Air Force families so that military members can fully concentrate on their assigned duties and job performance. Air Force Regulation 160-38, entitled "Family Advocacy Program," assigns specific tasks for all Family Advocacy Programs. These include identifying, reporting, assessing, and treating families with exceptional medical or educational needs, children who are at risk for injury, and families that are experiencing maltreatment (Mollerstrom, Patchner, & Milner, 1992).

The Army Program

The Army's program was conceived primarily as a medical program; however, the approach was broadened to cover social aspects. The original directive (AR 600-48), issued on November 26, 1975, made the Deputy Chief of Staff for Personnel directly responsible for program implementation. Under the directive, a child was defined broadly as a dependent younger than 18 years (Blanchard, 1992).

The program was subsequently placed under the auspices of the Army Community Services (ACS) program in October, 1978. At the headquarters level, the Surgeon General was required to support the program in providing health services, establishing a system for collecting data on cases of maltreatment, and supervising the medical and psychosocial aspects of identifying, preventing, and treating abuse. Ultimately, the Army's program was expanded to include spouse battering in accordance with Army Regulation 608-18.

Currently, the ACS has overall responsibility for managing the Army's Family Advocacy Program. Medical treatment personnel, Army lawyers,

military police, chaplains, and other Army staff personnel work with local
Child Protective Service agencies to ensure that Army families receive help.
The program identifies, reports, treats, prevents, and follows the progress of
abuse incidents. The services that are offered include community education
and awareness, primary prevention efforts to enhance good parenting and
family communication, crisis intervention, emergency shelter, and counseling (Blanchard, 1992).

The Navy Program

On February 4, 1976, the Navy Bureau of Medicine and Surgery issued
BUMED instruction 6320.53A, providing policies and guidance to establish
a Child Advocacy Program within the Navy Medical Department. This program serves both Navy and Marine Corps personnel. The need for a Navy-
wide child advocacy program with centralized control and guidance became
apparent after the proliferation of local initiatives at base medical facilities.
By 1975, all 14 regional navy medical centers had developed child maltreatment policies or advocacy regulations (Blanchard, 1992).

The BUMED instruction outlined procedures for protecting children who
were abused, neglected, or abandoned. It further directed commanders to
ensure that services for children receive careful evaluation and monitoring,
consistent with approved local standards. The Navy Surgeon General had
responsibility both for the Child Advocacy Program and for establishing a
headquarters Child Advocacy Committee to supervise the entire program.
Along with overseeing the program, the central committee was responsible
for establishing and maintaining a central registry of confirmed cases of child
abuse and neglect and for conducting rate analysis and future data retrieval
(Blanchard, 1992).

Similar to the Air Force and Army, the Navy expanded its program in the
mid-1980s, and the Child Advocacy Program became the Family Advocacy
Program after the Secretary of the Navy signed SECNAV Instruction
17523A. The Navy Family Advocacy Program addresses the prevention,
identification, intervention, treatment, followup, and reporting of child and
spouse maltreatment (Blanchard, 1992). The Navy's program includes the
following assumptions:

1. Family violence occurs within all communities, including the Navy
   community.
2. Family maltreatment and abuse are disruptive and interfere with the
   work performance of the service member and thus with the mission of
   the Navy.
3. Family violence and neglect are incompatible with the high standards
   of professional and personal discipline required of Navy members.

4. Most perpetrators of family violence are not deviant or incorrigible; many may be rehabilitated.
5. Victims and involved families often are best served when the perpetrators of family violence are placed in treatment and are available to participate in the family's general rehabilitation.
6. Perpetrators of family violence must be held accountable for their behavior.
7. Swift and certain intervention is a very effective deterrent.
8. The rehabilitation of a valued service member is cost effective for the Navy.

The Navy's comprehensive response to family violence is designed to prevent or stop the violence and minimize its impact on the family and the Navy mission.

CONCLUSION

To date, research points to military families as a particularly high-risk group for family violence (Montalvo, 1976; West el al., 1981; Neidig and Friedman, 1984; Schwabe & Kaslow, 1984; Neidig, 1985; Sonkin et al., 1985; Waldo, 1986; Cantos et al., 1993, 1994; Pan et al., 1994a, 1994b; Mercier, 1996). Thus, this book begins with the assumption that violence may too commonly occur in military families. Under government mandates, the military has established policies and agencies to address family violence, yet much work remains to be done in order to more fully understand and treat the complex nature of domestic abuse.

Because the military is a closed system, conducting research has never been easy. Obtaining data can be problematic for social scientists in their effort to identify those risk factors which specifically affect military families. Without adequate research, it is difficult to offer targeted treatment strategies and prevention programs for military families victimized by abuse. To this end, though not all inclusive, this collection identifies and examines some of the issues related to family violence within the military community, while several of the studies offer recommendations for treatment and prevention.

REFERENCES

Blanchard, R. (1992). *Protecting Children in Military Families: A Cooperative Response.* Washington, DC: Department of Health and Human Services.

Cantos, A. L., Neidig, P. H., & O'Leary, K. D. (1993). Men's and women's attributions of blame for domestic violence. *Journal of Family Violence, 8,* 289-302.

Cantos, A. L., Neidig, P. H., & O'Leary, K. D. (1994). Injuries of women and men in a treatment program for domestic violence. *Journal of Family Violence, 9*, 113-124.

Department of Defense. (1987). *Department of Defense Instruction 6400.2: Child and Spouse Abuse Report.* Washington, DC: Author.

Eastman, E. S. (1988). An investigation of the relationship between Naval deployment and indices of family functions. Ph.D. dissertation, Virginia Consortium for Professional Psychology, Norfolk, VA.

Elder, D. R. (1988). Differences in reported spouse abuse in military families when: (A) Spouses are interviewed separately or together (B) by a male or female interviewer. Ph.D. dissertation, Department of Human Behavior, United States International University, San Diego, CA.

Farrington, K. (1986). The application of stress theory to the study of family violence: Principles, problems, and prospects. *Journal of Family Violence, 1*, 131-147.

Gelles, R. J., & Cornell, C. P. (1990). *Intimate Violence in Families* (2nd ed.). Newbury Park, CA: Sage.

Griffin, W. A., & Morgan, A. R. (1988). Conflict in maritally distressed military couples. *The American Journal of Family Therapy, 16*, 14-22.

Julian, T. W., & McKenry, P. C. (1993). Mediators of male violence toward female intimates. *Journal of Family Violence, 8*, 39-56.

Langley, R., & Levy, R. C. (1977). *Wife Beating: The Silent Crisis.* New York: E. P. Dutton.

Mace, D., & Yoder, E. (Eds.). (1998). *Federal Employees Almanac* (45th ed.). Reston, VA: Federal Employees News Digest.

McCurdy, K., & Daro, D. (1993). *Current Trends in Child Abuse Reporting and Fatalities: The Results of the 1992 Annual Fifty State Survey.* Chicago, IL: National Committee for Prevention and Child Abuse.

McNelis, P. J. (1988). Military installation teams. In D. C. Bross, R. D. Krugman, M. R. Lenherr, D. A. Rosenberg, & B. D. Schmitt (Eds.), *The New Child Protection Team Handbook.* New York: Garland.

Mercier, P. J. (1996). Pounding seas against the shore: Wife battering in the U.S. Navy and its relationship to duty assignment. M.A. thesis, Department of Sociology and Criminal Justice, Old Dominion University, Norfolk, VA.

Mollerstrom, W. W., Patchner, M. A., & Milner, J. S. (1992). Family violence in the Air Force: A look at offenders and the role of the Family Advocacy Program. *Military Medicine, 157*, 371-374.

Montalvo, F. F. (1976). Family separation in the Army: A study of the problems encountered and the caretaking resources used by career Army families undergoing military separation. In H. I. McCubbin, B. B. Dahl, & E. J. Hunter (Eds.), *Families in the Military System* (pp. 147-173). Beverly Hills, CA: Sage.

Neidig, P. H. (1985). Domestic violence in the military, part I: Research findings and program implications. *Military Family, 5*, 3-6.

Neidig, P. H., & Friedman, D. H. (1984). *Spouse Abuse: A Treatment Program for Couples.* Champaign, IL: Research Press.

Neidig, P. H., Friedman, D. H. & Collins, B. S. (1986). Attitudinal characteristics of males who have engaged in spouse abuse. *Journal of Family Violence, 1*, 223-233.

Pan, H. S., Neidig, P. H., & O'Leary, K. D. (1994a). Male-female and aggressor-victim differences in the factor structure of the Modified Conflict Tactics Scale. *Journal of Interpersonal Violence, 9*, 367-382.

Pan, H. S., Neidig, P. H., & O'Leary, K. D. (1994b). Predicting mild and severe husband-to-wife physical aggression. *Journal of Consulting and Clinical Psychology, 62*, 975-981.

Rice, H. (1999). General responds to 60 Minutes program. *The Fort Eustis Wheel,* 6 February, p. 6.

Saunders, D. G. (1992). Woman battering. In R. T. Ammerman & M. Hersen (Eds), *Assessment of Family Violence: A Clinical and Legal Sourcebook* (pp. 208-235). New York: John Wiley.

Schumm, W. R., & Hammond, P. M. (1986). Self-reported marital quality of military families living off-post in a Midwestern community. *Psychological Reports, 59*, 391-394.

Schwabe, M. R., & Kaslow, F. W. (1984). Violence in the military family. In F. W. Kaslow & R. I. Ridenour (Eds.), *The Military Family* (pp. 125-146). New York: Guilford Press.

Sonkin, D. J., Martin, D., & Walker, L. E. (1985). *The Male Batterer: A Treatment Approach.* New York: Springer.

Straus, M. A. (1992). Social stress and marital violence in a national sample of American families. In M. A. Straus, R. J. Gelles, & C. Smith (Eds.), *Physical Violence in American Families: Risk Factors and Adaptations to Violence in 8,145 Families* (pp. 181-201). New Brunswick, NJ: Transaction.

Straus, M. A., Gelles, R. J., & Steinmetz, S. K. (1980). *Behind Closed Doors: Violence in the American Family.* Garden City, NY: Doubleday.

Waldo, M. (1986). Group counseling for military personnel who battered their wives. *Journal for Specialists in Group Work, 11*, 132-138.

West, L. A., Turner, W. M., & Dunwoody, E. (1981). *Wife Abuse in the Armed Forces.* Washington, DC: Center for Women Policy Studies.

Section I

WIFE BATTERING IN THE MILITARY

Section I, Wife Battering in the Military, contains five chapters written by criminal justice, medical, and military scholars; educators; and practitioners. This section addresses wife battering in the military through theoretical and empirical analyses. It begins with an examination of how theories of subculture offer a possible explanation of domestic violence involving Marines. In Chapter 2, David Marshall and Marilyn McShane build on early sociological literature concerning juvenile subcultures, Wolfgang and Ferracutti's subculture of violence, and the more recent work in the area of occupational subcultures to explore the mission and training of the Marine Corps in terms of its effects on the self-image of service members as well as their families. Marshall and McShane offer suggestions for prevention of domestic violence considering the nature and function of the Marine Corps.

Heath Graves and Laura Moriarty, in Chapter 3, measure partner violence in the Air Force, comparing incidence rates to known military and civilian rates. They determine whether violence between spouses in the Air Force is more prevalent than known military and civilian incidence rates.

Chapter 4 examines the severity of wife battering in the U.S. Navy and its relationship to duty assignments. Whereas limited research has focused its attention on wife battering in the military, virtually no research has been conducted in the Navy. This study utilizes Naval Base Police data on domestic disturbance calls, as well as ship deployment schedules, in order to compare the incidence of reported battering between sailors assigned to sea and shore duty. This research concludes that an intervention period prior to a sailor's return home or during a "honeymoon period" may be possible.

Phyllis Sharps, in Chapter 5, investigates the relationship between reported abuse, depressive symptoms, and self esteem among expectant active-duty and dependent military women. Data in her study include 298 pregnant women who received prenatal care at two East Coast military clinics and voluntarily completed an anonymous survey about abuse in the year

13

prior to and during their current pregnancy. Sharps' study determines that among the women surveyed, abuse victims were typically Hispanic, young, and often single; the perpetrator was more likely to be enlisted.

Lastly, as a unique occupation and lifestyle, military service has a great influence over the lives and behavior of its members. One important area of study is the possible influence that military and combat training have on domestic violence and types of crime. In Chapter 6, Leana Allen examines military experience and domestic violence among a sample of inmates in state correctional facilities in the United States. Her results indicate that military experience increases the likelihood of having been incarcerated for a violent crime and having victimized family members, particularly a spouse or a child.

Chapter 2

FIRST TO FIGHT: DOMESTIC VIOLENCE AND THE SUBCULTURE OF THE MARINE CORPS

DAVID H. MARSHALL AND MARILYN D. MCSHANE

INTRODUCTION

Controversial cases of domestic violence, including incidences involving sports heros, movie stars, and political figures, have done much to renew debate about the causes and solutions to this age-old problem. Although mandatory arrest policies were implemented in many jurisdictions following the results of research that suggested arrest reduced domestic violence recidivism (Sherman & Berk, 1984; Jaffe, Wolfe, Telford, & Austin, 1986), subsequent studies have not been able to support such a policy and several sociologists have raised serious concerns about the methodologies employed in this research.

Despite the fact that batterers and victims come from all walks of life, much research has been dedicated to isolating factors associated with risk and determining whether certain groups of people are more predisposed toward domestic violence than others. This study focuses on domestic battery and military service, specifically in the U.S. Marine Corps, using subculture theories to explain why Marines may show a tendency toward violence and a negative view of women. Although it is often difficult to obtain accurate information on the quality of domestic relationships, it may be possible to infer service members' attitudes toward women by examining their relationships with women in their work environment.

Literature on police and correctional officer subcultures describes how norms are institutionalized and enforced from within, particularly those that protect the group from the threat of membership diversity. The negative consequences of these subcultures have been blamed for many public and personnel-relations problems, including corruption, sexual harassment, excessive use of force, and the "code of silence." Administrators have addressed these problems with reform movements and study those individuals who are attracted to the job, those who are selected, and the processes of how they are trained and socialized (Parsons, 1996).

It is argued that some subcultures promote violence, as well as negative perceptions of women, in all aspects of life, including family and employment. Members of such subcultures are at higher risk of bringing violence into their personal relationships; therefore, they may be expected to have higher rates of domestic assault.

THE NATURE OF SUBCULTURES

The concept of subculture implies a group of peers who may not only share many of the same values of the greater society but also fashion separate and unique ideals that set them apart from the norm. Early subculture theories focused on how delinquent gang members bonded together to achieve a status they perhaps could not achieve in the larger, dominant culture (Cohen, 1955; Cloward & Ohlin, 1960). Cohen (1955) theorized that youths engaged in "negativistic, malicious, and non-utilitarian" behaviors as a result of the breakdown of effective family supervision and parental authority, as well as the hostility of the child toward the parents. The decision to join a subculture is viewed as a way to relieve the status-frustration lower-class youths experience. Cohen (1955) also suggested the existence of middle-class male delinquent subcultures, derived from masculine protest, which emphasized rowdy activities such as racing cars, drinking, and acting tough (Williams & McShane, 1994).

Literature related to subcultures describes them as homogenous, somewhat autonomous, socially isolated units characterized by similar world views and regulated by an internal system of discipline. The subculture of violence theory suggests that societies that value "machoism," or the equation of maleness with aggression, also have "frontier mores," in which the rule of the gun and the fist are idealized. This approach to subculture theory helps to explain how behavior is learned and shared in a cultural setting and becomes expected when given certain environmental stimuli (Shoemaker & Sherman, 1987). Therefore, the conduct of the individual is an external exhibition of shared values (Wolfgang & Ferracutti, 1967). These subcultural traits, as described by the literature, can be used to analyze the Marine Corps in terms of its potential to generate and promote its own subculture.

THE MARINE CORPS AS SUBCULTURE

Subcultures, characterized by a lack of dispersion, are often found in isolated geographic areas. The Marine Corps has only 18 installations, as compared to 82 Army posts, 86 Navy bases, and 97 Air Force bases (Presidio-Heartwork, 1992). Not only is the Marine Corps more isolated than any of the other services, but it is also smaller, with 174,507 personnel, which is less than half of any of the other branches. Because of the high concentration of service members in remote locations with smaller civilian populations, Marines may be less socially integrated in the larger surrounding community and perhaps less socially active than other service members. In addition, Marines will meet fewer people and be stationed at fewer installations than any of the other services' members. Marines and their families have a much greater chance of being stationed at the same base several times throughout a Marine's career. This means they are more likely to live near and work with the same people time and time again.

The Marine Corps is the only service to have twenty-four-hour-a-day military police presence at the entrances of all of their installations. This "closed gate" policy leads to a lack of socialization with the surrounding civilian communities, further isolating Marines and their families. This sends the message that the Corps is interested in keeping those not in the subculture away from those who are. This may be important because a 1988 study by Kirk Williams and Richard Hawkins (1989, p. 592) found that a lack of integration into the community and family is an indicator that domestic violence may be present in a relationship.

Homogeneity fosters the subculture's strength and durability (Wolfgang & Ferracutti, 1967), and members of a subculture are most often similar in regard to race, ethnicity, and gender. The Marine Corps has the lowest percentage of women (4.3%) of the entire military service, which averages 12 percent female (Marines, 1994).

The majority of Marines are in the lower pay grades, with 83 percent of enlisted Marines between the pay grades of E-1 to E-5. The evidence linking crime and economic inequality is strong, particularly when analyzing the subculture of violence. Wolfgang's study of youth crime in Philadelphia found that when the city's youths were divided into two economic status groups, higher and lower, the youths with the lower socioeconomic status committed substantially more criminal activity (Currie, 1985).

OCCUPATIONAL ROLES AND THE SUBCULTURE
OF VIOLENCE

Occupational subcultures are created by the jobs people perform. Although they are not necessarily deviant, they share many of the characteristics of criminal subcultures such as shared sentiments, beliefs, and customs. Occupational subcultures do not have the geographical boundaries often found in delinquent subcultures. Two such occupational subcultures, police officers and correctional guards, are particularly relevant to the Marine subculture because of similarities between criminal-justice organizations and the military. As Barker (1977, p. 360) explains:

> A typical police organization represents a form of social organization in which a continuing collectivity of individuals shares a significant activity (police duties); the individuals have a history of continuing interaction based on that activity (clannishness); they acquire a major portion of their identity from the closeness of this interaction (police solidarity); and they share special norms and values with a particular argot. In short, most police organizations possess the qualities of a subculture (Skolnick, 1966; Strecher, 1967).

Intensive training and indoctrination begin the recruit's experience within the subculture. Reiss and Bordua (1967) reported significant differences on personality trait scores between a group of police recruits at the beginning of training, but few significant differences as compared with a group of experienced police officers. Moreover, recruits' scores were similar across four geographically separate cities. Ekman, Friesen, and Lutzker (1960) found similar aggressive behaviors among military recruits. According to the results found by Ekman et al. (1960) and Reiss and Bordua (1967), personality traits, attitudes, and beliefs are developed in both the military and police occupations.

Steinmetz and Straus (1974) argue that the more normalcy placed on aggressive behavior in the occupational role, the greater the amount of violence. In the Marines, a pro-aggressive attitude is reinforced from the top of the rank structure to the bottom. As explained by Sergeant Major Lewis G. Lee, the highest ranking enlisted Marine, "Marines are naturally aggressive, and we have to encourage that" (Fast track: Quick updates on the major issues, 1994). The primary goal of the Marine Corps leadership is to instill in all Marines that they are warriors first (U.S. Department of Navy, 1995). These guiding beliefs and principles influence their attitudes and regulate their behavior.

Marines, like police, train and work in an environment that values bravery. In police work, the potential to become a victim of violence, the need for support by fellow officers during dangerous encounters, and the legitimate use of violence all contribute to the subculture's norms. As Barker (1977, p. 360) explains:

> Because of social isolation and withdrawal into their own group for support and approval, the police officer becomes subjected to intense peer group influence and control. The peer group can set up and maintain effective subcultural mechanisms of informal control through occupational socialization including prescribed deviant conduct.

In addition, police are generally homogenous groups of predominantly white males. Women represent only 10 percent of the country's current police force (McElrath, 1997; Martin, 1994) and as Doerner and Patterson (1996) note, it is mostly external forces such as the courts and lawsuits that have been responsible for the hiring of even that small percentage of women. Unlike police departments, the military has, for the most part, been exempt from the external legal pressures facing policing and corrections.

Both in the military and in police work, the major problem women face is their male counterparts. Janus, Lord, and Power (1988) determined that most female police officers reported that they had been assigned demeaning details solely because they were women. Larwood, Glasser, and McDonald (1980) found that women were viewed as less reliable than men in military specialities not traditionally assigned to women. Further, they discovered that the longer men were in the military, the more negative they became toward women.

A recent series of sex scandals associated with recruits in basic training have focused on the power military leaders have over their trainees, particularly women. One judge ruled that drill sergeants so dominated their charges that they did not have to use a weapon, threats, or force in order to commit rape (Associated Press, 1997). As hundreds of complaints ranging from sexual harassment to assault surface around the country, critics claim that the military's failure to address this conduct over time has created a permissive atmosphere that appears not only to tolerate but to condone such abuse (Richter, 1997; Knight, 1997). One could theorize that acts that attempt to intimidate and control women are consistent with the need to protect the subculture from their intrusion or at least to limit (and devalue) their role within it.

In the military, as well as in policing, promotional opportunities for women are limited and there are few women in leadership positions. According to Martin (1991), women represented only 3.3 percent of the supervisory ranks in policing (rank of sergeant or higher) at the end of 1986. Figures for the military are similar. In 1994, only two percent of all general officers were female, with the Marine Corps having only one female general officer (Marines, 1994).

The military shares several similarities with correctional officers. Interviewing correctional officers, Kauffman (1988) found that group solidarity was viewed as essential, not only to the accomplishment of the shared goals but to the officers' survival. As a group, correctional officers were willing and able to bring considerable pressure upon members to conform. The demographic characteristics of the correctional officers are similar to those of military members. Most of the officers Kauffman (1988) studied were young, white males who had no formal education beyond high school. Additionally, similar stressors affect both groups: low pay, family separation, isolation, and feelings of no support from the administration. When comparing correctional officers and Army personnel, Long, Shoudsmith, Voges, and Roache (1986) found the former more likely to suffer stress reactions. Like the military, many prison employees live in remote, rural areas with isolated living arrangements, shut off from the rest of society (Fox, 1983). Long et al. (1988) concluded that the correctional officer subculture was the reaction of the "person" to the "social environment" of the prison. This mimics the formation of military subcultures. As the military member enters the "institution," his life becomes the result of working and living within the subculture.

While the paramilitary structure of police and corrections agencies has been well-documented in management studies, the utility of such designs has only recently become controversial (Benton & Nesbitt, 1988; Gilbert, 1988; Menke, Zupan, Stohr-Gilmore, & Lovrich, 1990). The chain-of-command control model vests authority in rank and rewards officers on their ability to take and follow commands and to seek approval from supervisors rather than to solve problems at their own level of operation. While most critics do not dispute the success of the military model in accomplishing tasks, they view it as a serious impediment to effective personnel communications and employee development (McShane & Williams, 1993).

DOMESTIC VIOLENCE AND MARINE SUBCULTURE

Since 1988, the number of domestic violence cases reported to the Department of Defense has increased, even though the military population has declined each year (Fast track: Quick updates on the major issues, 1995). Interestingly, though, rates of child and spouse abuse are higher in the Marine Corps than any other of the service branches (see Figures 2-1 and 2-2).

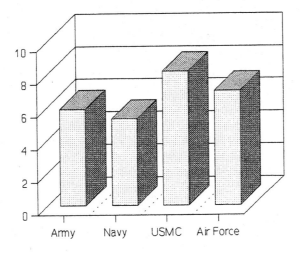

Figure 2-1. Rate per 100 of child abuse. Source: *Navy Times*, Fast track: Quick updates on the major issues. Feb. 27, 1995, p. 28.

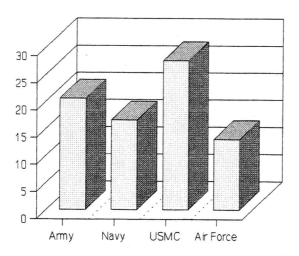

Figure 2-2. Rate per 100 of spouse abuse. Source: *Navy Times*, Fast track: Quick updates on the major issues. Feb. 27, 1995, p. 28.

According to military data, the average abuser is in pay grades E-4 to E-6; however, Marine Corps abusers were consistently more likely to be in the lower E-1 to E-3 grades. Forty-three percent of the Marine Corps is within these pay grades. Because almost all Marines are promoted above the E-3 paygrade within a four-year enlistment, and most enlist within a year or two of high school graduation, it can be assumed that these abusers are between 19 and 22.

As Table 2-1 indicates, Marine Corps abusers fit the age categories consistent with Wolfgang and Ferracutti's (1967) subculture of violence.

Table 2-2 suggests that Marine Corps abusers are of a lower socioeconomic status. Social class is an important factor in many studies of violent crime, as well as subculture theory. Assaultive crimes are overrepresented by members of the lower social strata (Wolfgang & Ferracutti, 1967).

Just as Marine Corps abusers tend to be younger, so do the victims of domestic assaults. More than two-thirds of Marine Corps spouse-abuse victims are 25 or younger, while about one-half of the victims in the Army, Navy, and Air Force combined were 25 or younger.

Because Marines are taught that violence is good, they may not feel deterred from using violence in the home. In most civilian communities, if an individual is arrested for domestic assault, he is taken to jail, at least for the night, and may face stiff penalties as well as the humiliation of going to jail. However, if a Marine is apprehended for a domestic assault, he is released that night to his unit representative, who will recommend that the Marine spend the night in the barracks. Usually, the domestic assault will be on the blotter the following day, and the unit commander will receive a copy of the incident report. At this point, it is left up to the unit commander to punish as he/she sees fit. However, often there is very little, if anything, done. The Marine may receive formal counseling, but most often there is no further disciplinary action taken.

Table 2-1
PERCENT OF ABUSERS BY AGE BY MILITARY SERVICE

Age	USMC	ARMY	NAVY	AIR FORCE
16-20	33	16	9	11
21-25	37	41	42	36
26-30	17	24	22	33
31-35	12	10	19	14
36+	1	8	8	6

Source: Caliber Associates (1994). *Analysis of the Marine Corps Spouse Abuse Responses to the Department of Defense Victim Intake Survey.* (Contract No. M00027-04-2658). Washington, DC: U.S. Government Printing Office.

Table 2-2
PERCENT OF ABUSERS IN PAY GRADE BY MILITARY SERVICE

Pay Grade	USMC	ARMY	NAVY	AIR FORCE
E1-E3	41	23	14	13
E4-E6	52	68	79	82
E7-E9	5	7	6	4
Officers	2	2	1	2

Source: Caliber Associates (1994). *Analysis of the Marine Corps Spouse Abuse Responses to the Department of Defense Victim Intake Survey.* (Contract No. M00027-04-2658). Washington, DC: U.S. Government Printing Office.

Article 128 of the Uniformed Code of Military Justice (UCMJ) entitled "Assault (Spouse and child abuse)" is available to charge and punish Marines who are accused of abusing their wives or children. Marines can be sanctioned by commanders with nonjudicial punishment (NJP), a form of plea bargaining commonly used for drunk and disorderly conduct, dereliction of duty, and unauthorized absences. At NJP, the commander is the judge, jury, and executioner. He/she determines guilt or innocence and may select from a limited range of punishments (U.S. Department of Defense, 1992). A Marine has the right to refuse NJP in lieu of a trial by courts-martial. This is a formal hearing, much like a normal civilian trial, but the jury is made up of senior enlisted and Marine officers. Marines usually accept NJP.

The United States Department of Defense Family Advocacy Committee's Research Subcommittee (1993) initiated action to complete a family violence survey of all of the branches of the military. The survey identified 19,281 substantiated domestic violence cases for 1992. From these, 482 service members were administratively separated, and 250 cases were prosecuted under the UCMJ. The data indicate that only a very small number of cases faced legal action. This lack of formal prosecution can be viewed from the symbolic interactionist perspective: service members as well as authorities define domestic violence as "normal," undeserving of intervention and any significant criminal labeling. Similarly, recent investigations into the Los Angeles Police Department determined that "LAPD officers were not prosecuted for domestic violence because of an unwritten practice that the department maintained of using internal disciplinary measures to handle such complaints, rather than the criminal justice system" (Lait, 1997, p. B1). Recent reports indicate that as many as 31 officers in the Los Angeles Sheriff's Department and 80 in the LAPD have domestic violence records, these figures uncovered only when federal legislation prohibited persons with domestic violence convictions from carrying firearms (Tobar, 1997).

VICTIM MISCONCEPTIONS SUPPORT THE SUBCULTURE

Often, victims who are dependents of Marine Corps abusers believe that if their spouse is identified as abusive, he/she will face stiff penalties. While very few Marines are formally punished for abusive behaviors, one analysis found Marine Corps victims to be more afraid of military consequences for their spouses than of any other consequence (Caliber Associates, 1994). A 1994 study examined victim intake surveys for perceptions of the consequences of reporting abuse, as well as the actual system responses. The data indicated a number of significant differences between the responses from Marine Corps spouse abuse victims and those of other services. About two-thirds of all Marine Corps victims were very or somewhat afraid that a spouse's military career would be in trouble: the spouse would be punished by the military, discharged from the Marine Corps, or face unpleasantness at work (Caliber Associates, 1994). When asked, "How afraid are you that any of the following will happen because your problem is known by the military?" Marine Corps' victims were much more likely to be afraid of the military consequences (Table 2-3). In addition, almost half of all Marine Corps victims feared that their spouse would hurt them, while only about one-third of those in other services felt that way. This may indicate that Marines exhibit aggressive tendencies at home much more frequently than the members of other services.

While Marine Corps' victims believed their spouses would suffer severe disciplinary action for abusing them, Department of Defense statistics on prosecution clearly show that this perception is false. Victims' fears may be related to other well-publicized cases in which Marines are punished swiftly and harshly for what may seem to be small lapses in duty or attention to detail. One of the most common punishments, garnishing wages, may serve as a deterrent to some women who already feel the effects of low incomes and economic hardships.

Table 2-3
VICTIM'S FEARS OF CONSEQUENCES BY MILITARY SERVICE

Victim's Fear	USMC	ARMY	NAVY	AIR FORCE
Things will get worse at home	52	40	34	31
Spouse will hurt her	47	33	27	22
Spouse will be kicked out of the military	63	54	45	54
Spouse will leave her	44	29	25	25
Will not be able to support self/kids	52	41	35	36
Family will think bad about her	33	12	9	13
Friends will think bad about her	32	15	6	7
Too many people will hear about it	57	43	29	40

Source: Caliber Associates (1994). *Analysis of the Marine Corps Spouse Abuse Responses to the Department of Defense Victim Intake Survey.* (Contract No. M00027-04-2658). Washington, DC: U.S. Government Printing Office.

APPLYING THEORIES OF VIOLENCE TO THE MARINES

Seemingly, there are two theoretical components regarding the Marine subculture and violence. The first points out that the violence exhibited by Marines is learned. This is consistent with social learning theory and occupational perspectives that suggest that the institution of the Corps assists in developing and creating violent behavior. The other point is that the high rate of domestic violence in the Marine Corps is correlated with recruiting practices. This "importation" explanation contends that the Marine Corps tends to recruit and enlist individuals who have a predisposition for violence. This theory is similar to Cohen's (1955) earlier thesis that juveniles join gangs in a process of rejecting traditional middle-class social systems in which they believe they do not fit. By disowning middle-class values, they are free to adopt alternative and often conflicting values such as violence, drug-taking, and dropping out of school. Reinforcement by the gang allows members to achieve a status that may seem unattainable outside the subculture. It is possible, then, that the Marine Corps recruits those with a predisposition for violence and then encourages and develops those traits even further. As reinforcement, those who readily adapt to the expectations and conduct norms of the subculture are rewarded, promoted, and given leadership roles. They are envied among their peers in a system designed to instill a competitive spirit.

In addition to police and correctional officers, other subcultural groups can be connected to the Marine Corps subculture. The extensive study of skinheads by Hamm (1993) found that the conduct norms of the skinhead subculture were transmitted through the intensity of peer relations. Violence is the norm, and nonviolence is considered deviant. Skinheads felt more comfortable committing acts of violence when other members were nearby. Violence became an act of imitation with group reinforcement. This is strangely parallel to Marine training where acts of violence are rewarded and praised, and nonviolence is considered weak and dangerous.

Marine Corps recruiting practices certainly support the importation explanation. While other services have changed their marketing strategies to stay competitive with civilian employment opportunities, the Marines have not. Though other branches advertise "learning a trade or skill," the Marine Corps continues to present the image of "warrior" or "knight" in most recruiting media. Individuals with a predisposition for violence may find this appealing. These advertisements and the images they promote not only attempt to legitimize violence but suggest that one should be rewarded for performing in such a manner.

PREVENTING DOMESTIC VIOLENCE IN THE MARINES

Sociologists have long recognized the existence of approved deviance in various organizational settings (Barker, 1977). Such approval is implicated when deviant conduct "does not reflect unfavorably on the individual's overall identity" (Schur, 1971, p. 25). Outside of combat, reacting quickly with anger and aggression should neither be acceptable nor tolerated. The Marine Corps needs to intervene with young couples who, fortunately, may not have established long-term patterns of chronic and escalating abuse. Primary prevention should sensitize young couples to the definitions, symptoms, and dynamics of abuse. Violence-prevention training should begin at induction, educating recruits about the dangers of domestic violence and the disciplinary consequences that would be involved. Training should help young Marines learn to separate combat- or job-related violence from family interactions and develop appropriate responses for each.

The Marine Corps itself should engage in a self-study that would examine whether its current recruiting practices result in the enlistment of those with predispositions for violence and domestic assault. Instruments that attempt to screen for or predict the potential for family violence already exist and could be used in the selection process. Research focused on intervention and prevention could use comparative samples of those already in other service branches, as well as those in police and corrections. As Guido (1996, p. 277) indicates, radical transformation is needed to move away from the "rank and file reactive style of policing and corrections." It has been recommended that such organizations revise the basic rank system, create nonmilitary titles for appropriate personnel grades, and eliminate a number of authority levels (Meese, 1993). The implication is that changes in the organizational structure will influence group norms and, potentially, subcultural values.

Along with some of these suggested reforms, the Marine Corps should also critically analyze its response to domestic violence and increase training for military police, commanders, and members of the Judge Advocates' Staff. Intervention and treatment programs should be accessible, and participation should be encouraged from the highest levels. By identifying factors that create or contribute to a subculture tolerant of domestic violence and working to eliminate them, the Marine Corps may be able to argue that they are first to "stop the fight."

REFERENCES

Associated Press. (1997, April 19). Army judge's rape opinion challenges sergeant's case. *Los Angeles Times*, sec. A, p. 16.

Barker, T. (1977). Peer group support for police occupational deviance. *Criminology*, 15(3), 353-366.

Benton, F.W. & Nesbitt, C. (Eds). (1988). *Prison Personnel Management and Staff Development*. College Park, MD: American Correctional Association.

Caliber Associates. (1994). Analysis of the Marine Corps spouse abuse responses to the Department of Defense victim intake survey. Washington, DC: U.S. Government Printing Offices.

Cloward, R. A., & Ohlin, L. E. (1960). *Delinquency and Opportunity: A Theory of Delinquent Gangs*. New York: Free Press.

Cohen, A. K. (1955). *Delinquent Boys: The Culture Conflict of the Gang*. New York: Free Press.Currie, B. (1985). *Confronting Crime: An American Challenge*. New York: Pantheon.

Doerner, W., & Patterson, E. (1996). The influence of race and gender upon rookie evaluations of their field training officers. In D. Kenney & G. Cordner (Eds.), *Managing Police Personnel* (pp. 79-91). Cincinnati: Anderson.

Ekman, P., Friesen, W. V., & Lutzker, D. R. (1961). Psychological reactions to infantry basic training. *Journal of Consulting Psychology, 26*(1), 103-104.

Fast Track: Quick updates on the major issues. (1995, February 27). *Navy Times*, p. 28.

Fox, V. (1983). *Correctional Institutions*. Englewood Cliffs, New Jersey: Prentice-Hall.

Gibson, W. G. (1994). *Warrior Dreams: Paramilitary Culture in Post-Vietnam America.* New York: Hill and Wang.

Gilbert, M. (1988). Supervision. In F. W. Benton & C. Nesbitt (Eds.), *Prison Personnel Management and Staff Development* (pp. 95-105). College Park, MD: American Correctional Association.

Guido, R. (1996). Organizational change and workforce planning: Dilemmas for criminal justice organizations for the year 2000. In R. Muraskin & A. Roberts (Eds.), *Visions for Change: Crime and Justice in the Twenty-First Century* (pp. 272-282). Upper Saddle River, NJ: Prentice-Hall.

Hamm, M.S. (1993). *American Skinheads: The Criminology and Control of Hate Crime.* Westport, CT: Pregaer.

Jaffe, P., Wolfe, D. A., Telford, A., & Austin, G. (1986). The impact of police changes in incidents of wife abuse. *Journal of Family Violence, 1*(1), 37-49.

Janus, S. S., Lord, L. K., & Power, T. (1988). Women in police work: Annie Oakley or Little Orphan Annie? *Police Studies, 11*(3), 124-127.

Kauffman, K. (1988). *Prison Officers and Their World.* Boston: Harvard University Press.

Knight, H. (1997, April 30). Civilian panel sought to probe sex abuse. *Los Angeles Times*, sec. A, p. 20.

Lait, M. (1997, April 29). LAPD to review domestic abuse investigations. *Los Angeles Times*, sec. B, pp. 1 and 8.

Larwood, L., Glasser, E., & McDonald, R. (1980). Attitudes of male & female cadets toward military sex integration. *Sex Roles, 3*, 381-390.

Long, N., Shouksmith, G., Voges, K., & Roache, S. (1986). Stress in prison staff: An occupational study. *Criminology, 24*(2), 331-343.

Marines. (1994, January). *Almanac '94 Special Edition.* Washington, DC: U.S. Government Printing Office.

Martin, S. E. (1994). "Outsider within" the station house: The impact of race and gender on black women police. *Social Problems, 41*(3), 383-400.

Martin, S. E. (1991). The effectiveness of Affirmative Action: The case of women in policing. *Justice Quarterly, 8*(4), 489-504.

McElrath, K. (1997). Careers in law enforcement. In P. Cromwell & R. Dunham (Eds.), *Crime and Justice in America: Present Realities and Future Prospects* (pp. 171-179). Upper Saddle River, New Jersey: Prentice Hall.

McShane, M., & Williams, F. P. (1993). *The Management of Correctional Institutions.* New York: Garland.

Meese, E. (1993). *Community Policing and the Police Officer: NIJ Perspectives on Policing.* Washington, DC: U.S. Department of Justice.

Menke, B. A., Zupan, L., Stohr-Gilmore, M. K., & Lovrich, N. P. (1990, September). Human resource development: An agenda for jail research. Paper presented at the National Institute of Corrections Conference. Denver, CO.

Parsons, D. A. (1996). Police officers' perceptions: A comparative study by gender and organization. Ph.D. dissertation, Department of Humanities and Social Sciences, University of California, Irvine, CA.

Presidio–Heartwork. (1992). Base closure evaluation project. San Francisco, Ca.

Reiss, A. J., & Bordua, D. J. (1967). *Environment and Organization: A Perspective on the Police.* New York: John Wiley and Sons.

Richter, P. (1997, April 30). Drill sergeant guilty of 18 charges of rape. *Los Angeles Times*, sec. A, pp. 1 and 21.

Schur, E. M. (1971). *Labeling Deviant Behavior.* New York: Harper and Row.

Sherman, L. W., & Berk, R. A. (1984). The specific deterrent effects of arrest for domestic assault. *American Sociological Review, 49*(2), 261-272.

Shoemaker, D. J., & Sherwood, W. J. (1987). The subculture of violence and ethnicity. *Journal of Criminal Justice, 15*, 461-472.

Skolnick, J. (1966). *Justice Without Trial: Law Enforcement in Democratic Society.* New York: John Wiley.

Steinmetz, S. K., & Straus, M. A. (1974). *Violence in the Family.* New York: Mead.

Strecher, V. (1967). When subcultures meet: Police-Negro relations. In S. Yefsky (Ed.), *Science and Technology in Law Enforcement* (pp. 52-57). Chicago: Thompson.

Tobar, H. (1997, May 1). Three deputies go to court, regain right to carry guns. *Los Angeles Times*, sec. B, pp. 1 and 3.

U.S. Department of Defense. (1992). *Military Justice Study Guide.* Newport, RI: Naval Justice School.

U.S. Department of Defense. (1993). *Family Advocacy Committee's Research Subcommittee: Prosecution of Domestic Violence Perpetrators Within the Military Services.* San Diego: Author.

U.S. Department of Navy. (1995). *FMFM 1-0: Leading Marines.* Washington, DC: Headquarters United States Marine Corps.

Williams, F., & McShane, M. (1994). *Criminological Theory* (2nd ed). Englewood Cliffs, NJ: Prentice-Hall.

Williams, K., & Hawkins, R. (1989). Controlling male aggression in intimate relationships. *Law and Society Review, 23*(45), 591-612.

Wolfgang, M., & Ferracutti, F. (1967). *The Subculture of Violence.* London: Social Science.

Chapter 3

PARTNER VIOLENCE IN THE AIR FORCE: ESTIMATING INCIDENCE RATES

E. Heath Graves and Laura J. Moriarty

With numerous media reports alleging the persistent problem of domestic violence in the military and often concluding an over representation of military domestic violence reports, the question remains, to what extent is domestic violence a problem in the military? Moving away from the more anecdotal evidence, this research attempts to measure one facet of domestic violence, that is, partner violence among Air Force family members. Research on domestic violence is substantial; however, there is a dearth of research on military domestic violence in general, and partner violence, in particular.

Based on research conducted by Peter Neidig, Thompson (1994) reported that one in every three Army couples has experienced an incident of spouse abuse in the last year. This contrasts drastically with the one in eight figure found in the more heterogeneous sample of the 1985 National Family Violence Survey (Gelles, 1993). This overrepresentation also appeared prominently when Berk and his colleagues replicated the Minneapolis survey in Colorado Springs. They found military couples accounted for 24 percent of domestic calls, while comprising only seven percent of the population (Berk, Campbell, Klap, & Western, 1992).

Some researchers believe military spouses are less likely to report (officially or in surveys) domestic violence than their civilian counterparts due to a military family's social isolation and the fact that such reports may result in loss of rank (pay) or unemployment for the offender (Caliber Associates, 1996a; West, Turner, & Dunwoody, 1981). This means that, even if military-family violence rates are higher, the hypothesized decreased tendency to report may make this increased rate hard or impossible to discover.

Cronin (1995) used a unique approach to bypass this problem. Using a sample of college students from military and civilian households in Germany, he asked them to report violence in their parents' relationships and found, in several categories, a significantly higher incidence of partner violence in the military couples. Further, he reported a much higher incidence of violence in commissioned officers than spouse- or self-report studies have found (Cronin, 1995). If this research is accurate, it would seem there is also a difference in the likelihood of reporting (at least on surveys) between enlisted and commissioned members and spouses. However, Cronin's samples were very small: 116 military and 86 civilian couples.

Two recent studies have examined abuse in the Air Force and Army. The self-report Army study concluded that 228 per 1000 active duty males and 311 per 1000 active duty females reported committing moderate or severe aggressive acts on their spouses in the past year. In contrast, the rate of officially reported partner violence during this period was around 18 per 1000 active duty members (Caliber Associates, 1996a).

A similar Air Force study was conducted by Caliber Associates (Caliber Associates, 1996a, 1996b, 1996c). This self- and victim-report instrument was included as part of an Air Force Needs Assessment. It showed that 132 per 1000 active duty males and 205 per 1000 active duty females reported perpetrating moderate to severe violence in the last year. This is compared to an official report rate of 8.7 per 1000.

These two studies clearly delineate the military into separate (Army and Air Force) subgroups, raising the questionable merit of the frequent research practice of conducting "military" studies without specifying a branch of the service. Also, they tend to confirm that there is a significant lack of reporting domestic violence incidents. In both cases, the highest possible reporting rate that can be deduced from the figures is still under eight percent.

Explanations for the military domestic violence rate range from simply the demographic makeup of the armed forces (Caliber Associates, 1996c; West et al., 1981) to the types of training soldiers receive (Grossman, 1995). One of the primary explanations for the overrepresentation of the military population in spouse abuse statistics is demographics. That is, the military has more (1) young people, (2) new couples, (3) young couples with low incomes, and (4) people with approximately 12 years of education. As each of these has been proposed as correlates of spouse abuse, a higher rate of spouse abuse in the military would be expected from these facts alone (Caliber Associates, 1996c; Fagan, 1996; West et al., 1981).

There are other factors, though, that have been hypothesized to contribute to this problem. First, because of military deployments or temporary duty assignments (TDY) away from home, couples are often separated. Thus, at the end of a deployment, the military member will have to reintegrate back into the family, disrupting the patterns and the structure established during his/her absence. In families where military spouses take a traditional leadership role, reintegration means reassuming that leadership role, taking it back from the spouse who carried it for the duration of the deployment. Even if the family does not use a traditional leadership role, there will likely be a redivision of household tasks, which may produce much of the same tension. Power and control issues in this situation fit well into a feminist model explaining domestic violence (Ylllö, 1993).

Second, most military couples are reassigned and must relocate every two to three years. Heightening stress, such moves can produce periods of increased isolation, especially for young couples living off the military installation who may have only one car, which the military member uses for work (Caliber Associates, 1996c; Nielson, Endo, & Ellington, 1984; West et al., 1981).

A social control approach can also be used to look at military couples' situation. The military exerts a concerted effort to bond soldiers to their units and to the people with whom they work. Relatively unforgiving compared to the civilian world when societal norms are broken, the military uses the Uniform Code of Military Justice (UCMJ), which are not necessarily laws or statutes. Violations of the UCMJ could include gross displays of poor judgment or "conduct unbecoming." Based on this social control approach, an airman can be expected to readily conform in a social setting. However, the isolation of the family may serve to distance the airman from this control system while at home, contributing to the *family-only* cycle of abuse described in some studies (Straus & Gelles, 1990).

Although the military is relatively unforgiving when certain norms are violated, it can be and has been argued that mild violence may not be outside of some military subgroups' norms. It should come as no surprise that the focus of some military training is to prepare soldiers for violence and that "killing people and breaking things" is a necessary condition of the military (Grossman, 1995). There are two reasons often proposed for a higher acceptance of violence in the military. First, people who accept or like violence may be attracted to the military image or lifestyle and join. Second, violence as a necessary condition is characteristic of military training and socialization. Both of these theories may, in part, be correct.

Thus, using a "subculture of violence" explanation, criminological theory would suggest that there are higher rates of mild violence among military members than in a civilian population, but that such violence, once it exceeds a certain group-acceptability level, will be less likely (Williams & McShane, 1994). A cursory look at the 1985 National Family Violence Survey (Straus & Gelles, 1990) and Caliber Associates (1996b) data seems to indicate that this may be true, as the amount of severe violence as a percent of total violence is less in the military data. However, this is far from conclusive.

It can also be argued that military members, because of the security, retirement benefits, and uncertainty of employment if discharged, will also have a high stake in conformity (Sherman, Smith, Schmidt, & Rogan, 1992). This has implications for this study as well. An individual's high stake in conformity, together with the social control of the unit, would predict a desire for avoidance with disciplinary agencies, hence producing either a deterrent effect or an under-reporting effect.

In the present research, the authors measure domestic violence incidence among active duty Air Force members using both reported and unreported incidents. These rates are compared to the civilian data (National Family Violence Survey) and the military data (Caliber Study) to test whether military domestic violence, and in particular, Air Force partner violence, is higher (i.e., more prevalent) than civilian incidence rates and/or known military incidence rates. Explanations for the Air Force rates are provided.

METHODOLOGY

Currently, there are approximately 299,000 active-duty Air Force members stationed in the continental United States. Another 81,000 are stationed overseas. The sample for this study was drawn from those in the United States.

The names and home addresses of 975 Air Force spouses were drawn from the database maintained by the Defense Manpower Data Center in California to create the sample. The first three digits of the home zip code were compared to the first three digits of the zip code of the base recorded as the Air Force member's current duty station. This procedure is necessary because it is estimated that up to 40 percent of the home addresses in this database are outdated; however, current base information is correct for well over 95 percent of the entries. Comparing these two zip codes reduces the possibility of losing a large portion of the sample to bad addresses.

Due to the structure of this database, true random selection was not possible. Instead, a substitute stratified selection procedure was used to ensure that the records were not selected in a way that would bias the resulting sample. A more detailed explanation of the methodology can be found in endnotes 1 through 4.

Of the 910 surveys mailed, twenty-six were returned by the post office because the forwarding order had expired; however, a forwarding address was provided. Second packages were sent to these 26 respondents at their new addresses. A total of 67 packages were returned by the post office with no forwarding address. Therefore, the maximum number contacted by the survey was 843. Of this number, 261 were returned, of which 6 were unusable. The final sample size, 255, results in a 30.2 percent response rate. For the sample size obtained (255), we can be 95 percent confident that the actual percentages fall within ±6.1 percentage points.

To gauge the representativeness of the sample to the Air Force population, we compared the sample to the population examining key demographic variables (Potter, 1997; Air Force Personnel Center, 1996). As Table 3-1 shows, the sample is mostly white (87%), male (97%), with some college (27%), and holding an enlisted (E5-E6) rank (35%). While the percentages are slightly different, the population statistics indicate the same profile: that is, white (82%) males (86%) with some college (51%) holding the enlisted (E5-E6) rank (36%).

Table 3-1.
DEMOGRAPHIC PROFILE OF FINAL SAMPLE

Race	USAF	Sample	Age	USAF	Sample
Hispanic	4.2%	3.9%	19-20	2.0%	1.0%
White	81.5%	86.9%	21-22	5.6%	2.9%
Black	8.6%	6.8%	23-24	7.4%	5.2%
Other	5.7%	2.4%	25-26	8.3%	9.0%
			27-29	12.9%	11.4%
			30-32	13.5%	12.4%
			33-36	21.0%	23.3%
			37-40	17.0%	21.9%
			41-44	8.7%	8.6%
			45-49	3.1%	4.3%
			50+	0.5%	0.0%

Education Level	USAF	Sample
Hold advanced degree	15.5%	23.5%
Four year college graduate or more	12.8%	16.4%
Associate degree	13.3%	13.9%
Some college	50.5%	27.1%
High school	7.9%	19.1%

Military Ranks	USAF	Sample
E1-E4	26.6%	14.3%
E5-E6	36.2%	34.3%
E7-E9	14.5%	18.6%
O1-O3	12.5%	14.3%
O4-O6	10.2%	18.1%

Table 3-1. Continued

Religion	USAF	Sample		Gender	USAF	Sample
Catholic	26.9%	22.6%		Male	85.5%	96.6%
Jewish	0.3%	0.0%		Female	14.5%	3.4%
Protestant	43.1%	53.4%				
Muslim	0.0%	0.0%				
Buddhist	0.0%	0.0%				
Atheist	0.0%	0.0%				
Other	13.2%	12.8%				
None	16.5%	11.3%				

Number of Children	USAF	Sample
None	41.7%	24.2%
One	20.7%	22.5%
Two	25.6%	36.0%
Three	9.6%	11.4%
Four or more	2.5%	5.9%

Partner Violence Measures

In order to maintain consistency with this and many other reported studies, the measurement tool for violent incidents was a slightly modified version of the Revised Conflict Tactics Scale or CTS2. The CTS2 is a recent revision of the Conflict Tactics Scale (CTS1) that has been used extensively in the field of spouse abuse research for the last 15 years (Schafer, 1996; Straus, Hamby, Boney-McCoy, & Sugerman, 1996; Gelles & Straus, 1988). This study used the complete psychological aggression (preliminary alpha=.97) and physical assault (preliminary alpha=.86) subscales of the CTS2. It also included the complete injury scale, except that items 55 and 23 were combined (preliminary alpha=.95). The Cronbach alphas listed for each scale are from the initial psychometric evaluation of this scale using a sample of college students (Straus et al., 1996). This published revised edition was the version used in the present research, with the modifications noted below.

The physical assault scale was put back in the hierarchical order of the CTS1 where the tactics become less socially acceptable the further the respondent goes in the survey (the CTS2 is in random order). This was necessary because the survey asked respondents who answered yes to any of the questions in the physical assault scale to give further information. In an ordered form, this is easily done by asking respondents if they have answered "never" to all questions in a certain range. Another modification was made to the CTS2. One of the frequent complaints about the C1 was that it failed to capture the reasons for and results of assaults on a partner (Schaefer, 1995; Yllö, 1993). The CTS2 solves the second of these objections by including an injury subscale. The modification used in this survey is an attempt to improve the first issue. For each tactic on the CTS2 physical assault scale, the respondents were first asked if they ever "used this tactic" and then asked if their partner had ever used it. Moreover, respondents were asked how many of the total times they used these tactics for self-defense. This was also asked of the partner.

Hypotheses

There are several hypotheses tested in this research. They are all related to incidence rates. First, we expect to find higher incidence rates among the Air Force sample than found in the civilian population and military as a whole. (We will use existing data, i.e., National Family Violence Survey and the Caliber Study, and the results of our study to test this hypothesis). Second, we expect to find differences among the sample between males and females when using violent tactics in self-defense. Third, we expect females to have a higher injury rate than males. Finally, in order to explain the incidence rates found, we expect the following variables to be correlated with incidence rates: acceptance of slapping, partner's age, involvement with other spouses, household income, frequency of the partner becoming drunk, temporary duty assignments (TDY), recentness of a move, and use of violence.

Domestic Violence Incidence Rates

The domestic violence incidence rates were measured as the percent of the couples that had experienced each type of violence. These rates were first computed using only the raw CTS2 data (ignoring the self-defense answers) for occurrences in the last 12 months, so that they could be compared to the other studies, i.e., the 1985 National Family Violence Survey (NFVS) and the 1995 Air Force Needs Assessment Survey.

As Table 3-2 reports, the rates of minor violence (e.g., throwing something at partner, twisting arm or hair, pushing or shoving, grabbing, or slapping) in the last 12 months were slightly higher in the present study compared to the other studies. However, these observed differences, while consistent, were within the margin of error of this study and hence cannot be considered statistically significant. Also, as expected, the incidence rates found in this study matched those of the Needs Assessment Survey within the margins of error for the study. In several cases, most obviously in the husband to wife serious abuse[1] rate, the Needs Assessment Survey reported somewhat lower incidence rates. This seems logical because the Caliber Needs Assessment Survey was not anonymous. Again, however, these differences were within the margin of error of this study.

Table 3-2.
PREVALENCE OF VIOLENCE IN THE LAST 12 MONTHS

	This Study	1985 NFVS	1995 Needs Assessment	Aprox. margin of error
Any Violence	17.9%	16.1%		+/-4.7%
Violence by the USAF member	15.1%		14.7%	+/-4.4%
Husband to wife violence	15.3%	11.6%	11.1%	+/-4.3%
Wife to husband violence	*	12.4%	11.5%	*
Violence by the spouse/respondent	15.1%		16.8%	+/-4.4%
Husband to wife violence	*	11.6%		*
Wife to husband violence	14.8%	12.4%		+/-4.3%
Any serious abuse	6.0%	6.3%		+/-2.9%
Serious abuse by the USAF member	4.4%			+/-2.5%
Husband to wife severe abuse	4.7%	3.4%	2.2%	+/-2.5%
Wife to husband severe abuse	*	4.8%	9.0%	*
Serious abuse by the spouse	3.2%			+/-2.2%
Husband to wife severe abuse	*	3.4%		*
Wife to Husband severe abuse	3.4%	4.8%		+/-2.2%

As mentioned earlier, the present study included the option of classifying certain instances of partner violence as self-defense. The next two tables (Table 3-3 and Table 3-4) report the incidence rates when adjusted by removing the self-defense tactics. Table 3-3 reports the rates for the 12-month period preceding the survey administration. Table 3-4 reports incidence rates for the duration of the couple's relationship.

---

1. Serious abuse includes stabbed with a knife, punched or hit with something that could hurt, choked, slammed into a wall, burned or scalded, kicked, or beat up partner.

Table 3-3
TWELVE MONTH PREVALENCE RATES ADJUSTED FOR SELF-DEFENSE

	Normal CTS2 Prevalence Rate	Adjusted Self-defense	Margin of error
Any Violence	17.9%		+/-4.7%
Violence by the USAF member	15.1%	13.3%	+/-4.4%
Husband to wife violence	15.3%	13.7%	+/-4.3%
Wife to husband violence	*	*	*
Violence by the spouse/respondent	15.1%	13.3%	+/-4.4%
Husband to wife violence	*	*	*
Wife to husband violence	14.8%	13.7%	+/-4.3%
Any serious abuse	6.0%		+/-2.9%
Serious abuse by the USAF member	4.4%	3.6%	+/-2.5%
Husband to wife severe abuse	4.7%	3.8%	+/-2.5%
Wife to husband severe abuse	*	*	*
Serious abuse by the spouse	3.2%	2.8%	+/-2.2%
Husband to wife severe abuse	*	*	*
Wife to Husband severe abuse	3.4%	3.0%	+/-2.2%

Table 3-4
PREVALENCE OF VIOLENCE OVER THE ENTIRE RELATIONSHIP

	Normal CTS2 Prevalence Rate	Adjusted Self-defense	Margin of error
Any Violence	30.0%		+/-5.7%
Violence by the USAF member	23.5%	20.9%	+/-5.2%
Husband to wife violence	23.7%	20.9%	+/-5.1%
Wife to husband violence	*	*	*
Violence by the spouse/respondent	25.5%	24.2%	+/-5.4%
Husband to wife violence	*	*	*
Wife to husband violence	25.4%	24.5%	+/-5.3%
Any serious abuse	12.7%		+/-4.1%
Serious abuse by the USAF member	10.0%	9.2%a	+/-3.7%
Husband to wife violence	11.0%	9.8%b	+/-3.8%
Wife to husband violence	*	*	*
Serious abuse by the spouse	6.4%	4.8%a	+/-3.0%
Husband to wife violence	*	*	*
Wife to Husband violence	6.7%	5.1%b	+/-3.0%

ᵃ,ᵇ when considered by couple, the differences between men and women (hence, USAF members and spouses) were significant at p=.028 (using Wilcoxon Signed Ranks Test).

As is obvious from the tables, eliminating uses of physical tactics delineated as self-defense does not seem to move many offenders into the nonviolent realm. Perhaps most significantly, there does not seem to be a huge difference between men and women in the use of physical tactics in self-defense across most of the categories. However, self-defense did seem to play a significant role in female spouse use of serious abuse tactics in self defense over the duration of the relationship. Considering couples as related samples, a Wilcoxon Signed Rank Test confirmed a significant difference in the number of serious abuse tactics used by men and women in self defense over the duration of the relationship (p=.028). The significance of this relationship is further confirmed using dichotomous coding for the occurrence or nonoccurrence of violence comparing male and female self-defense tactics (p=.043).

The next incident rate evaluated was the injury rate. As indicated in Tables 3-5 and 3-6, violent acts do seem to result in injury more often when perpetrated by the husband. Again, conceptualizing couples as paired samples, Wilcoxon Signed Rank and McNemar tests yielded statistically significant results. In assessing physical injury in the past 12 months, when numbers of injury measures reported are evaluated, the Wilcoxon test indicates significance (p=.003). If the variables are re-coded to make them dichotomous measures of whether or not injury has occurred, the McNemar test is significant (p=.022). A similar McNemar analysis for physical injury over the course of the relationship indicates significance (p=.008). This means that women are more likely than males to be injured in the last 12 months and over the duration of the relationship.

Table 3-5
PREVALENCE OF INJURY IN THE LAST 12 MONTHS

	Injury rate	Margin of error
Any injury	6.5%	+/-3.1%
Injury caused by the USAF member	5.7%[a]	+/-2.9%
Husband caused injury	6.0%[b]	+/-2.9%
Wife caused injury	*	*
Injury caused by the respondent	2.0%[a]	+/-1.7%
Husband caused injury	*	*
Wife caused injury	2.1%[b]	+/-1.7%
Any serious injury	0.8%	+/-1.1%

[a,b] When considered by couple, the differences between men and women were significant at p=.003 (using Wilcoxon Signed Ranks Test).

Table 3-6
PREVALENCE OF INJURY OVER THE DURATION OF THE RELATIONSHIP

	Injury rate	Margin of error
Any injury	10.2%	+/-3.7%
Injury caused by the USAF member	8.9%[a]	+/-3.5%
Husband caused injury	9.4%[b]	+/-3.5%
Wife caused injury	*	*
Injury caused by the respondent	4.1%[a]	+/-2.4%
Husband caused injury	*	*
Wife caused injury	4.3%[b]	+/-1.7%
Any serious injury	2.0%	+/-1.7%

[a,b] When considered by couple, the differences between men and women were significant at p=.008 (using McNemar's Test)

What explains the partner violence incidence rates found among the Air Force members? Employing logistical regression models to find out, we used variables measuring family separation or recent moves, interaction/involvement with other spouses, demographics, acceptance of violence, drinking behaviors, and use of violence not in self defense to help explain any violence and serious violence in the last 12 months. Focusing first on any violence in the past year and then on serious abuse in the past year, we found that the acceptance of slapping, the partner's age and involvement with other spouses, the household income, and the frequency of the partner becoming drunk all aid in the prediction of violence. With these variables in the model, slightly over 30 percent of the variance is accounted for (Cox and Snell R^2=.309 or 31%) and 91 percent of the cases in the sample are correctly predicted. The chi-square test of the change in log likelihood was significant (X^2=82.33; p=.0001).

The model for the serious abuse found only three variables to be substantially helpful in predicting this occurrence. However, these three variables—use of violence by the respondent (not in self-defense), frequency of the partner becoming drunk, and partner age—explained 18 percent of the variance (Cox and Snell R^2=.180 or 18%). The chi square was significant (X^2=48.32; p=.0015).

DISCUSSION AND CONCLUSION

As always in a study of domestic violence, the rate of incidence is a major concern. In this research, many similarities with previous civilian studies were found. However, most of the minor abuse measures were consistently (but not significantly) elevated in the military sample. Since correlations were not found with family separation or recent moves, the possibility remains that this increase is either random or an artifact of demographics. It is also possible that minor violence may be more accepted in the military subculture. However, since age did correlate significantly and strongly with abuse in the sample and that a large portion of the sample was young (42% were 32 or under), this increase in abuse may have been as result of randomization.

The fact that the separation and movement of families (and their subsequent reintegration) did not correlate significantly with abuse failed to provide the expected support for power and authoritarianism theories as a central causative factor in such abuse.

Discrepancies in serious abuse rates were found when comparing the Caliber Associates Air Force results to the present research. Our findings indicate a higher serious abuse rate. One reason for this difference may be the anonymity of the surveys: ours was anonymous while the Caliber Associates study was confidential. Further, the Caliber study omitted several of the items from the serious abuse section of the CTS, while we included them, and several respondents indicated such abuse. Therefore, the discrepancies may be the result of a conceptual problem (internal validity) measuring serious abuse differently in each study may explain the differences found or a reporting problem, more honest replies are found in anonymous surveys than in confidential surveys.

The use of a self-defense measure allowed us to look at adjusted incidence rates as well. Very little of the violence that occurred was reported as self-defense. However, when comparing males to females, a significant difference was found in the use of serious abuse tactics used in self-defense. Women were more likely to use serious abuse tactics in self-defense. This gives some credence to the argument that the equal incidences between men and women often found in this area are at least partly a result of the smaller member of the couple resorting to more serious tactics in self-defense. This more one-sided view of serious abuse was also supported by the finding of a significant difference between men and women in rates of injury from domestic violence. However, it should be noted that the vast majority of the men were USAF members and the vast majority of the women were civilian spouses. Thus, these differences could also be viewed as military versus non-military differences; however, demographics could not support this. Further, the fact that most of the incidence rates closely parallel civilian-study rates would make this a hard proposition to accept. Nevertheless, that this effect was a combination of these two factors is possible and even somewhat plausible. However, because of the great similarity in the overall military rates to the civilian data, gender differences seem more likely the main effect.

The limited examination of abuse using logistic regression yielded very few surprises, finding most of the same correlates to abuse frequently found in the literature. However, the finding that use by the respondent of physical tactics not in self-defense was the largest predictor of receiving serious abuse is significant. Although this concept has certainly been proposed elsewhere, separating violence used in self-defense and not in self-defense had been a problem. There was some amount of auto-correlation expected when self-defense could not be separated out since victims of severe abuse would be more likely to use physical tactics in self-defense than others. The separation of these two types of use of physical tactics eliminated this auto-correlation effect and showed the relationship between violence not in self-defense and serious abuse more clearly.

FUTURE RESEARCH

The role self-defense plays in domestic violence in terms of the infliction of serious abuse and subsequent injury must be explored further, not only with military populations but also with civilian populations. Researchers have found it difficult to separate violent acts into abuse and self-defense. The modifications to the CTS2 proposed in this study begin to highlight the impact of using serious-abuse tactics in self-defense. Our findings need to be replicated to determine if women are putting themselves in more dangerous situations by fighting back.

ENDNOTES

1. The sample was drawn from Air Force members in the United States for the following reasons: first, the mail to overseas areas is slow and unpredictable; second, since military members move frequently and almost always rotate through overseas assignments, there is no reason to believe these members will differ significantly from those in the states, except in certain demographic measures; and third, many members stationed overseas, although married, are not accompanied by their families on these tours and so have been separated from their spouses for many months. Including the spouses of these members would likely hurt validity as it artificially deflates prevalence. Since the database used in this study to select the sample cannot easily distinguish if family members are on assignment with the Air Force member, all overseas couples were eliminated.

2. The substitute stratified selection procedure used for this study sorted the sample as follows: 8th digit of the Social Security Number (SSN), day of birth, month of birth, name, and 6th digit of the SSN, to create a sample that was not biased in any predictable way. To ensure no recognizable bias, the resulting sample was profiled by the first three digits of the Social Security Number (geographic origin) and base of assignment. The profile showed no bias in these categories. Sixty-five of the addresses were then randomly eliminated to result in the final desired sample size of 910.

3. Surveys were mailed first class using stamps instead of metered postage. Although most studies have shown these two items to have minimal effect, studies which have shown a difference favor this type of postage except when compared to registered or certified mail (Bailey, 1994), which was not feasible in this study. Unfortunately, the only 78 cent stamp available at the time of the study was a Women's Suffragist stamp. Since the possibility of presenting a perceived research bias existed if this stamp was used, two normal (U.S. Flag) 32 cent and one (Blue Jay) 20 cent stamps were used. The survey was mailed with a cover letter including an Air Force and academic institution signature block to show sponsorship by both. Military members are often inundated with surveys, and this was an attempt to differentiate this survey from the many "quality of life" and "customer service" surveys these families often receive.

4. Gift certificates for free small frosty desserts were donated by Wendy's International to use as an incentive to reply. The surveys were mailed from Richmond, Virginia, beginning August 1, 1997. A staggered mailing was done to maximize the possibility that the survey packages would arrive in the middle of the week. A follow-up letter, mailed eight days after the initial mailing to the entire sample, did not include the survey. Instead, respondents were asked to call collect if they needed another survey.

REFERENCES

Air Force Personnel Center. (1997). *Active Air Force Demographics*. Available: http://www.afpc.af.mil/analysis/demograf [1997, Aug 30].

Bailey, K. D. (1994). *Methods of Social Research* (4th ed.). New York: Macmillan.

Berk, R. A., Campbell, A., Klap, R., & Western, B. (1992). Bayesian analysis of the Colorado Springs spouse abuse experiment. *Journal of Criminal Law and Criminology, 83,* 170-200.

Caliber Associates. (1996a). *Abuse Victims Study Final Report.* Unpublished manuscript.

Caliber Associates. (1996b). *The Study of Spousal Abuse in the Armed Forces: Analysis of Spouse Abuse Incidence and Recidivism Rates and Trends.* Unpublished manuscript.

Caliber Associates. (1996c). *Final Report on the Study of Spouse Abuse in the Armed Forces.* Unpublished manuscript.

Cronin, C. (1995). Adolescent reports of parental spousal violence in military and civilian families. *Journal of Interpersonal Violence, 10*(1), 117-122.

Fagan, J. (1996). The Criminalization Of Domestic Violence: Promises And Limits. Paper presentation at the 1995 Conference on Criminal Justice Research and Evaluation, Washington, DC.

Gelles, R. J. (1993). Through a sociological lens: Social structure and family violence. In R. J. Gelles & D. Loeske (Eds.), *Current Controversies on Family Violence* (pp. 31-46). London: Sage.

Gelles, R. J. & Straus, M. A. (1988). *Intimate Violence: The Causes and Consequences of Abuse in the American Family.* New York: Simon and Schuster.

Grossman, D. A. (1995). *On Killing: The Psychological Cost of Learning to Kill in War and Society.* Boston: Little, Brown.

Nielsen, J. M., Endo, R. K., & Ellington, B. L. (1992). Social isolation and wife abuse: A research report. In E. Viano (Ed.), *Intimate Violence* (pp. 49-60). Washington: Hemisphere Publishing.

Potter, A. (1997). Personal Interview. September 18.

Schafer, J. (1996). Measuring spousal violence with the Conflict Tactics Scale: Notes on reliability and validity issues. *Journal of Interpersonal Violence, 11*(4), 572-585.

Sherman, L. W., Smith, D. A., Schmidt, J. D., & Rogan, D. P. (1992). Crime, punishment and stake in conformity: Legal and informal control of domestic violence. *American Sociological Review, 57,* 680-690.

Straus, M. A., Hamby, S. L., Boney-McCoy, S., & Sugarman, D. B. (1996). The revised Conflict Tactics Scale (CTS2): Development and preliminary psychometric. *Journal of Family Issues, 17*(3), 283-316.

Straus, M. A., & Gelles, R. J. (1990). *Physical Violence in American Families.* London: Transaction Publishers.

Thompson, M. (1994). The living room war. *Time, 143,* May 23, 48-51.

West, L. A., Turner, W. M., & Dunwoody, E. (1981). *Wife Abuse in the Armed Forces.* Washington, DC: Center for Women Policy Studies.

Williams, F. P., & McShane, M. D. (1994). *Criminological Theory.* Englewood Cliffs: Prentice-Hall.

Yllö, K. A. (1993). Through a feminist lens: Gender, power, and violence. In R. Gelles & D. Loeske (Eds.), *Current Controversies on Family Violence* (pp. 47-63). London: Sage.

Chapter 4

DOMESTIC VIOLENCE IN THE NAVY: EXPLORING THE RELATIONSHIP BETWEEN SEVERITY OF ABUSE AND DUTY ASSIGNMENT

PETER J. MERCIER

Past studies indicate that the demographic make-up of military families closely parallels that of violent families in the general population (Montalvo, 1976; West, Turner, & Dunwoody, 1981; Neidig & Friedman, 1984; Schwabe & Kaslow, 1984; Neidig, 1985; Sonkin, Martin, & Walker, 1985; Waldo, 1986; Cantos, Neidig, & O'Leary, 1993, 1994; Pan, Neidig, & O'Leary, 1994a, 1994b). Generally, wife battering is believed to occur in younger families and those with lower socioeconomic status (Straus, Gelles, & Steinmetz, 1980; West et al., 1981). Additionally, certain stressors identified with the increased occurrence of wife battering in the general population are regularly experienced by Navy families (West et al., 1981; Eastman, 1988). These findings alone may justify the military population as a significant constituency for domestic violence research. Although there is a paucity of empirical studies on spousal abuse in the military, virtually no research has been conducted in the U.S. Navy. As such, this study examines the severity of wife battering in the Navy and attempts to determine if duty assignment has an impact on its occurrence.

Active-duty military personnel, regardless of branch, may experience separations from their families as a result of overseas assignments, temporary duty assignments, or isolated duty tours (Sonkin et al., 1985). Yet the Navy's mission routinely requires that sailors serve extended periods of time at sea. During these tours, Navy personnel may have limited communication with their families, unlike most Army and Air Force personnel temporarily stationed away from home.

Note: The views, opinions, and findings contained in this chapter are those of the author and should not be construed as official Department of Navy positions, policies, or decisions, unless so designated by other official documentation.

The following study seeks to determine what impact sea duty may have on the severity of wife battering in Navy families and specifically addresses the following questions: *Is the severity of wife battering more prevalent in Navy families in which husbands are assigned to sea duty? Are incidents of severe wife battering more prevalent immediately following the deployed sailor's return home?*

REVIEW OF THE LITERATURE

Although numerous theories have been postulated over the years to explain family violence, the most frequently mentioned are the *family stress theory* (Hill, 1949; Hansen & Johnson, 1979; McCubbin & Patterson, 1983; Farrington, 1986), the *frustration-aggression theory* (Dollard, Doob, Miller, Mowrer, & Sears, 1939; Etzioni, 1971; Gelles & Straus, 1979), the *resource theory* (Gelles & Straus, 1979; Bersani & Chen, 1988; Gelles & Cornell, 1990), the *social learning theory* (Bandura, 1973, 1977; Gelles & Straus, 1979; Straus et al., 1980), the *social-structural theory* (Gelles & Straus, 1979; Thorman, 1980), and the *theory of patriarchy* (Dobash & Dobash, 1979; Gelles & Cornell, 1990). These six theories share similar propositions and support the notion that male Navy members may suffer a great deal of stress and frustration due to their low status and low pay. These levels of stress and frustration are amplified for male Navy members assigned to sea-duty commands, such as ships, because they may spend a great deal of time away from home. Upon their return, they may feel somewhat estranged from their wives who have had complete parental and family budgetary responsibilities during their absences. The male Navy member may perceive that he has lost the family leadership role (head of the household) and may attempt to regain his patriarchal authority upon his arrival home. As a result of these factors, a male Navy member who is prone to violence may demonstrate abusive behavior towards his wife in order to alleviate stress, frustration, and disappointment. Though none of the factors identified in the theories cause violence, they may contribute to violent behavior when a person is already prone to violence.

Research comparing domestic violence in the military family to that of the civilian population has produced inconclusive results, yet some studies have attempted to identify differences between these two communities. In a comparison study of distressed military and civilian couples receiving marital therapy, William Griffin and Allison Morgan (1988) found that military wives were more likely to be physically battered than civilian wives. In a more recent comparative study, Christopher Cronin (1995), examining both military and civilian children's reports of parental spousal abuse, found that children from military families reported a higher percentage of parental spousal abuse than children from civilian families. In an effort to more fully understand family violence in the military, the most comprehensive study to date, that of Peter Neidig and his associates (Cantos et al., 1993, 1994; Pan et al., 1994a, 1994b), determined that nearly one-third of male Army soldiers reported that either they and/or their spouses engaged in at least one episode of violence during the previous year; nine percent of the episodes were categorized as severe violence.

Although research suggests that military families are at a particularly high risk for family violence due to various stressors affecting the family unit (Montalvo, 1976; West et al., 1981; Neidig & Friedman, 1984; Schwabe & Kaslow, 1984; Neidig, 1985; Sonkin et al., 1985; Waldo, 1986; Cantos et al., 1993, 1994; Pan et al., 1994a, 1994b), a comprehensive examination of the literature has not disclosed any research relative to family violence and/or wife battering with respect to duty assignments or ship deployments. However, other research has been conducted with Navy members and their wives to see how they cope with stress during periods of long deployments (Patterson & McCubbin, 1984; Eastman, 1988). According to Patterson and McCubbin (1984, p. 95), "separations of a duration of eight months to a year . . . are likely to involve changes in family roles, processes, and relationships in order to manage family life." During these periods, Navy wives have complete household management and budgetary responsibilities during their husbands' absences. Such separations may increase the likelihood of trauma and family dysfunction.

Additionally, in a study examining life stress events and deployment-specific attitudes within Navy families, Edward Eastman (1988) found that Navy couples assigned to shore-duty assignments had significantly lower levels of mean life stress scores as compared to those with sea-duty assignments. Furthermore, Eastman (1988) discovered that Navy personnel assigned to ships, but not deployed, also had significantly lower stress levels as compared to those sailors who had just returned from a deployment.

As a result, the Navy Family Advocacy Program, speculating that a short "honeymoon" period may exist upon a sailor's return home from deployment, notes an increase in reported wife-abuse cases approximately two to three weeks after their husbands' ships return home (Thomas, 1995).

Based on the theoretical arguments, a review of the literature, and Family Advocacy reports, this study makes the following hypotheses: (1) *Severity of wife battering by male Navy members is higher for those with sea-duty assignments;* (2) *Male Navy members assigned to ships deployed the longest are more likely to inflict severe battering;* and (3) *Male Navy members who batter their wives upon returning from deployments will follow a transition model: incidents of wife battering will be low for those home less than eight days; high for those home from eight to 30 days; and low for those home more than 30 days.*

METHODOLOGY

The Navy population considered for this study includes all active-duty enlisted male batterers residing in five base-housing complexes at an East Coast Naval installation. These housing complexes have 5445 units, and only enlisted personnel are assigned to them. Eighteen (18) percent of the allocations at these complexes are either enlisted Marine Corps personnel or active-duty enlisted Navy females, while the remaining 82 percent is evenly divided between active-duty enlisted Navy males assigned to shore and sea-duty commands.

This study utilizes records provided by the Naval Base Police on domestic disturbances at these housing complexes for 1992, 1993, and 1994. All record incidents of domestic violence requiring police intervention. The initial police data include 519 domestic disturbance-related calls such as husband-wife and parent-child conflicts. This data set does not include domestic homicides, rapes, or sexual assaults.

Of the 519 domestic disturbance calls, a total of 176 incomplete cases or cases involving incidents related to Marine Corps personnel, siblings, or parent-child conflicts were excluded from analysis. In addition, 50 cases were omitted because the enlisted perpetrator was either a female or a dependent husband. Therefore, 293 Naval Base Police reports on domestic disturbance calls are retained for analysis.

The Naval Base Police data have the following fields: date of incident; type of domestic disturbance (categorized by base police as either a *nonassault*, *simple assault*, or *aggravated assault*); gender, race, and birth date of the perpetrator; pay grade of the perpetrator; the commands to which perpetrators are assigned; and whether the incident was a repeat episode of marital violence.

In addition to the Naval Base Police data, ship deployment schedules were obtained from the Naval Historical Center in Washington, DC. This information allowed an analysis of correlations between the length of deployment and incidents of wife battering. Data from the deployment schedules were coded for each battering incident case (sea duty only) in the Naval Base Police data set.

Dependent Variable: Wife Battering

Naval Base Police classify domestic violence disturbances into three categories: nonassault, simple assault, and aggravated assault. The first of these, nonassault, is generally defined as some type of disorderly conduct, disturbance, or dispute between two spouses, but neither party is physically assaulted. This category includes verbal arguments and disagreements, verbal threats, and throwing or hitting inanimate objects due to anger. Even nonassault disturbances qualify for consideration because as Bell (1988, p. 92) has noted, "a domestic dispute is any quarrel, altercation, or strife . . . between household members." Usually, a family member (a spouse, child, other relative) or a neighbor will notify police to report domestic disturbances or disputes of this type.

The second category used by the Naval Base Police, simple assault, involves some type of physical violence or aggression against a spouse and includes hitting, slapping, pushing, biting, or kicking.

The third category of domestic-related calls, aggravated assault, relates to the intentional infliction of serious bodily injury with or without a weapon. Aggravated assaults include injuries caused by a knife or gun; physical abuse that results in broken bones or other serious injuries which require medical treatment; and threats made with a weapon, even if the abusive behavior is not consummated.

Utilizing the three categories of domestic-related disturbance calls identified by the Naval Base Police, this study measures wife battering as mild (verbal disputes or arguments between a husband and a wife and may include the throwing of objects–nonassault), moderate (simple assault), and severe (aggravated assault). The distinction between moderate and severe battering "parallels the legal one between simple and aggravated assault" (Smith, 1987, p. 179).

Independent Variable: Duty Assignment

Duty assignment, a dichotomous variable, is measured and defined as shore duty and sea duty. Shore duty includes all duty performed within the 48 contiguous states where Navy personnel are assigned to land-based activities and commands; sea duty includes an assignment to any ship (Mack & Paulsen, 1988; U.S. Department of Navy, 1993). Naval Base Police data identify the names of the commands to which the perpetrators are assigned for each domestic disturbance call. The names of these commands were evaluated as either shore-based activities or ships and were coded as shore duty or sea duty.

Intervening Variables: Deployment and Transition

This study considers two intervening variables. The first, length of deployment, is defined as the length of time a sailor assigned to a ship has been continuously deployed prior to a battering incident. This is measured by calculating the number of days deployed by examining the dates of departure from and arrival to the homeport on deployment schedules for the ships listed in the data. The dates of departure and arrival closest to the battering incident dates are used to determine the length of deployment. Since research suggests that long deployments can contribute to various stressors which may already affect the family unit and which can cause other family dysfunction (Patterson & McCubbin, 1984), the length of deployment was coded into four categories: 45 days or less, 46 to 90 days, 91 to 135 days, and more than 135 days. The length of deployment in this data set ranged from 2 days to 180 days.

The second intervening variable is transition period or what has been referred to as the "honeymoon period" (Thomas, 1995). Transition period is measured and defined as the number of days between a sailor's return home from a deployment and a battering incident. As Thomas (1995) notes, Navy Family Advocacy social workers observe an increase in reported wife-battering cases approximately two to three weeks after ships return home from deployments. Therefore, the transition period between the sailor's return home from deployment and a battering incident is further coded into three categories: less than 8 days, 8 to 30 days, and more than 30 days.

Analysis of Data

The statistical program SAS was used to analyze the data, and four procedures were utilized: frequencies, cross-tabulations, chi-square, and measures of association. Frequencies and descriptive statistics were used to examine each variable. Secondly, a cross-tabulation of the independent and dependent variables was conducted.

To test the hypotheses, chi-square was used to determine the statistical significance of the relationship between the independent and dependent variables. The frequency of wife battering severity was examined and compared for those assigned to sea and shore duty.

RESULTS

Wife Battering and Duty Assignment

The first hypothesis in this study states that the severity of wife battering by male Navy members is more prevalent among those with sea-duty assignments. Table 4-1 examines the severity of wife battering, comparing sea and shore-duty assignments. Utilizing chi-square, the differences between sea duty and shore duty are nearly significant at the .05 level (p=.087). Because the critical value to test the hypothesis is .05, the first research hypothesis is rejected. Also, gamma (.130) suggests that this is a weak relationship. However, within these data, 70 percent of those who battered their wives were assigned to sea duty, while only 30 percent of the batterers were assigned to shore duty. Further examination of Table 4-1 reveals that 18 percent of those assigned to sea duty committed severe battering and 40 percent committed moderate battering. In comparison, only eight percent of the shore-duty sailors inflicted severe battering, while the percentages of the mild and moderate wife battering categories are comparable between shore and sea-duty assignments. It is noted that twice as many of the sea-duty sailors engaged in severe battering as compared to the shore-duty sailors.

Because a problem may exist with the recording of nonassault domestic disturbances by the Naval Base Police, the mild category was temporarily eliminated from the data for further testing. Table 4-2 demonstrates a statistically significant relationship between wife battering severity and duty assignment when only the physical abuse categories are examined. Seventy-one percent of the sailors who physically assaulted their wives were assigned to sea duty, while 29 percent were assigned to shore duty. Additionally, 30 percent assigned to sea duty committed severe battering as compared to 14 percent of the shore-duty sailors. Thus, gamma (.449) indicates that a moderate relationship exists between the physical abuse categories of wife battering and duty assignment.

Table 4-1
PERCENTAGE DISTRIBUTION OF WIFE BATTERING SEVERITY
BY DUTY ASSIGNMENT

Wife Battering	Duty Assignment	
	Shore	Sea
Mild	42.7	40.2
Moderate	49.4	42.1
Severe	7.9	17.7
Total	100.0	100.0
(n)	(89)	(204)

Chi-square (df=2)=4.875
p>.05
Gamma=.130

Table 4-2
PERCENTAGE DISTRIBUTION OF WIFE BATTERING SEVERITY BY DUTY
ASSIGNMENT (MINUS THE MILD CATEGORY)

Wife Battering	Duty Assignment	
	Shore	Sea
Moderate	86.2	70.5
Severe	13.8	29.5
Total	100.0	100.0
(n)	(51)	(122)

Chi-square (df=1)=4.797
p<.05
Gamma=.449

Wife Battering and Length of Deployment

The second hypothesis states that male Navy members assigned to ships who have been deployed the longest are more likely to inflict severe battering. As Table 4-3 reflects, there is a clear pattern of relationship between wife battering and length of deployment. For the sailors deployed between two and 45 days, 78 percent of the battering is mild and none is severe. At the other extreme, for deployments between 136 and 180 days, only five percent of the battering is mild while 84 percent is severe. Furthermore, the majority, 56 percent of the sailors deployed between 91 and 135 days, engaged in severe battering. These results are statistically significant at the .0001 level; therefore, the research hypothesis is accepted. Additionally, gamma (.971) suggests that this is a strong relationship. Table 4-3 reveals that sailors who are deployed for more than 90 days are more likely to inflict severe battering.

Table 4-3
PERCENTAGE DISTRIBUTION OF WIFE BATTERING SEVERITY BY LENGTH
OF DEPLOYMENT, SEA DUTY ONLY

Wife Battering	Length of Deployment			
	2 to 45 days	46 to 90 days	91 to 135 days	136 to 180 days
Mild	77.9	0.0	0.0	5.3
Moderate	22.1	97.9	44.1	10.5
Severe	0.0	2.1	55.9	84.2
Total	100.0	100.0	100.0	100.0
(n)	(104)	(48)	(34)	(19)

Chi-square (df=6)=226.668
p<.0001
Gamma=.971

Wife Battering and Transition Period

The last hypothesis states that male Navy members who batter their wives upon returning home from deployments will follow a transition model: incidents of wife battering will be low for those home less than eight days; high for those home from eight to 30 days; and low for those home more than 30 days. Table 4-4 provides information about wife battering and transition period for sailors assigned to sea-duty commands; that is, this table illustrates the relationship between the number of days since a sailor has returned home from a deployment and a battering incident.

Clearly, 84 percent of the battering incidents occurred between eight and 30 days after sailors returned home from deployments. If battering occurs within the first week, it tends to be mild, 75 percent. Severe battering is most likely to occur after the first week but within the fist month, 20 percent. Only 10 percent of the sea-duty sailors battered their wives after being home less than eight days, and only six percent battered after being home more than 30 days from the end of their deployments. These results are statistically significant at the .05 level; therefore, the research hypothesis is accepted.

Table 4-4
PERCENTAGE DISTRIBUTION OF WIFE BATTERING SEVERITY BY
TRANSITION PERIOD, SEA DUTY ONLY

	Time Since Returning From Deployment		
Wife Battering	Less than 8 days	8 to 30 days	More than 30 days
Mild	75.0	35.3	50.0
Moderate	25.0	44.5	41.7
Severe	0.0	20.2	8.3
Total	100.0	100.0	100.0
(n)	(20)	(173)	(12)

Chi-square (df=4)=13.803
p<.05
Gamma=-.528

DISCUSSION

The primary objective of this study is to determine whether duty assign-ment affects wife battering. Among batterers included in this data set, most are assigned to sea duty, yet chi-square suggests that the severity of wife bat-tering is not related to duty assignment. As mentioned earlier, however, these results may reflect a problem in the way the Naval Base Police docu-mented domestic disturbance in their reports when there was no evidence of physical violence. For example, police officers responding to a housing unit on a domestic disturbance in which the husband and wife were arguing and/or were verbally abusive to each other will generally mediate the dis-pute and document the incident. The problem arises in that the officer arbi-trarily determines the perpetrator of the argument and completes an inci-dent/complaint report with the alleged perpetrator identified as the subject and the other spouse identified as the victim. In other words, the inclusion and coding of the mild category may be faulty because no physical evidence of abuse exists.

On the other hand, the police officer can more accurately determine the perpetrator of the incident when visual bruises or other forms of physical violence are evidenced. Consequently, moderate and severe battering may present a better picture of serious wife battering in relation to duty assignment. Upon eliminating the mild category of wife battering from the data, there is a relationship between the severity of wife battering and duty assignment.

Yet, because this study accepts the definition of wife battering as including both physical and verbal aggressiveness (Straus et al., 1980; Edleson, Eisikovits, & Guttman, 1985; Gelles, 1992), the mild category of batterers was retained and examined throughout this study in an effort to assess a more comprehensive picture of marital conflict within this sample.

Although there have been no studies conducted in the U.S. Navy to assess the prevalence of wife battering, other research suggests that stress-related factors, such as duty assignment, are associated with family violence (West et al., 1981; Neidig & Friedman, 1984; Sonkin et al., 1985). This may be true for the Navy more than the other military services, because an assignment to a ship may be more stressful than an assignment to a land-based command. Generally, sailors assigned to ships, as well as their families, have to adjust to the unpredictability of deployments (Patterson & McCubbin, 1984). Deployments do not just consist of six to eight-month tours; Navy ships routinely deploy for two to six weeks at a time for what is known as "workups." These "workups" prepare the Navy ships and their crews for longer deployments. Even when these ships are at the piers, the crews put in long hours by "standing watches," participating in various types of training, and maintaining their ships for battle. Therefore, sailors assigned to sea duty may be isolated from their families due to long hours and not just from long deployments. This may cause stress which could lead to wife battering if a sailor is prone to violence (Sonkin et al., 1985). Because stress seems to be a consistent theme in most family violence theories, it can not be ruled out as a possible mediating factor, especially for sailors assigned to sea duty.

Similarly, although there is no literature on the severity of wife battering in relationship to the length of deployment on Navy ships, other evidence suggests that prolonged frustration and stress may increase one's aggressive behavior (Dollard et al., 1939). Navy personnel deployed for long periods of time are isolated from their families, deprived of opportunities of self-expression, and lack any sense of privacy due to their living and sleeping arrangements (up to 30 or more sailors may live in a berthing area where they sleep on bunks, maintain their personal possessions in footlockers, and share communal rest rooms). Long deployments, seeming endless at times, may exaggerate these frustrations. As a result of increased frustration, sailors who return home from long deployments and are already prone to violence may engage in aggressive behavior toward their wives by severely battering them.

The third hypothesis, that the incidents of wife battering will be high from eight to 30 days after a sailor returns home from a deployment, is intended to identify a window of opportunity in which intervention can take place prior to the occurrence of a battering incident. As Table 4-4 reflects, the incidence of wife battering is high from eight to 30 days after sailors return home from deployments. Although the literature does not address wife battering and Navy deployments, representatives from the Navy Family Advocacy Program indirectly support this result because counselors notice an increase in wife-battering cases approximately two to three weeks after ships return from deployments (Thomas, 1995).

Regrettably, this research has some limitations, the primary one being in its design; only male batterers living in five Navy housing complexes were examined. Therefore, a determination of potential factors leading to battering can not be made. Additionally, these results can not be generalized. Overall, this research would have benefited if demographic information, such as age, pay grade, race, and duty assignment, could have been obtained for all male Navy members living in these housing complexes in order to compare the differences between batterers and nonbatterers.

Although additional research in this area is necessary, there appears to be a relationship between wife battering and duty assignment among those Navy members who batter. For sailors who batter, more are assigned to sea duty than to shore duty. Furthermore, battering sailors who have been deployed the longest appear to batter their wives with greater severity as compared to those with relatively short deployments. Finally, there is a short transition or "honeymoon" period between the time battering sailors return home from deployments and the first incidents of battering.

But what does all of this mean for the Navy? The Navy will always have ships, and sailors will always be assigned to these ships. In fact, the Navy has recently considered the implementation of longer deployments for economic reasons. Instead of six month deployments, the Navy is considering the possibility of extending these deployments to nine months. Weighing the results of this study and the potential for longer deployments, the Navy may need to address reasonable attempts to deter wife battering, particularly in relationship to duty assignments.

Currently, Navy Family Service Centers have programs in which teams of deployment education specialists fly out to the returning ships and provide return and reunion homecoming presentations. These teams conduct a variety of workshops focusing on personal relationships, financial concerns, and readjustment issues. Specific topics include the overall impact of sailors' return home for those who are married or in relationships; the re-establishment of physical and emotional intimacy in a relationship; adaptation to a new baby for the sailors who became fathers while deployed; basic information and practical advice on financial matters; and the most current information on helping agencies and resources available to assist Navy personnel who experience problems upon their return home (U.S. Department of Navy, 1992). However, this program neither addresses marital conflicts that may emerge, nor the potential root of these conflicts, and it does not deal with domestic violence issues.

In recent years, the Navy has adopted a "no tolerance" attitude about certain issues such as drug use, alcohol abuse, and sexual harassment. However, the Navy has virtually ignored domestic violence because of its private nature, though problems on the "home front" could lead to problems and various distractions at work, proving disastrous to an operational ship if the distracted sailor works in a critical area. The Navy should consider implementing domestic violence awareness seminars, which could be incorporated into the Navy Family Service Center's return and reunion homecoming program.

Finally, this study identifies a time frame when domestic violence seems to escalate after sailors return home from deployments. Knowing that there may be a window of opportunity for intervention prior to the occurrence of a battering incident is useful for the development of a program to combat wife battering. To borrow an adage from the business community, there is a bottom line. The Navy, as an organization, needs to become proactive in its approach to dealing with wife battering. Much of this can be accomplished through additional research and Navy-wide training programs and awareness seminars.

REFERENCES

Bandura, A. (1973). *Aggression: A Social Learning Analysis*. Englewood Cliffs, NJ: Prentice-Hall.

Bandura, A. (1977). *Social Learning Theory*. Englewood Cliffs: Prentice-Hall.

Bell, D. J. (1988). The victim-offender relationship: A determinant factor in police domestic dispute dispositions. *Marriage and Family Review, 12*, 87-102.

Bersani, C. A., & Chen, H. (1988). Sociological perspectives in family violence. In V. B. Van Hasselt, R. L. Morrison, A. S. Bellack, and M. Hersen (Eds.), *Handbook of Family Violence* (pp. 57-86). New York: Plenum Press.

Cantos, A. L., Neidig, P. H., & O'Leary, K. D. (1993). Men's and women's attributions of blame for domestic violence. *Journal of Family Violence, 8*, 289-302.

Cantos, A. L., Neidig, P. H., & O'Leary, K. D. (1994). Injuries of women and men in a treatment program for domestic violence. *Journal of Family Violence, 9*, 113-124.

Cronin, C. (1995). Adolescent reports of parental spousal violence in military and civilian families. *Journal of Interpersonal Violence, 10*, 117-122.

Dobash, R. E., & Dobash, R. P. (1979). *Violence Against Wives: A Case Against the Patriarchy*. New York: Free Press.

Dollard, J., Doob, L. W., Miller, N. E., Mowrer, O. H., & Sears, R. R. (1939). *Frustration and Aggression.* New Haven: Yale University Press.

Eastman, E. S. (1988). An investigation of the relationship between Naval deployment and indices of family functions. Ph.D. dissertation, Virginia Consortium for Professional Psychology, Norfolk, VA.

Edleson, J. L., Eisikovits, Z., & Guttman, E. (1985). Men who batter women: A critical review of the evidence. *Journal of Family Issues, 6,* 229-247.

Etzioni, A. (1971). Violence. In R. K. Merton & R. Nisbet (Eds.), *Contemporary Social Problems* (3rd ed.) (pp. 709-741). New York: Harcourt Brace Jovanovich.

Farrington, K. (1986). The application of stress theory to the study of family violence: Principles, problems, and prospects. *Journal of Family Violence, 1,* 131-147.

Gelles, R. J. (1992). Methodological issues in the study of family violence. In M. A. Straus, R. J. Gelles, & C. Smith (Eds.), *Physical Violence in American Families: Risk Factor and Adaptations to Violence in 8,145 Families* (pp. 17-28). New Brunswick, NJ: Transaction.

Gelles, R. J., & Cornell, C. P. (1990). *Intimate Violence in Families* (2nd ed.). Newbury Park, CA: Sage.

Gelles, R. J., & Straus, M. A. (1979). Determinants of violence in the family: Toward a theoretical integration. In W. R. Burr, R. Hill, F. I. Nye, & I. L. Reiss (Eds.), *Contemporary Theories About the Family,* vol. 1 (pp. 549-581). New York: Free Press.

Griffin, W. A., & Morgan, A. R. (1988). Conflict in maritally distressed military couples. *American Journal of Family Therapy, 16,* 14-22.

Hansen, D. A., & Johnson, V. A. (1979). Rethinking family stress theory: Definitional aspects. In W. R. Burr, R. Hill, F. I. Nye, & I. L. Reiss (Eds.), *Contemporary Theories About the Family,* vol. 1 (pp. 582-603). New York: Free Press.

Hill, R. (1949). *Families Under Stress.* New York: Harper and Row.

Mack, W. P., & Paulsen, T. D. (1988). *The Naval Officer's Guide* (9th ed.). Annapolis, MD: Naval Institute Press.

McCubbin, H. I., & Patterson, J. M. (1983). Family transitions: Adaptation to stress. In H. I. McCubbin & C. R. Figley (Eds), *Stress and the Family,* vol. 1 (pp. 5-25). New York: Brunner/Mazel.

Montalvo, F. F. (1976). Family separation in the Army: A study of the problems encountered and the caretaking resources used by career Army families undergoing military separation. In H. I. McCubbin, B. B. Dahl, & E. J. Hunter (Eds.), *Families in the Military System* (pp. 147-173). Beverly Hills, CA: Sage.

Neidig, P. H. (1985). Domestic violence in the military, part I: Research findings and program implications. *Military Family, 5,* 3-6.

Neidig, P. H., & Friedman, D. H. (1984). *Spouse Abuse: A Treatment Program for Couples.* Champaign, IL: Research Press.

Pan, H. S., Neidig, P. H., & O'Leary, K. D. (1994a). Male-female and aggressor-victim differences in the factor structure of the Modified Conflict Tactics Scale. *Journal of Interpersonal Violence, 9,* 367-382.

Pan, H. S., Neidig, P. H., & O'Leary, K. D. (1994b). Predicting mild and severe husband-to-wife physical aggression. *Journal of Consulting and Clinical Psychology, 62,* 975-981.

Patterson, J. M., & McCubbin, H. I. (1984). Gender roles and coping. *Journal of Marriage and Family, 46,* 95-104.

Schwabe, M. R., & Kaslow, F. W. (1984). Violence in the military family. In F. W. Kaslow & R. I. Ridenour (Eds.), *The Military Family* (pp. 125-146). New York: Guilford Press.

Smith, M. D. (1987). The incidence and prevalence of woman abuse in Toronto. *Violence and Victims, 2,* 173-187.

Sonkin, D. J., Martin, D., & Walker, L. E. (1985). *The Male Batterer: A Treatment Approach.* New York: Springer.

Straus, M. A., Gelles, R. J., & Steinmetz, S. K. (1980). *Behind Closed Doors: Violence in the American Family.* Garden City, NY: Doubleday.

Thomas, A. (1995). Personal interview, August 23, Norfolk, VA.

Thorman, G. (1980). *Family Violence.* Springfield, IL: Charles C Thomas.

U.S. Department of Navy. (1992). *Navy Family Deployment Guide.* Norfolk, VA: Navy Family Service Center.

U.S. Department of Navy. (1993). *Enlisted Transfer Manual.* Washington, DC: Bureau of Naval Personnel.

Waldo, M. (1986). Group counseling for military personnel who battered their wives. *Journal for Specialists in Group Work, 11,* 132-38.

West, L. A., Turner, W. M., & Dunwoody, E. (1981). *Wife Abuse in the Armed Forces.* Washington, DC: Center for Women Policy Studies.

Chapter 5

ABUSE AND MENTAL HEALTH OUTCOMES IN MILITARY PREGNANT WOMEN

PHYLLIS W. SHARPS, LORETTA CEPIS, AND BETH GERING

INTRODUCTION

Violence threatens the health and well-being of more than 1.8 million women of childbearing age annually (Gelles & Straus, 1990). Previous research has demonstrated that pregnancy does not assure women protection from abuse (Campbell & Humphreys, 1993); in fact, for some women pregnancy may increase their risk for abuse. As many as 16 percent of women in the general population report battering during pregnancy (Smith, 1995). Moreover, violence has become a leading cause of mortality for women during the childbearing years and the immediate postpartum period (Bachman, 1994). Fildes, Reed, and Jones (1993) found that trauma accounted for 46 percent of the deaths for pregnant women in an urban sample. The mechanism of injury for maternal traumatic deaths was attributed to gunshot wounds, motor vehicle crashes, stab wounds, strangulation, blunt head wounds, burns and falls. In the majority of incidences of violence against women, the perpetrator was her intimate partner. These women suffered the consequences of both physical and mental harm to themselves and physical harm to their unborn children.

A growing body of research has documented the prevalence of abuse during pregnancy in the general population of women. However, to date there have been no published studies that have documented the prevalence of battering during pregnancy among military spouses, dependent daughters, and/or active duty military pregnant females.

LITERATURE REVIEW

Abuse Defined

Abuse or intimate partner abuse is defined as repeated physical or sexual assault from an intimate partner within the context of coercive control (Campbell & Humphreys, 1993). Across all domestic violence incidents, approximately 90 percent of the violence is battering of the female partner by her male partner, with 6–7 percent being mutual violence and 2–3 percent that of females battering male partners (Campbell & Humphreys, 1993). In most cases, female battering of the male is self-defense. In cases of males battering females and mutual male-female battering, the violence threatens the health and well being of women (Smith, 1995).

Abuse in Pregnancy

Pregnancy may stimulate the first episode of domestic violence or escalate an already abusive relationship (Campbell, Poland & Walker, 1992). Prevalence rates of domestic violence reported during pregnancy reveal a range from 0.9 percent to 25 percent among women seeking prenatal care (Saltzman & Johnson, 1996; Gielen, O'Campo, Faden, Kass, & Xue, 1994; Amaro, Fried, & Cabral, 1990). Helton, McFarlane, and Anderson (1987) reported a prevalence rate of 23 percent, which was obtained by personal interviews with women enrolled in prenatal clinics. O'Campo, Gielen, Faden, and Kass (1994) studied prevalence and categorized violence into moderate (threats) and severe (reported battering). They found that 20 percent of the women entering prenatal care reported abuse. Parker, McFarlane, and Soeken (1994) and Gielen et al. (1994) have reported similar rates (19%) of women reporting abuse during pregnancy. In one of the few large ethnically diverse samples (N=691), Parker et al. (1994) reported that 19 percent of the African American and Caucasian women and 14 percent of the Hispanic women reported abuse during the current pregnancy. While most studies of abuse during pregnancy are cross-sectional or end with delivery, Gielen et al. (1994) reported that 19 percent of the women reported moderate to severe abuse during pregnancy, while 25 percent of the women reported severe abuse during the first six months postpartum. These studies demonstrate that while for some women pregnancy and the birth of an infant are protective periods from abuse, for others, pregnancy and/or birth may increase their risk for battering.

There are several conditions that have been found to increase a woman's risk for abuse during pregnancy. A primary predictor of abuse during pregnancy is abuse prior to pregnancy. Helton (1987) found that 87.5 percent of women who were abused during the current pregnancy had been abused prior to becoming pregnant. Stewart and Cecutti (1993), in their study of women who were 20 or more weeks pregnant, found similar results: 86 percent of their sample had been abused before the current pregnancy.

Other researchers have found that as the level of both the husband's and wife's education increases, abuse decreases (Campbell, Poland, & Walker, 1992; Sampselle, Petersen, & Murtland, 1992). Unplanned pregnancy, younger age (<20 years), and being unmarried are other variables that have been associated with increased risk for abuse during pregnancy (Medical Association, 1992). From qualitative studies, there is also an indication that male-partner jealousy, of the unborn child or if the male partner thinks the baby is someone else's, is a factor in abuse during pregnancy (Campbell et al., 1992).

Abuse and Perinatal Outcomes

Abuse during pregnancy has been associated with both poor maternal and pregnancy outcomes. It is a hazard to the health of the mother and the developing fetus. Poor outcomes have included traumatic injuries to the mother which have resulted in preterm labor, preterm birth miscarriages, and low birth-weight infants (Donovan, 1995; Dye, Tollivert, & Kenney, 1995). Additionally, physical abuse during pregnancy has been associated with inadequate or late entry into prenatal caring (Campbell et al., 1992; Sampselle et al., 1992). Additionally, both abused teen and adult women are 2–3 times more likely to enter prenatal care during the third trimester (Sampselle et al., 1992). In all cases and across all ethnic groups, both abused teen and adult women were found to be at greater risk for delivering infants who weighed less. These women also showed lower pregnancy weight gains, shorter intervals (<24 months) between pregnancies, and the use of substances such as cigarettes, alcohol, or drugs during the current pregnancy (Sampselle et al., 1992). All of these conditions found among women who are abused and pregnant contribute to poor maternal health and birth outcomes.

Abuse and Mental Health Outcomes in Perinatal Populations

There is a growing body of research that provides evidence of the link between perinatal abuse and maternal mental health. Several researchers (Smith, 1995; Hall, Gurley, Sachs, & Kryscio, 1991; Sampselle et al., 1993) have shown that abuse during pregnancy is correlated with mental health outcomes such as anxiety, depression, isolation, and substance abuse.

Previous research studies suggest that these poor mental health outcomes are linked with poor prenatal weight gain, increased use of alcohol, cigarettes, and cocaine. Such health behaviors are associated with adverse neonatal outcomes in the general population of women (Berenson, Stiglich, & Wilkinson, 1989; Zuckerman, Amaro, Bauchner, & Cabral, 1989). There is also evidence of a direct relationship of abuse during pregnancy with prenatal substance use/abuse and adverse infant outcomes such as low birthweight (Parker et al., 1994).

Depression and low self-esteem are the two mental-health outcomes that have been most often studied among abused women. Depression is a syndrome of complex symptoms, characterized by dysphoric mood or loss of interest or pleasure in all or most usual activities or pastimes (Beck, 1970; Shaver & Brennan, 1991). Self-esteem is defined as the evaluation an individual makes and customarily maintains with regard to self, usually expressed as an attitude of approval or disapproval (Rosenberg, 1965). Whether measured as depressive symptoms or as psychiatric diagnosis, abused women have consistently been found to be more depressed than nonabused women, and abused woman are often depressed more than any other psychiatric diagnosis in a variety of studies (Campbell, Kub, & Rose, 1996; Gleason, 1993). Although less often measured in studies of abuse during pregnancy, the pattern of depression as the primary mental-health response in battered women seems to be consistent. Torres (1992) found higher levels of depressive symptoms in abused pregnant women than nonabused pregnant women in a convenience sample of 65 women in their third trimester of pregnancy. Campbell et al. (1992) also found abuse during pregnancy was associated with depressive symptoms at the time of delivery in a controlled study of 400 low-income urban women in Detroit.

Additionally, women's self-esteem has also been shown to be affected by domestic violence, with the majority of studies revealing that abused women have lower self-esteem than those not abused (Cascardi & O'Leary, 1992). Torres (1992) found significantly lower self-esteem in pregnant women who were abused than those who were not.

Abuse in Military Perinatal Populations

Several studies document the prevalence of domestic abuse in military families. These studies have attempted to look at environmental and military contexts and their relationships to abuse in military families. To date, these studies' limitations involve samples which are not representative of all ranks in the Armed Forces, samples that prevent representation of all military populations, or samples that include only substantiated cases from married couples (Hurlbert, Whitaker, & Munoz, 1991; Neidig, 1985). Researchers conclude that abuse exists in the military, and more studies are needed (Miller & Veltkamp, 1993). As yet, there have been no population-based or random-sample studies published that examine self-reported abuse and its relationship to depressive symptoms and self-esteem in military perinatal populations.

PURPOSE OF THE STUDY

This preliminary study examines the relationship of self-reported abuse and self-reported depressive symptomatology and low self-esteem in military perinatal populations. Several assumptions were made for this study: that military pregnant women are not immune to abuse, that military pregnant women face threats to their health and well-being similar to women in the general population, and that the results of this study would be useful in the development of future research protocols, as well as in the development of interventions suitable to the special needs of military women.

METHODOLOGY

This study is a cross-sectional, nonexperimental survey of military pregnant women. The obstetrical-gynecological clinics of two military hospitals (Air Force and Navy) on the East Coast were used to recruit women for the study. The two sites selected had a combined delivery rate of 2000 deliveries annually.

Sample

The convenience sample consisted of 298 pregnant women. The subjects were either active-duty military women or dependent wives or daughters of an active-duty military member from all branches of the Armed Forces. The only criterion for inclusion in the sample was that the women received prenatal care at either study site between November, 1995 and January, 1996. All women were invited to participate in the study regardless of age, gestation, socioeconomic status, race, or rank. Women were excluded from the sample if they had literacy problems which prevented them from reading or responding to the survey instruments. Written informed consent was obtained prior to giving the women the surveys to complete.

Instruments

The Women's Pregnancy Well Being Assessment Survey (Figure 5-1) was developed by the investigators using three existing measures of abuse, depressive symptomatology, and self-esteem: the Abuse Assessment Screen (AAS), Beck Depression Inventory (BDI), and the Rosenberg Self-Esteem Scale (RSE). The survey also contained 20 items designed to elicit demographic background data about the women and their partners. Seemingly, these data are pertinent to understanding domestic abuse in a military population.

Abuse Assessment Screen (AAS)

The Nursing Research Consortium on Violence and Abuse (Parker & McFarlane, 1991; Parker, McFarlane, Soeken, Torres, & Campbell, 1993) developed the Abuse Assessment Screen (AAS). The five-item AAS has been widely used to establish the prevalence of abuse during pregnancy (Norton, Peipert, Zieler, Lima, & Hume, 1995; McFarlane, Parker, Soeken, & Bullock, 1992; Parker et al., 1993; Parker et al., 1994). The AAS consists of five questions to determine the severity, frequency, perpetrator, and sites of bodily injury which occurred during a stated period of time. The content validity for the AAS screen has been established by a panel of 12 nurse researchers of White, African American, and Hispanic ethnicities who have both worked with and studied abused woman. Questions 2, 3, and 4 have well established criterion-related validity ($p < .001$). The scores for these 3 questions were also compared with the Conflict Tactics Scale of the Index of Spouse Abuse (ISA) and the Danger Assessment Scale (DAS) (Soeken, McFarlane & Parker, 1995). Test-retest reliability was established for the AAS using an ethnically stratified cohort of women (n=48; n=40). The test-retest reliability assessment resulted in 83 percent and 100 percent agreement for the two samples respectively (Soeken et al., 1995). For this study, women who answered yes to either question 2, 3, or 4 were considered "abused." Also, women answering yes to question 3 were considered abused during pregnancy.

Figure 5-1a

Woman's Perinatal Well-Being Assessment Survey
(Phase I)
Please fill in or circle the answers to the following questions as best you can

How many times have you been pregnant? _____ Living Children? _____

How far along are you in your pregnancy?
   1st Trimester (less 12 weeks), 2nd Trimester (12-23 weeks), 3rd Trimester (24-42 weeks)

Marital Status: Married   Single   Separated   Divorced

Age: (self) _____ (partner)_____

Race (Circle)
   (self) American Indian or Alaska Native   (partner) American Indian or Alaska Native
          Asian or Pacific Islander   Asian or Pacific Islander
          Black, not of Hispanic origin   Black, not of Hispanic origin
          Hispanic   Hispanic
          White, not of Hispanic origin   White, not of Hispanic origin

Are you a U.S. Citizen? YES   NO   If you answered No, what country are you from? _____

Rank/Grade: (self)   Air Force, Army, Coast Guard, Marine Corps, Navy, Public Health Service
              (partner)   Air Force, Army, Coast Guard, Marine Corps, Navy, Public Health Service

How long have you been with your current partner? < 1 year, 1-3 yrs, 5-7 yrs, 8-10 yrs. >10 yrs.

Is your current partner the baby's father? YES   NO

Circle the HIGHEST level of education you have achieved:
   Some High School, High School Graduate, Some College, College Degree, Graduate Degree

I am a Dependent YES   NO   I work outside the home   YES   NO

How long have you lived at your current duty station? <1 year, 1-2 yrs, 3-4 yrs, 5-6 yrs, <7 yrs.

Do you live on base? YES   NO

How many times have you or your partner been separated due to the military (e.g. Deployment, training) in the last three years? None, 1-3 times, 4-6 times, 7-10 times, > 10 times

Total months separation: None, 1-3 months, 4-6 months, 7-10 months, 11-12 months, >1 years

Do you have supportive family members or close friends who live in the local area (within 100 miles)? YES   NO

Do you have friends/or peers within your community (military) who you suspect are abused by their significant other? YES   NO

Were your ever a victim of abuse in your family of origin? YES   NO
If YES, was the abuse: Emotional, Physical or Sexual

Would it bother/offend you if a health care provider asked you if you had ever been hit by your partner? YES   NO

Prior to today, were you aware of abuse services in your local community? YES   NO

Did your significant other accompany you to your prenatal appointment today? YES   NO

Figure 5-1b

On this questionnaire are groups of statements. Please read each group of statements carefully. The pick out the one statement in each group which best describe the way you have been feeling in the PAST WEEK, INCLUDING TODAY! Circle the number beside the statement you picked. If several statements in the group seem to apply equally well, circle each one. Be sure to read all the statements in each group before making your choice.

1. 3 I have not appetite at all anymore.
    2 My appetite is much worse now.
    1 My appetite is not as good as it used to be.
    0 My appetite is no worse than usual.

2. 3 I feel that the future is hopeless and that things cannot improve.
    2 I feel I have nothing to look forward to.
    1 I feel discouraged about the future.
    0 I am not particularly pessimistic or discouraged about the future.

3. 3 I feel I am a complete failure as a person (parent, parent, partner, wife).
    2 As I look back on my life, all I can see is a lot of failures.
    1 I feel I have failed more than the average person.
    0 I do not feel like a failure.

4. 3 I am dissatisfied with everything.
    2 I don't get satisfaction out of anything anymore.
    1 I don't enjoy things the way I used to.
    0 I am not particularly dissatisfied.

5. 3 I feel as though I am very bad or worthless.
    2 I feel quite guilty.
    1 I feel bad or unworthy a good part of the time.
    0 I don't feel particularly guilty.

6. 3 I hate myself.
    2 I am disgusted with myself.
    1 I am disappointed in myself.
    0 I don't feel disappointed in myself.

7. 3 I get too tired to do anything.
    2 I get tired from doing anything.
    1 I get tired more easily than I used to.
    0 I don't get any more tired than usual.

8. 3 I have lost all of my interest in other people and don't care about them at all.
    2 I have lost most of my interest in other people and have little feeling for them.
    1 I am less interested in other people than I used to be.
    0 I have not lost interest in other people.

9. 3 I can't make any decisions at all anymore.
    2 I have great difficulty in making decisions.
    1 I try to put off making decisions.
    0 I make decisions about as well as ever.

10. 3 I feel that I am ugly or repulsive-looking
    2 I feel that there are permanent changes in my appearance and they make me look unattractive.
    1 I am worried that I am looking old or unattractive.
    0 I don't feel that I look any worse than I used to.

11. 3 I can't do any work at all.
    2 I have to push myself very hard to do anything.
    1 It takes extra effort to get started at doing something.
    0 I can work about as well as before.

12. 3 I would kill myself if I had a chance.
    2 I have definite plans about committing suicide.
    1 I feel I would be better off dead.
    0 I don't have any thoughts of harming myself.

13. 3 I am so sad or unhappy that I can't stand it.
    2 I am blue or sad all the time and I can't snap out of it.
    1 I feel sad or blue.
    0 I do not feel sad.

Used with permission of Aaron T. Beck, M.D.

Read the statements below. Circle the answer that BEST expersses/describes your feelings about the statement.

SA=Strongly Agree   A=Agree   D=Disagree   SD=Strongly Disagree

	SA	A	D	SD
1. I feel that I am a person of worth, at least on equal basis with others.	SA	A	D	SD
2. I feel that I have a number of good qualities.	SA	A	D	SD
3. All in all, I am inclined to feel that I am a failure.	SA	A	D	SD
4. I am able to do things as well as most other people.	SA	A	D	SD
5. I feel I do not have much to be proud of.	SA	A	D	SD
6. I take a positive attitude toward myself.	SA	A	D	SD
7. On the whole, I am satisfied with myself.	SA	A	D	SD
8. I wish I could have more respect for myself.	SA	A	D	SD
9. I certainly feel useless at times.	SA	A	D	SD
10. At times I think I am not good at all.	SA	A	D	SD

Figure 5-1c

(Circle YES or NO for each question)

1. Have you ever been physically hurt by someone? YES   NO

2. Within the last year, have you been hit, slapped, kicked, or otherwise physically hurt by someone? YES   NO
   If YES, by whom (circle all that apply) Husband   Ex-husband   Boyfriend   Stranger   Other   Multiple
   Total number of times _____

3. Since you've been pregnant, have you been hit, slapped, kicked, or otherwise physically hurt by someone?
   YES NO
   If YES, by whom (circle all that apply) Husband   Ex-husband   Boyfriend   Stranger   Other   Multiple
   Total number of times _____

Mark (with an X) the area of injury on the body map then place a   SCORE
score next to each incident according to the following scale:

1=Threat of abuse including the use of a weapon
2=Slapping, pushing; no injuries of lasting pain
3=Punching, kicking, bruises, cuts and/or lasting pain
4=Beating up, severe contusions, burns, broken bones
5=Head injury, internal injury, permanent injury
6=Use of a weapon; wound from weapon

(If any of the descriptions for the higher number apply,
us the higher number)

4. Within the last year, has anyone forced you to have sexual activities? YES   NO
   If YES, by whom (circle all that apply) Husband   Ex-husband   Boyfriend   Stranger   Other   Multiple
   Total number of times _____

5. Have you ever been hit, slapped, kicked or otherwise physcially hurt by someone since delivering your baby?
   YES NO
   If YES, by whom (circle all that apply) Husband   Ex-husband   Boyfriend   Stranger   Other   Multiple
   Total number of times _____

6. Are you afraid of your current partner or anyone listed above? YES   NO

7. During the 12 months before this pregnancy, have you been slapped, kicked, or otherwise physcially hurt by
   someone? YES   NO
   If YES, by whom (circle all that apply) Husband   Ex-husband   Boyfriend   Stranger   Other   Multiple
   Total number of times _____

8. During the 12 months before this pregnancy has anyone forced you to have sexual activities? YES   NO
   If YES, by whom (circle all that apply) Husband   Ex-husband   Boyfriend   Stranger   Other   Multiple
   Total number of times _____

Beck Depression Inventory (BDI)

The short form of the BDI (Figure 5-1b) was used to study the relationship between depressive symptomatology and abuse during pregnancy in military women. The BDI is the most recognized and frequently used self-report measure of depressive symptomatology. The short form of the BDI, consisting of 13 items, addresses four domains of depression: behavioral, affective, cognitive, and physiological. The short form of the BDI is designed to assess the intensity of depressive symptomatology in terms of the following 13 symptom-attitude categories: mood, pessimism, sense of failure, lack of satisfaction, feelings of guilt, self-dislike, suicidal wishes, social withdrawal, indecisiveness, distortion of body image, work inhibition, fatigability, and loss of appetite (Shaver & Brennan, 1991). Each statement is rated in terms of the severity of the symptom; whereas a "0" indicates the absence of a symptom-attitude, a "3" indicates maximum severity. Beck and Beck (1972) have suggested the following cut-off scores for the short BDI: 0–4 none or minimal; 5–7 mild; 8–15 moderate; and 16 and above severe depressive symptomatology. These cut-off scores were used to interpret the findings from this study. The short form of the BDI is considered to be as reliable and valid as the more widely used 21 symptom-attitude BDI (Shaver & Brennan, 1991). The short form is highly correlated with the longer BDI (.96). Convergent validity of the short BDI has been reported to range from .60 to .90 (Shaver & Brennan, 1991).

Rosenberg Self-Esteem Scale (RSE)

This scale was used to examine the relationship between abuse and self-esteem. The RSE (Figure 5-1b), designed to measure one's global feelings of self worth or self-acceptance (Rosenberg, 1979), is one of the most widely used measures of global self-esteem (Blascovich & Tomaka, 1991). In addition, the instrument has been extensively used in nursing research to assess self-esteem in pregnant women (Curry, Campbell, & Christian, 1994; Kemp & Page, 1987; Mercer & Ferketrich, 1988; Norbeck & Tilden, 1983). The instrument has proved to be reliable with test-retest coefficients ranging from .84 to .87 (Norbeck & Tilden, 1983; Mercer & Ferketrich, 1988) and a coefficient alpha of 0.88 (Flemming & Courtney, 1988). For the current study, the Cronbach's coefficient alpha was 0.90. Additionally, the RSE has been deemed valid because of its correlation with several other self-esteem concepts and positively correlated with measures of low-esteem such as depression and anxiety (Flemming & Courtney, 1984). The scale consists of ten statements, half (5) of which are positively worded and include statements related to feeling worthwhile, having a positive attitude, and self-satisfaction. The other five statements are negatively worded and include statements related to feelings of uselessness or failure. The response categories range from 1 (Strongly Disagree) to 4 (Strongly Agree). Statements 1, 2, 4, 6, and 7 are positively worded and scored as described above. Statements 3, 5, 8, 9, and 10 are negatively worded and are reverse scored. The RSE scores can range from 10–40, with higher scores representing increased self-esteem (Rosenberg, 1965; Rosenberg, 1979).

Procedures

Prior to data collection for the study, approval was obtained from the institutional review boards at the two military hospital sites and from the University of Maryland. All pregnant women at the two clinic sites were asked to participate. Women who agreed to participate completed the surveys in a quiet location in the clinic away from their partners. Of the 317 women who were approached during the study period, 298 completed the surveys, yielding an overall response rate of 94 percent. Five women (1.5%) declined to participate, and four women were ineligible to participate because of literacy problems. Another 10 women (3.1%) did not return surveys. The surveys, which were distributed in a self-sealed envelope, also contained a plain white business card that had the telephone number for the national domestic violence hot-line and local community domestic violence resources. Women were encouraged to take the cards and keep them in a safe place or to return them in the sealed envelope with the completed study instruments. Anecdotally, it was learned that many women took the cards to pass on to friends or neighbors.

The data were analyzed using descriptive statistics, Pearson's correlation, t-tests, and chi-square. The level of significance set for all analysis procedures was 0.05.

RESULTS

The demographic characteristics of the sample are presented in Table 5-1. The sample was diverse in both the ethnicity and military status of the women. The ethnic groups of the women included in the sample were as follows: White (71.2%); black, not Hispanic (18.2%); Hispanic (5.5%); Asian American (3.4%); and Native American Indian (1.7%). The mean age of women was 26 (range 16 to 42 years); 89.6 percent were married (on average of 3.8 years), and 97.3 percent reported having at least a high-school diploma. Among the women returning surveys (Table 5-2), 73.3 percent were dependents of active-duty members, 21 percent active-duty enlisted personnel, and 5.4 percent active-duty officers. All branches of the Armed Forces were included in the sample: Air Force (38%), Navy (25.8%), Army (22.2%), Marine Corps (8.6%), Coast Guard (3.9%), and Public Health Service (1.4%).

Table 5-1
DEMOGRAPHIC CHARACTERISTICS OF THE SAMPLE

Variable	Mean	(SD)
Age (self)	26.97 years	5.43
Age (partner)	29.12 years	5.98
Length of Current Relationship	3.88 years	1.65
Number of Pregnancies	2.41	1.27
Gestational Age	27.3 weeks	8.64
Children	.84	.82

Table 5-2
SOCIODEMOGRAPHIC CHARACTERISTICS OF THE SAMPLE

Variable	Number (n)	Percent(%)
Race (Self)		
Asian American	10	3.4
Black, not Hispanic	53	18.2
Hispanic	16	5.5
Native American	5	1.7
White, not Hispanic	208	70.1
Marital Status		
Married	266	89.6
Not Married	31	10.4
Branch of Service of Family		
Air Force	106	38.0
Army	62	22.2
Coast Guard	11	3.9
Public Health	4	1.4
Marines	24	8.6
Navy	72	25.8
Rank		
Dependent of Active Duty	217	73.3
Enlisted	62	21.0
Officer	19	5.7

Education (Self)		
Some high school	8	2.7
High school graduate	64	21.5
Some College	119	39.9
College Graduate	77	25.8
Graduate Degree	30	10.1

Table 5-3 presents the abuse status of the women. Fifty-four women (18.3%) reported abuse in their family of origin. The abused women included active-duty women (43%/12), dependent wives (43%/12), and dependent daughters (14%/4). Among the women included in the sample, 27 women (9.1%) reported being abused in the last year, and five women (1.7%) indicated that they had been forced to have sex in the last year. Ten women (3.4%) reported being abused during the current pregnancy. In all cases of reported abuse or forced sex, the husband was reported as being the most frequent perpetrator (48%–50%), followed by boyfriends (25%–50%). When asked about the frequency of abuse, women described being physically hurt on the average of three times within the last year and two times during the current pregnancy. Women reported being forced into sexual activities about two times during the last year. The most common forms of physical abuse reported by the women were punching and kicking, with bruises and cuts having lasting pain (48%/12), and slapping and pushing with no lasting pain (36%/9).

Table 5-3
PREVALENCE OF ABUSE IN THE SAMPLE USING THE AAS

Question	Number (n)	Percent (%)
Physically hurt by someone in the last year		
No	271	90.9
Yes	27	9.1
If hurt, by whom		
Husband	12	48
Boyfriend	9	36
Other	5	12
Multiple	1	4
Physically hurt since pregnant		
No	288	96.6
Yes	10	3.4
Forced sexual activities in the last year		
No	293	98.3
Yes	5	1.7

If forced, by whom		
Husband	2	50
Boyfriend	2	50

Table 5-4
DEMOGRAPHICS OF ABUSED AND NONABUSED WOMEN

Variable	Abused (n)	Nonabused (n)
Family Military Rank*		
Enlisted	22	155
Officer	2	94
Marital Status**		
Married	18	248
Single	9	22

*Chi-square=8.30 (df=1), p<.01
**Chi-square=16.65 (df=1), p<.001

The chi-square analysis revealed that there were two demographic characteristics that were significantly different among the abused and nonabused women: military rank and marital status (Table 5-4). Identified abusers were most likely to be enlisted personnel (n=21, E–1 to E-6). In one case, the perpetrator was identified as a noncommissioned officer and in two cases as officers. The abused women were also unmarried (30% vs. 7%).

The specific mental-health outcomes examined in this study were self-reported depressive symptomatology and self-esteem (Table 5-5). The Beck Depression Inventory (BDI) was used to assess depressive symptomatology. The mean BDI score for the total sample was 3.61. Scores falling between 0 to 4 on the short BDI are considered to indicate no or minimal depressive symptomatology (Beck & Beck, 1972). Scores between 5 and 7 on the short BDI are indicative of mild depressive symptomatology. The mean BDI score for the nonabused women was 3.25 compared to the abused women's mean score of 7.0. The t-test analysis of the scores between abuse was significantly different (t=5.23, p<.001). There was also a significant positive correlation between abuse as identified with the AAS and the BDI score (r=.2931, p<.001).

The Rosenberg Self-Esteem Scale (RSE) was used to examine self-esteem in the sample of women participating in the study. The mean score for the nonabused women was 34.58 compared to the abused women's mean score of 30.50. Scores on the RSE can range between 10 and 40 with higher scores indicating higher self-esteem (Rosenberg, 1965; 1979). The t-test analysis revealed the differences were significant (t=3.71, p<.001). Pearson's correlation revealed a significant negative relationship (r=.2377, p<.01) between abuse and self-esteem.

Table 5-5
MENTAL HEALTH OUTCOMES AND ABUSE

Variables	r	P – Value
AAS/Self-Esteem	–.2377	< .01
AAS/BDI	.2931	< .001

DISCUSSION

In this preliminary study of 298 pregnant women, the Abuse Assessment Screen (AAS) was found to be an effective, anonymous, self-reporting, screening measure among military women for the identification of abuse during pregnancy. Using the AAS screen, 9.1 percent of the women reported physical abuse in the last year, and 3.4 percent were abused during the current pregnancy. There are no comparable military studies of abuse during pregnancy. However, in civilian populations, many studies have reported the prevalence of abuse in pregnancy to range from 0.9 to 25 percent (Amaro et al., 1990; Anderson, McFarlane, & Helton, 1986; Bullock & McFarlane, 1989; Campbell et al., 1992; Gazmararian, et al., 1996; Gielen et al., 1994; Helton, 1986; Helton, McFarlane, & Anderson 1987a, 1987b; Helton & Snodgrass, 1987; McFarlane et al., 1991, 1992; Stewart & Cecutti, 1993). The variations in prevalence rates reported is most often related to methods used to assess abuse. Studies that use personal interviews and systematic assessment of abuse throughout the pregnancy yield the highest prevalence rates (Parker et al., 1994). Therefore, although the 3.4 percent of the women reporting abuse during the current pregnancy fall within the lower prevalence-rate ranges, it is likely to be the result of underreporting of abuse during pregnancy among military women. On the other hand, it may indicate that pregnancy is a protective period for some women and if this is the case, it reinforces the need for continued screening before and after pregnancy, including the postpartum period.

Other research studies support the finding of 9.1 percent of women in this study who reported abuse prior to pregnancy. Studies of abuse prior to pregnancy have reported at prevalence ranges from three to nine percent (Adams-Hillard, 1985; Amaro et al., 1990; Berenson et al., 1991; Campbell et al., 1992; Helton et al., 1987a; McFarlane et al., 1992). This finding from the current study further supports the reliability and validity of the AAS for identifying abuse. On the other hand, the self-report method used to identify abuse for this sample may have resulted in an under-reporting of abuse. Some researchers have suggested that the personal interview yields the most accurate assessment of abuse among women, which further supports the need for additional research using personal interview methods for screening military women for abuse (Helton et al., 1987a, 1987b; McFarlane, et al., 1991; Parker et al., 1994).

Caliber Associates (1994a) conducted a survey study composed of all cases of spouse abuse reported to the Family Advocacy Programs in the Air Force, Army, Navy, and Marine Corps. The cases are categorized by the severity of abuse reported. According to this report, 57 percent of the cases were classified as mild abuse, 33 percent as moderate, and 3 percent as severe. Using the AAS classification of severity of abuse, 36 percent of the women were characterized as having suffered mild abuse, 56 percent having suffered moderate abuse, and eight percent having suffered severe abuse. This study reports a higher proportion of women experiencing moderate to severe forms of abuse.

The demographic differences between abused and nonabused women related to age, ethnicity, and marital status, in general, have been supported by other research. The younger ages of the abused women, 16–20 years (42%) and 21–25 (36%), have also been supported by other researchers. These studies have substantiated that the younger the age of women, the greater the risk for being abused (Parker et al., 1993, 1994; Stewart & Cecutti, 1993). The significant finding of a higher proportion of Hispanic (31.25%) women being abused compared to Whites (6.25%) and African Americans (13.2%) differs from other findings. Parker et al.'s (1994) large ethnically diverse sample of 691 women find that Whites and Blacks had similar rates of abuse (19%) compared to Hispanic women (14%). Across most studies of abuse in women, ethnic/racial background has not been found to be consistently related to abuse (Flitcraft & Stark, 1996; Plichta, 1993). Therefore, care must be taken not to attribute ethnic background as a cause of abuse. A larger, more ethnically diverse sample is needed among military populations to understand the relationship of ethnicity and abuse in pregnancy. In this study, abused women were less likely to be married as compared to nonabused, 33 percent vs. 8 percent respectively. Divorced or separated women face the same risk of abuse as married women (Stark & Flitcraft, 1996).

Cailber Associates (1994a) found no significant differences in the distribution of reported abuse among the Air Force, Army, Navy, or Marine Corps.

However, this study found significant differences in the rank and pay grade of the perpetrators, as did the Department of Defense Abuse Victims Study (Caliber Associates, 1994b). The Abuse Victims Study found that the majority (69%) of spouse offenders were in the E-4 to E-6 pay grades, 23 percent in the pay grades E-1 to E-3, five percent in E-7 to E-9, and two percent officers. In general, the DOD study disclosed that 98 percent of the male abusers were enlisted personnel, and two percent were officer personnel. This finding differs from the findings of this study in that 41.7 percent were in the E-1 to E-3 pay grades, 45.8 percent in pay grades E-4 to E-6, 4.2 percent in pay grades E-7 to E-9, and 8.3 percent officers. Overall, this study reflects that 91.7 percent of the abusers were enlisted, and 8.3 percent were noncommissioned and commissioned officers. It is interesting to note that the findings from this study revealed a higher proportion of abusers among the mid-range of enlisted ranks and pay grades and among the officer ranks. These men are generally older, more established in their careers, and at a higher pay grade. In addition, that the proportion of officers as perpetrators of abuse is higher in this study than in the other military studies may reflect an underreporting among officer ranks. The Family Advocacy Programs believe that there is an underreporting of abuse among officer military families (Caliber Associates, 1994c), which also supports this perception. Reasons given by the respondents for not reporting the abuser included: fear of further abuse, potential disruption of the abuser's military career, concerns for well-being of the family, financial concerns, shame, sense of isolation, loss of privacy, perceived lack of appropriate services, distrust of the military, cultural norms and values (Caliber Associates, 1994a, 1994b, 1994c).

Findings of significantly higher depressive symptomatology and lower self-esteem among abused women compared to nonabused women are similar to findings from other studies of abuse during pregnancy. Moreover, other studies have linked the finding of higher depressive symptomatology among abused women with poor pregnancy outcomes such as intrauterine growth retardation, preterm labor and birth, and low-birthweight infants (Parker et al., 1993, 1994). The findings of lower self-esteem among abused women were similar to Torres (1992), who found lower levels of self-esteem and higher depressive symptomatology among abused women. Also, not all abused women in this study reported low self-esteem. Further studies are needed to identify what strategies military women may use to cope with abuse during pregnancy. Often the findings of low self-esteem and high depressive symptomatology and poor pregnancy outcomes are found among poor women whose economic situation is frequently a barrier to prenatal care. Clearly more studies are needed to determine the perinatal outcomes in military women for whom access to prenatal care is often not a barrier, in order to understand how abuse and mental health status may influence perinatal outcomes.

SUMMARY

This preliminary study of 298 military pregnant women found that 3.4 percent experienced abuse during the current pregnancy, and 9.1 percent were abused in the year before the pregnancy. Abused women reported higher levels of depressive symptomatology and lower levels of self-esteem compared to nonabused women. In addition, abuse during pregnancy was positively correlated with depressive symptomatology and negatively correlated with self-esteem. This study demonstrates that military women, pregnant military women, and dependent women are not immune to abuse. The findings in this population were similar to other studies of abuse in pregnant civilian populations.

Major limitations of the study were the use of a small convenient sample, a cross-sectional design, and the use of a self-report measure as the only means to assess abuse. Therefore, more research using a systematic, personal interview with multi-assessment points during pregnancy and the postpartum period among military populations is needed to accurately identify the prevalence and magnitude of the problem in the military. Further studies need to explore abuse among pregnant military women and the consequences for pregnancy outcomes. Furthermore, additional studies are needed to understand the complex relationships of demographic and institutional variables unique to the military, how these variables may influence abuse, and how these variables could be modified to reduce abuse among pregnant military women.

REFERENCES

Adams–Hillard, P. J. (1985). Physical abuse in pregnancy. *Obstetrics and Gynecology, 66*, 185-190.

Amaro, H., Fried, L., & Cabral, H. (1990). Violence during pregnancy and substance use. *American Journal of Public Health, 80*, 575-589.

Anderson, E., McFarlane, J., & Helton, A. (1986). Community as client: A model for practice. *Nursing Outlook, 34*, 220-224.

Bachman, R. (1994). *Violence against women: A national crime victimization survey report.* Washington, DC: Department of Justice.

Beck, A. T. (1970). *Depression: Causes and Treatment.* Philadelphia: University of Pennsylvania Press.

Beck, A. T., & Beck, R. W. (1972). Screening depressed patients in a family practice: A rapid technique. *Postgraduate Medicine, 52*, 81-85.

Berenson, A., Stiglich, N. J., & Wilkinson, G. (1991). Drug abuse and other risk factors for physical abuse during pregnancy among non-Hispanic, Black and Hispanic women. *American Journal of Obstetrics and Gynecology, 164*, 491-499.

Blascovich, J., & Tomaka, J. (1991). Measures of self-esteem. In J. P. Robinson, P. R. Shaver, & L. S. Wrightsman (Eds.), *Measures of Personality and Social Psychological Attitude* (pp. 115-160). San Diego, CA: Academic Press.

Caliber Associates. (1994a). *Victims Survey Preliminary Report.* Fairfax, VA: Department of Defense.

Caliber Associates. (1994b). *Abuse Victims Study Final Report.* Fairfax, VA: Department of Defense.

Caliber Associates. (1994c). *Preliminary Process Report Study.* Fairfax, VA: Department of Defense.

Campbell, J. C., & Humphreys, J. (1993). *Nursing Care of the Survivors of Family Violence.* St. Louis: Mosby.

Campbell, J. C., Kub, J. E., & Rose, L. (1996). Depression in battered women. *Journal of American Women's Medical Association, 51,* 106-110.

Campbell, J. C., Poland, M., & Walker, J. (1992). Correlates of battering during pregnancy. *Research in Nursing and Health, 15,* 219-226.

Casardi, M., & O'Leary, K. D. (1992). Depressive symptomatology, self-esteem and self-blame in battered women. *Journal of Family Violence, 7,* 249-259.

Curry, M. A., Campbell, R. A., & Christian, M. (1994). Validity and reliability testing of the prenatal psychosocial profile. *Research in Nursing and Health, 17,* 127-135.

Department of Defense. (1995). *Almanac: Defense 95 (Issue 5).* Alexandria, VA: American Forces Information Services.

Donovan, P. (1995). Physical violence toward pregnant women is more likely to occur when pregnancy is unintended. *Family Planning Perspectives, 27,* 222-223.

Dye, D. D., Tollivert, R. V., & Kenney, C. J. (1995). Violence, pregnancy and birth outcomes in Appalachia. *Pediatric and Perinatal Epidemiology, 9,* 53-47.

Fildes, J., Reed, L., & Jones, N. (1992). Trauma: The leading cause of maternal death. *Journal of Trauma, 32,* 643-645.

Flemming, J. S., & Courtney, B. E. (1984). The dimensionality of self-esteem: Hierarchical facet model for revised measurement scales. *Journal of Personality and Social Psychology, 46,* 404-421.

Gazmararian, J. A., Lazorick, S., Spitz, A. M., Ballard, T. J., Saltzman, L. E., & Marks, J. S. (1996). Prevalence of violence against pregnant women. *JAMA, 275*(24), 1915–1920.

Gelles, R. J., & Straus, M. A. (1990). The medical and psychological cost of family violence. In M. A. Straus & R. J. Gelles (Eds.), *Physical Violence in American Families: Risk Factors and Adaptations to Violence in 8,145 Families* (pp. 425-430). New Brunswick: Transaction.

Gielen, A., O'Campo, P., Faden, R., Kass, N. & Xue, X. (1994). Interpersonal conflict and physical violence during the childbearing years. *Social Science Medicine, 39*(6), 781-787.

Gleason, W. J. (1993). Mental disorders in battered women: An empirical study. *Violence and Victims, 8,* 53-68.

Helton, A. (1986). Battering during pregnancy. *American Journal of Nursing, 86,* 910-913.

Helton, A. (1987). *Protocol of Care for the Battered Woman.* White Plains, NY: March of Dimes Birth Defects Foundation.

Helton, A., McFarlane, J., & Anderson, E. (1987a). Battered and pregnant: A prevalence study. *American Journal of Public Health, 77,* 1337-1339.

Helton, A., McFarlane, J., & Anderson, E. (1987b). Prevention of battering during pregnancy: Focus on behavioral change. *Public Health Nursing, 4,* 166-174.

Helton, A., & Snodgrass, F. G. (1987). Battering during pregnancy: Intervention strategies. *Birth, 14,* 142-147.

Hurlbert, D., Whitaker, K., & Munoz, C. (1991). Etiological characteristics of abusive husbands. *Military Medicine, 156,* 670-675.

Kemp, V., & Page, C. (1987). Maternal self-esteem and prenatal attachment in high-risk pregnancy. *MCN, 16,* 195-206.

McFarlane, J., Christoffel, K., Bateman, C., & Bullock, L. (1991). Assessing for abuse: self-report versus nurse interview. *Public Health Nursing, 8*(4), 245–250.

McFarlane, J., Parker, B., Soeken, K., & Bullock, L. (1992). Assessing for abuse during pregnancy. *JAMA, 267,* 3176-3178.

Medical Association. (1992). American Medical Association Diagnostic and treatment guidelines on domestic violence. *Archives of Family Medicine, 1,* 39-47.

Mercer, R., & Ferketrich, S. (1988). Stress and social support as predictors of anxiety and depression during pregnancy. *Advances in Nursing Science, 10*(2), 26-39.

Miller, T., & Veltkamp, L. (1993). Family violence: Clinical indicators among military and post-military personnel. *Military Medicine, 158,* 766-771.

Neidig, P. H. (1985). Domestic violence in the military: Research findings and program implications. *Military Family, 5,* 3–6.

Norbeck, J., & Tilden, V. (1983). Life stress, social support and emotional disequilibrium in complications of pregnancy. *Journal of Health and Social Behavior, 24,* 30-46.

Norton, L. B., Peipert, J. F., Zieler, S., Lima, B., & Hume, L. (1995). Battering in pregnancy: An assessment of two screening methods. *Obstetrics and Gynecology, 85,* 321-325.

O'Campo, P., Gielen, A., Faden, R., & Kass, N. (1994). Verbal abuse and physical violence among a cohort of low income pregnant women. *Women's Health institute, 4,* 1-9.

Parker, B., & McFarlane, J. (1991). Nursing assessment of battered pregnant women. *The American Journal of Maternal Child Nursing, 16*(3), 161-164.

Parker, B., McFarlane, J., & Soeken, K. (1994). Abuse during pregnancy: Effects of maternal complications on birth weight in adult and teenage women. *Obstetrics and Gynecology, 84,* 323-328.

Parker, B., McFarlane, J., Soeken, K., Torres, S., & Campbell, D. (1993). Physical and emotional abuse in pregnancy: A comparison of adult and teenage women. *Nursing Research, 42,* 173-178.

Plichta, S. B. (1996). Violence, health and use of health care services. In *Women's Health Care Seeking Behavior* (pp. 237-270). Baltimore: Johns Hopkins Press.

Rosenberg, M. (1965). *Society and the Adolescent Self-Image.* Princeton, NJ: Princeton University Press.

Rosenberg, M. (1979). *Conceiving the Self.* New York: Basic Books.

Saltzman, L. E., & Johnson, D. (1996). CDC's family and intimate violence team: Basing programs on science. *Journal of American Medical Womens Association, 51*(3), 83-86.

Sampselle, C., Petersen, B. A., Murtland, T. L., and Oakley, D. J. (1992). Prevalence of abuse among pregnant women choosing a certified nurse-midwife or physician providers. *Journal of Nurse Midwifery, 37,* 269-273.

Shaver, P. R., & Brennan, P. A. (1991). Measures of depression and loneliness. In J. P. Robinson, P. R. Shawer, & L. Wrightman (Eds.), *Measures of Personality and Social Psychological Attitudes* (pp. 195-289). San Diego, CA: Academic Press.

Smith, G. S. (1995). Injury to women in the military. Proposal funded by Women's Health Research Program, DAMD I 7-940BAA (DWIW).

Soeken, K., McFarlane, J., & Parker, B. (1995). Development and testing of a clinical instrument to measure frequency. Unpublished manuscript, University of Maryland.

Stark, E., & Flitcraft, A. (1996). *Women at Risk: Domestic Violence and Women's Health.* London: Sage.

Stewart, D. E., & Cecutti, A. (1993). Physical abuse during pregnancy. *Canadian Medical Association Journal, 149,* 1257-1262

Torres, S. (1992). Battering during pregnancy: An exploratory study. Unpublished manuscript, University of Rochester.

Zuckerman, B., Amaro, H., Bauchner, H., & Cabral, H. (1989). Depressive symptoms during pregnancy: Relationship to poor health behaviors. *American Journal of Obstetrics and Gynecology, 160*(5), 1107-1111.

Chapter 6

THE INFLUENCE OF MILITARY TRAINING AND COMBAT EXPERIENCE ON DOMESTIC VIOLENCE

LEANA C. ALLEN

INTRODUCTION

The military is not merely an occupation; it is a lifestyle. As such, it influences the lives and behavior of all those connected with it. Currently, the military employs about 1.5 million active-duty men and women (World Almanac Books, 1996). In addition to the number of people currently in the military, the American population includes nearly 26.5 million veterans, with 77 percent having wartime experience (World Almanac Books, 1996). Since current and former military personnel constitute a large portion of society, the influence of military experience on behavior seems an important research topic. Unfortunately, little research has actually been conducted on the influence of military service on violence, particularly domestic violence.

Generally, there exists divergent opinions about the possible influence that military training and lifestyle can have on an individual's behavior. The military has been used to modify preservice behavior problems, such as crime and delinquency, by providing a structured, disciplined lifestyle. However, theorists believe that a military background may influence criminal behavior, because certain aspects of the military experience, such as training or combat, may encourage or teach individuals to become conditioned to violence. It is also possible that the military employs those who are predisposed to criminal behavior.

While early studies indicate that some individuals with a previous criminal record adjust well to military service, the question of the influence of military training on behavior has not been satisfactorily addressed in the research. A review of literature exploring the possibility that military training or lifestyle has a beneficial influence on deviant behavior finds that these factors have little or no effect in reducing recidivism (MacKenzie & Souryal, 1995; Morash & Rucker, 1990). An alternative hypothesis suggests that individuals either in the military or with military experience are more likely than their civilian counterparts to be involved in criminal activity. In recent years, the growing number of high-profile crimes committed by those having had military experience seems to support this hypothesis. Such crimes include the murder of a black couple as an initiation into a skinhead group (Galvin, 1995); attacks of "gay-bashing" against homosexual servicemen (Sterngold, 1993); the murders committed by Jeffrey Dahmer, who spent three years in the Army and was discharged for a drinking problem; and the Oklahoma City bombing by Timothy McVeigh, who was deployed during Operation Desert Storm and later failed in an attempt to make the elite Special Forces (Hackworth, 1995).

It seems that, at least recently, there exists some relationship between military experience and criminal behavior, particularly acts of extreme violence. Yet few studies have actually explored this relationship. Limited literature tends to be narrow, its focus on the sample being studied (Bryant, 1979). Examples include studies limited to only World War II veterans (Grinker & Spiegel, 1963; Hakeem, 1946), Vietnam veterans (see Borus, 1973; Jordan et al., 1992; Yager, Laufer, & Gallops, 1984), or veterans with psychiatric problems (Petrik, Rosenberg, & Watson, 1983; Resnick, Foy, Donahoe, & Miller, 1989; Yager, 1976; Yesavage, 1983a, 1983b).

LITERATURE REVIEW

Research suggests that certain characteristics of the military, such as lifestyle, training, or combat experience, may lead an individual to be criminal and that this behavior may carry over into later civilian life. Criminal behavior by military personnel may be due to the influence of basic training, the stresses of military life, combat training in general, or combat experience. Some studies that have examined the impact of basic training on behavior have found an increase in aggression and impulsivity among military individuals in basic training (Morash & Rucker, 1990). These two factors, valued in the military organization, may be related to criminal behavior and violence.

The development of criminal behavior in the military may also be due to stresses and characteristics of the lifestyle that are unique to the military. Research has suggested that stressors unique to military life, such as frequent moving, deployment, separation from family and from civilian society in general, may lead to violence within the home (Bohannon, Dosser, &

Lindley, 1995). Additionally, because military society is segregated from civilian society, it creates a sense of separation from and competition with the civilian world (Bryant, 1979). Though few studies have focused on the influence of these lifestyle stressors on domestic violence, Bohannon et al. (1995) suggest that the higher rates of violence observed in military couples may be related to these stresses, leading to conflicts within the home and violent methods of resolving such conflicts.

After attending basic training or boot camp, soldiers continue training for battle throughout their military service. For the purpose and efficient functioning of the military, rigid discipline and intense drills are necessary to train soldiers to instinctively do things which they might not otherwise do, namely killing the enemy in battle (Bryant, 1979). The argument has been made that this training teaches normally peaceful people how to fight and kill, and even after they leave the training or combat situation, these individuals may continue to behave aggressively and violently (Hakeem, 1946). In the military, individuals are taught to idealize aggression. Many studies have depicted the military as a "school for violence," a place where those who already accept the military values of masculinity and aggression instill those same values in new recruits (Martin, 1976). This explanation is more specifically known as the "sergeant syndrome," the idea that men learn to behave aggressively and violently through military socialization and training (Dubanoski & McIntosh, 1984). Dubanoski and McIntosh (1984) also argue that training in aggression and violent methods of problem- solving may generalize to child-care situations and conflict-resolution tactics between spouses.

Yet studies, having looked at the impact of military training on violence, conclude that there is little or no support for the hypothesis that military training leads individuals to commit more violent crimes (Beckerman & Fontana, 1989; Hakeem, 1946; Worthington, 1978; Yager et al., 1984). In a study of incarcerated offenders, those with military training showed no significant difference from those without military experience in terms of the types of crimes they committed (Hakeem, 1946). However, evidence that military training results in more criminal behavior and more violence does exist. In addition to the suggested influence of training on general violent behavior, some research has found that military training may particularly influence violence in the family setting. While little research has looked at the possible influence of military training on violence in the family, these studies do indicate a higher rate of violence in military families (Jensen, Lewis, & Xenakis, 1986). Dubanoski and McIntosh (1984), finding no significant differences between military and civilian families overall, did discover that more military fathers abused their children than expected. In a study of military families, Bohannon et al. (1995) compared the rates of violence in the military to civilian rates from previous studies and concluded that there is a much higher rate of violence in military families. Among individuals seeking marital therapy, military wives were more likely to report physical abuse than civilian wives (Griffin & Morgan, 1988). Other studies have found that a significantly large proportion of battering husbands had either been in the military prior to the abuse or were in the military at the time of the abuse (Martin, 1976). Children of military families also report more violence between their parents than children of civilian families, indicating a greater prevalence of spousal violence among military families (Cronin, 1995). Cronin (1995) does, however, state that it is difficult to determine from these studies whether the military environment leads to spousal violence or whether the military attracts individuals who are predisposed to violence.

The influence of combat experience on criminal behavior is described by the violent-veterans model, which explains crime committed by veterans as a result of a wartime resocialization process. Like the "sergeant syndrome," the violent-veterans model argues that combat training, specifically the use of that training in a combat situation, conditions soldiers to use violence in conflict resolution (Bebber, 1994). During combat, soldiers develop a greater acceptance of and greater skill in violence (Archer & Gartner, 1976). In a wartime situation, soldiers develop a new set of values and bring those values back to civilian society where they continue to behave aggressively (Martin, 1976).

One study of incarcerated Vietnam veterans found no significant difference between veterans and nonveterans in the incidence of violent crimes (Bureau of Justice Statistics, 1981), yet other studies have found a significant effect of combat on later violence. Yesavage (1983b, p. 384) states that "the violent reactions of Vietnam veterans appear to be something learned in Vietnam rather than long-standing personality traits." Combat veterans, more likely to be violent than noncombat veterans, are involved in more fights, use weapons more often, and cause serious injury (Boulanger, 1986). Petrik et al. (1983) argue that while there may be a relationship between combat experience and later general violence, there is no relationship between combat and violence specifically toward the female partners of veterans. However, some studies have found that as many as half of the wives of Vietnam veterans report having been physically abused by their husbands (Jordan et al., 1992).

PRESENT STUDY

As seen in this review, there is limited research on the relationship between military training and criminal behavior, particularly violence within the family, and what little research there is has produced inconclusive and contradictory evidence. Some authors have found that postservice violence is a result of premilitary characteristics (Hakeem, 1946; Schneider & LaGrone, 1945; Worthington, 1978). Others have found that individuals with military experience are more likely to commit crimes because of the influence of the military environment (see Bohannon et al., 1995; Boulanger, 1986; Cronin, 1995; Dubanoski & McIntosh, 1984; Jensen et al., 1986). There are also studies which found no relationship between military service and criminal behavior (see Beckerman & Fontana, 1989; Bureau of Justice Statistics, 1981; Yager et al., 1984). The difficulty in drawing conclusions from the literature may be due to a number of factors. First, few studies have included control variables, and few have included other variables reflecting military experience. One variable overlooked in the literature is a measure of exposure to training. The literature which has found no relationship between military training and criminal behavior is generated from studies which ignore the amount of time spent in military training, an important consideration.

Second, research findings differ depending on when the study was conducted and the composition of the sample. Most early studies found no evidence that military training increases the likelihood of criminal behavior (Hakeem, 1946; Worthington, 1978). However, research which has been done since the mid-1980s has tended to find a significant effect of military training on violence (Boulanger, 1986; Cronin, 1995; Jordan et al., 1992; Resnick et al., 1989). This corresponds with the observation that there are increasing numbers of individuals with military experience involved in criminal activity in recent years.

Perhaps related to the difference in results by time period, research with Vietnam veterans is also more likely to identify an effect of the military or combat on violence (Boulanger, 1986; Jordan et al., 1992; Resnick et al., 1989; Yesavage, 1983a, 1983b). The only study having looked at those in the military since the Vietnam War reveals a significantly greater likelihood of spousal violence in military families as compared to civilian families (Cronin, 1995), demonstrating the continued importance of exploring the relationship between military training and domestic violence.

The primary goal of this study is to identify the influence of military training or combat experience on violence. Prior research has suggested that military training leads an individual to become more violent. Specifically, those individuals with military experience will have a greater likelihood of having been incarcerated for a violent offense as compared to those without military experience. Additionally, the type of military experience may be important, such that combat experience should have an even greater impact on violence. For individuals with combat experience, the likelihood of being incarcerated for a violent crime should be greater than those with military non-combat experience and those without military experience. Research evidence would also suggest that because of the masculine, aggressive values of the military environment, violence within the family is more prevalent among those with military experience as compared to those without. This study seeks to determine whether those with military or combat experience are more likely to have committed crimes against family members than those without military experience.

Several previous studies have not identified the influence of military service; however, it is possible that these findings are due to an incomplete consideration of military factors. This study operates under several assumptions: that the influence of military training is not necessarily the same for all individuals; that individuals who receive more training will be more likely to commit a violent crime—individuals who spend more time in the military are presumably exposed to more combat training and therefore more influenced by that training; that individuals who have spent more time in military service will be more likely to commit violent crimes; that certain members of military service (Army and Marine Corps) may participate in more combat training and should thus have a greater likelihood of having been incarcerated for violent offenses.

METHODS

Procedure

The data for this study were taken from the *Survey of Inmates of State Correctional Facilities, 1991: United States.* This survey was conducted by the U.S. Bureau of the Census for the Bureau of Justice Statistics and provided a representative sample of individuals held in state prisons throughout the United States in 1991. For full information on the methods used in collecting these data, refer to the *Survey of Inmates of State Correctional Facilities, 1991: United States* (Bureau of Justice Statistics, 1991).

The original sample was obtained using a stratified, two-stage selection process. In the first stage, 277 prisons were selected from a population of 1,239 state facilities. In the second stage, the population included all inmates who had a bed in the selected facilities during June, July, or August of 1991. From this population of inmates, a systematic, random sample was selected, resulting in a sample (n=13,986) of inmates of state correctional facilities representative of the entire population of state prisoners. A personal interview was conducted with each inmate selected, and data were collected on individual characteristics, such as military history, current offenses, criminal history, and other background information.

This dataset was extremely large, so for the purpose of this study, a subsample of cases was selected from the original sample. Only 53 females (1.9% of the original sample) had ever served in the military, and of these, only three had seen combat. Since this sample size was inadequate for statistical analyses and because the military is considered to be a predominantly male institution, this study will only look at the impact of military training and combat experience on criminal behavior among men. The female cases in the original sample were excluded, and of the remaining male cases (n=11,163), a subsample was randomly selected. This selection process resulted in a sample of males incarcerated in state prisons about half the size of the original sample (n=5,170).

Subjects

The sample used in this study (n=5,170) was randomly selected from the original sample and included only male cases. Ages of inmates in the subsample ranged from 14 to 81, with 62.2 percent between 21 and 35 years of age. The distribution of race was nearly evenly divided between white (48.7%) and black (47.5%). Most individuals in the subsample (83.4%) had a prior criminal record, and most had attended some high school (72.4%). Most inmates (85%) had not served in the military, and of those who had, 15.4 percent served in a combat situation. Individuals in the subsample had committed a variety of offenses, 7.1 percent misdemeanor and public order offenses, 19.7 percent drug offenses, 24.4 percent property offenses, and 48.9 percent violent offenses.

This subsample showed the same general characteristics of the original sample, and the absolute differences in proportions between the two samples were very small (see Table 6-1). Though a z-statistic for the difference between proportions indicated that nearly all of the differences were statistically significant, this was likely due to the very large sample sizes. Most absolute differences were less than two percentage points, and the largest difference between the original sample and the subsample was three percentage points for employment. Practically speaking, these differences were not large enough to cause concern. Thus, with the exception of gender, the sample randomly selected was very similar to the original sample.

Table 6-1
DIFFERENCES IN PROPORTIONS BETWEEN ORIGINAL
SAMPLE AND SUBSAMPLE

Variable	Original Sample (n = 13,986)	Subsample (n = 5,170)	Z*
Male	79.8	100.0	-34.83***
Age			
Younger than 21	9.4	7.7	3.70***
Between 21 and 35	61.6	62.2	-0.80
Older than 35	29.0	30.1	-1.49
Arrest record prior to current offense	82.2	83.4	-1.94*
Education			
Less than high school	12.4	13.1	-1.30
Some high school	72.0	72.4	-0.55
More than high School	15.3	14.0	2.24*
Race			
White	48.8	48.7	0.12
Black	47.5	47.5	0.00
Asian	0.8	0.8	0.00
American Indian	2.1	2.1	0.00
Military service	14.1	15.0	-1.58
Combat service			
Yes	1.7	2.3	-2.73**
No	0.6	0.7	-0.77

*Z-statistic for differences in proportions
*p<.05; **p<.01; ***p<.001

Variables

Variables capturing the demographic information for each subject included age, education, and race. Age was a continuous variable measuring chronological age in years. Education was also a continuous variable reflecting the number of years of education. Race was a categorical variable with categories of White, Black/African American, Asian, and American Indian. Since a very small proportion of individuals (no more than 5% of individuals in each sample) fell into a category other than white or black, this variable was collapsed into a dichotomous measure of white and nonwhite.

Military experience was measured by a number of variables including military service, combat service, amount of time in military service, amount of time in combat, and branch of service. The two experience variables were dichotomous, indicating whether the individual had ever served in the military and whether the individual was involved in combat during the Vietnam War. Length of time in military service and length of time in combat were both continuous variables. Length of time in military service was defined as the number of years between entering the military and being discharged. Length of time in combat measured the number of months spent in a combat situation while stationed in Vietnam. Branch of service was a categorical variable indicating the branch of the military in which the individual may have served: Army, Navy, Marine Corps, Air Force, or Coast Guard. For some analyses, a dummy variable was used to indicate whether the individual had served in either the Army or Marines.

Information about the offense included the type of crime committed, offense and victim characteristics, and criminal history. Type of offense was measured in a categorical variable divided into numerous different offenses. These data were combined into a variable with only four categories—violent, property, drug, and public-order offenses. For statistical analyses, these were further divided into four dummy variables, one for each category of offense. Victim information was captured in several variables. A categorical variable indicated the gender of the victim(s): male or female in the case of a single victim; all male, all female, or both male and female in the case of multiple victims. For some analyses, a dichotomous variable identified whether the perpetrator had victimized at least one female. A set of dummy variables indicated the exact relationship between the offender and victim, whether the victim was a spouse, ex-spouse, parent/stepparent, child/stepchild, brother/sister, other relative, boyfriend/ex-boyfriend, girlfriend/ex-girlfriend, friend, or other nonrelative. Several of these variables were combined to create an additional dichotomous variable measuring whether the victim was a family member. Dummy variables also indicated whether the offender used a weapon and whether the victim(s) were injured during the offense. Information about an offender's prior criminal record was captured in a continuous variable measuring the chronological age at which he was first arrested.

RESULTS

Influence of Military Service on Violence

This study hypothesized that individuals with military training had a greater likelihood of violence compared to those without military experience. The primary variable of interest for measuring violence was incarceration for a violent crime. Both groups with military experience had a greater proportion of individuals who were incarcerated for a violent offense compared to those without military experience (see Table 6-2). The differences between the military groups and the nonmilitary group were significant (p<.01). However, there was no significant difference between the noncombat and combat groups.

A chi-square analysis found that there was a significant relationship between military experience and incarceration for a violent crime. In this sample, more individuals than expected from both the noncombat and the combat groups were incarcerated for committing a violent offense (X^2=38.63; p<.001). Though the chi-square value indicated a significant relationship for type of military experience, the measure of the proportionate reduction in error, Somer's d, was relatively small (d=0.12, p<.001), suggesting a weak relationship. Using the type of military experience variable resulted in a 12 percent reduction in error in the prediction of the commission of a violent crime.

The use of a weapon and injury to the victim were hypothesized as measures of violence similar to the commission of a violent offense, so they should be similarly related to military experience. Both variables were significantly related to the commission of a violent crime as indicated by chi-square analyses. Individuals who committed a violent offense were significantly more likely to use a weapon during the offense (X^2=1374.97; p<.001) and were also significantly more likely to cause injury to the victim (X^2=337.16; p<.001). Though these variables were strongly related to the commission of a violent offense, they were not significantly related to military experience. With one exception (the percent of individuals using a weapon in the nonmilitary and noncombat groups), differences in the proportion using a weapon and injuring the victim during the crime were not significant (see Table 6-2). A chi-square analysis supported these findings. The relationship between type of military experience and the use of a weapon only approached significance (X^2=4.75; p<.10), and the relationship between type of military experience and injury to the victim was insignificant (X^2=0.63; p=.730). Thus, the influence of military training and combat experience was limited to the commission of a violent crime rather than to a general level of violence.

Table 6-2
PROPORTION VIOLENT FOR DIFFERENT GROUPS

Group	% with violent offense[a]	% using weapon[a]	% injuring victim[a]
Nonmilitary[1]	46.6	21.2	7.1
Military Noncombat[2]	58.9	24.2	6.3
Combat[3]	58.0	26.9	7.6
	$Z^{12} = -5.87$*** $Z^{13} = -2.46$** $Z^{23} = 0.18$	$Z^{12} = -1.74$* $Z^{13} = -1.50$ $Z^{23} = -0.63$	$Z^{12} = -0.75$ $Z^{13} = 0.21$ $Z^{23} = 0.53$

[a] n = 4397 for nonmilitary; n = 654 for military noncombat;
n = 119 for combat
*$p < .05$; ** $< .01$; ***$p < .001$

To further explore the influence of military training and combat experience on violence, regression models, using incarceration for a violent offense as the dependent variable, were estimated. This was a dichotomous variable, so logistic regression was the most appropriate method of analysis. Preliminary bivariate regressions found positive and significant effects of both military experience (b=0.488; p<.001) and combat experience (b=0.394; p<.05) individually. However, when both were included as independent variables in a multivariate regression, the effect of combat became insignificant (b=-0.036; p=.857). Controlling for the influence of having had military experience, *having been in combat* had no significant effect on the commission of a violent crime. On the other hand, controlling for *having seen combat*, military experience significantly increased the likelihood of having been incarcerated for a violent crime (b=0.494; p<.001).

Age, education, race, and prior record are considered to be important control variables in analyses of criminal behavior, so these variables were included in the full regression model. Specifically, age, education, and age at first arrest were continuous variables, and race was a dichotomous variable with categories of white and nonwhite. The independent variables of interest, according to the hypotheses, were military experience and combat experience. In this model, age and race were significantly related to the likelihood of having been incarcerated for a violent offense (see Table 6-3). Controlling for these variables, *level of education* and *age at first arrest*, having combat experience did not have a significant effect on the likelihood of having been incarcerated for a violent offense. The effect of military service, however, was positive and significant (b=0.292; p<.01). Controlling for age, race, level of education, age at first arrest, and combat experience, *having been in the military* significantly increased the likelihood of having committed a violent offense. Comparing the Wald statistics for each of the independent variables, military experience had a stronger effect than any other variable except for age.

Table 6-3
SUMMARY OF LOGISTIC REGRESSION ANALYSIS FOR VARIABLES
PREDICTING THE COMMISSION OF A VIOLENT OFFENSE (n = 5,041)

Variable	B	Wald
Military experience	0.292	9.900**
Combat experience	0.012	0.004
Age	0.019	28.865***
Education	-0.015	1.560
Race	0.155	7.180**
Age at first arrest	0.006	2.235

*p<.05; **p<.01; ***p<.001

It is possible that previous research found no significant effect of military experience on criminal behavior because the effect of exposure to military training was not measured. It may be that most individuals serve for a short period of time, during which the influence of training is negligible. With longer periods of service, the influence of military training may increase. The use of a dichotomous variable indicating merely the presence of military experience may mask this true effect. To test this, a second logistic regression model, which replaced the dichotomous military and combat variables with continuous variables measuring the number of years in military service and the number of months spent in combat, was estimated. The same control variables, age, education, race, and age at first arrest, were included.

Results from this analysis confirmed the previous findings. As seen in Table 6-4, controlling for age, education, race, age at first arrest, and military experience, the number of months in combat had no significant influence on the likelihood of having been incarcerated for a violent offense. However, the effect of length of time spent in the military was positive and significant (b=0.076; p<.001). Controlling for age, education, race, age at first arrest, and combat experience, an increased time in military service increased the likelihood of having been incarcerated for a violent offense.

In order to determine which measure reflects the true effect of military service, an additional model measured the effect of time in military service only with the military sample. If this continuous variable is a better predictor than the dichotomous measure, its effects should remain in this estimation. Table 6-4 also presents the results for this analysis. In the military group, when controlling for age, education, race, and age at first arrest, the length of time spent in combat had no significant effect on the likelihood of having been incarcerated for a violent offense. The effect of time spent in the military was also insignificant. Among individuals with military experience, the length of time spent either in military service or in combat had no effect on the likelihood of having been incarcerated for a violent crime.

Although the effect of age at first arrest was not significant in the full sample, it became significant when the regression was run only on the military group, suggesting a possible interaction of the two variables. An additional logistic regression model was estimated, including the dichotomous military experience variable and the interaction of military experience and age at first arrest. In this model, the effects of the control variables remained the same as in previous analyses. Though the direction of the effect of combat experience changed, it was still insignificant. However, including the interaction term changed both the direction and the significance of the effect of military experience (b=-0.352; p<.10). Controlling for the interaction between military experience and age at first arrest, having military experience decreased the likelihood of having been incarcerated for a violent offense, and this effect only approached significance. The effect of the interaction term, however, was positive and significant (b=0.028; p<.001). For those with military experience, being older at the first arrest significantly increased the likelihood of having been incarcerated for a violent offense.

Table 6-4
SUMMARY OF LOGISTIC REGRESSION ANALYSIS FOR VARIABLES
PREDICTING THE COMMISSION OF A VIOLENT OFFENSE IN THE FULL
SAMPLE AND IN THE MILITARY GROUP

Variable	Full Sample (n = 5003)		Military Group (n = 717)	
	B	Wald	B	Wald
Time in military	0.076	10.586***	0.040	1.557
Time in combat	-0.000	0.000	0.001	0.009
Age	0.019	29.539***	0.004	0.260
Education	-0.014	1.385	-0.034	0.788
Race	0.160	7.582**	-0.302	3.670
Age at first arrest	0.004	1.130	0.026	9.906**

*p<.05; **p<.01; ***p<.001

Another important consideration in determining the influence of military training on criminal behavior is the branch of the military in which an individual served. This study hypothesized that individuals who were in the Army or Marine Corps, because they had more exposure to hand-to-hand combat training, would be more violent than those in other branches of the military or those with no military experience. A logistic regression model was estimated which included a dummy variable indicating service in the Army or Marine Corps along with the independent variables from the previous models. Since the dichotomous measure of military service was determined to be more accurate and the interaction of military experience and age at first arrest was significant, these variables were included in the model. Most of the relationships among the independent variables and the commission of a violent offense remained the same as in previous analyses. However, the inclusion of the interaction term and the dummy variable for service in the Army or Marines caused the effect of military service to become insignificant. The effect of service in the Army or Marine Corps approached significance (=-0.299; p<.10). Contrary to this hypothesis, having served in the Army or Marines decreased the likelihood of having been incarcerated for a violent offense.

Influence of Military Service on the
Victimization of Family Members

In this study, military service and combat experience were both hypothe-sized to increase the victimization of family members. A greater proportion of individuals in both military groups victimized a family member compared to those in the nonmilitary group (see Table 6-5). The differences between the nonmilitary group and both the noncombat and the combat groups were significant ($p<.01$). However, as with the measure of violence, there was no significant difference between the combat and noncombat groups.

Table 6-5
PROPORTION VICTIMIZING A FAMILY MEMBER FOR DIFFERENT GROUPS

Group	Family Member[a]	% Victimizing: Spouse or Girlfriend[a]	Child or Step-Child[a]
Nonmilitary[1]	3.6	0.8	2.1
Military Noncombat[2]	10.7	1.7	7.5
Combat[3]	8.4	1.7	5.9
	$Z12 = -8.16$***	$Z12 = -2.25$*	$Z12 = -7.83$***
	$Z13 = -2.73$**	$Z13 = -1.07$	$Z13 = -2.79$**
	$Z23 = 0.76$	$Z23 = 0.00$	$Z23 = 0.62$

[a]n=4397 for nonmilitary; n=654 for military noncombat;
n=119 for combat
*$p<.05$; **$p<.01$; ***$p<.001$

Chi-square analysis found a significant relationship between the victim-ization of a family member and type of military experience. More than twice as many individuals as expected with both noncombat and combat experi-ence victimized a family member ($X^2=68.08$; $p<.001$). The measure of the proportionate reduction in error was small ($d=.07$; $p<.001$), indicating that type of military experience significantly reduced the error in predicting the victimization of family members by about 7 percent. Though significant, this relationship was relatively weak.

A logistic regression model, predicting the victimization of family mem-bers, was estimated. In this model, the same variables as those used in the analysis of violence and the interaction of age at first arrest and military experience were included, as it was significant in the first analysis. Controlling for age, education, race, and age at first arrest, combat experience was not significantly related to the victimization of a family member (see Table 6-6). However, the coefficient for military experience was positive and significant (b=1.205; p<.001). Military experience increased the likelihood of having victimized a family member. The interaction of age at first arrest and military experience was also significant, but negative (b=-0.026; p<.05). For those with military experience, being older at the first arrest decreased the likelihood of having victimized a family member. In this model, a comparison of the Wald statistics showed that military experience was a stronger predictor than combat experience, education, and the interaction term.

Table 6-6
SUMMARY OF LOGISTIC REGRESSION ANALYSES FOR VARIABLES
PREDICTING THE VICTIMIZATION OF FAMILY MEMBERS

	Family Members[a]		Victimization of: Spouse or Girlfriend[a]		Child or Step-child[a]	
Variable	B	Wald	B	Wald	B	Wald
Military Experience	1.205	12.366***	1.076	5.732*	1.454	12.424***
Combat Experience	-0.364	1.009	0.030	0.004	-0.385	0.815
Age	0.037	23.827***	0.020	4.858*	0.039	17.691***
Education	0.049	3.828*	0.006	0.042	0.061	4.008*
Race	-1.092	47.740***	0.026	0.025	-1.305	37.570***
Age at First Arrest	0.034	17.084***	0.030	9.235**	0.036	13.216***
Interaction Term	-0.026	5.914*	-0.033	4.684*	-0.030	5.755*

[a]n = 5,041 for all models
*p<.05; **p<.01; ***p<.001

Service in the Army or Marines was also hypothesized to be related to the victimization of family members, but a logistic regression model which included the dummy variable for service in one of these branches refuted this hypothesis. Service in the Army or Marine Corps had no significant effect on the victimization of a family member (b=0.216; p=.438). The inclusion of this variable also had no impact on the effect of the other variables in the model.

The victimization of family may involve many different types of members, including spouses, children, siblings, parents, or other relatives. To explore the issue of domestic violence, this study examined the relationship of military and combat service to the victimization of spouses and children. In this sample, very few individuals victimized a spouse (n=49), so this variable also included an ex-spouse or a girlfriend. This expanded the definition of domestic violence slightly, but the variable was still able to measure crimes committed against intimate partners. As seen in Table 6-5, there was a significant difference between the nonmilitary and noncombat groups (p<.05). The differences between the nonmilitary and combat groups and between the noncombat and combat groups, however, were not significant.

Chi-square analysis found that the relationship between type of military experience and the victimization of an intimate partner approached significance (X^2=5.22; p<.10). More individuals than expected with military experience and with combat experience victimized a spouse or girlfriend. The statistic measuring the strength of this relationship, however, found it to be very weak (d=.008; p<.10). Using type of military experience reduced the error in predicting the victimization of an intimate partner by less than 1 percent. Though this relationship was statistically significant, it was practically meaningless. Logistic regressions confirmed these results.

A logistic regression model was estimated with the victimization of a spouse or girlfriend as the dependent variable. The same control variables as in previous analyses were included. In this model, combat experience did not have a significant effect on the victimization of an intimate partner (see Table 6-6). However, the effect of military experience was positive and significant (b=1.076; p<.05). Military experience increased the likelihood of having victimized a spouse or girlfriend. As in the analysis of the victimization of a family member, the interaction term in this model was also significant (b=-0.033; p<.05). For those with military experience, being older at the first arrest decreased the likelihood of having victimized a spouse. A comparison of the Wald statistics showed that military experience was a stronger predictor than most other variables, including age, education, race, combat experience, and the interaction term. Including the dummy variable for service in the Army or Marines did not change the effects of the other variables, and this variable had no significant effect on the victimization of a spouse or girlfriend (b=0.167; p=.674).

In addition to partner or spouse abuse, violence in the home may also include the victimization of children. Specifically, aggressive conflict resolution tactics learned during military training may generalize to child care. In this data, there were significant differences between noncombat, combat, and nonmilitary individuals in the proportion victimizing a child (see Table 6-5). A significantly larger proportion of both the noncombat and the combat group victimized a child compared to the nonmilitary group (p<.01). Again, there was no significant difference between the noncombat and combat groups.

Chi-square analysis found a significant relationship between the victimization of a child and type of military experience. More individuals than expected with both combat and noncombat experience victimized their own child or a step-child (X^2=63.70; p<.001). This relationship, though stronger than that for the victimization of an intimate partner, was still relatively weak. For type of military experience, there was only a small reduction in error, about 5 percent, in predicting the victimization of a child (d=0.05; p<.001).

As seen in Table 6-6, a logistic-regression analysis with the victimization of a child as the dependent variable produced similar results. Controlling for age, education, race, and age at first arrest, combat experience was not significantly related to the victimization of a child. The effect of military experience, however, was positive and significant (b=0.697; p<.01). Having military experience increased the likelihood of having victimized a child. The interaction between military experience and age at first arrest was also significant in this model (b=-0.030; p<.05). For those with military experience, being older at the first arrest decreased the likelihood of having victimized a child. As with the previous analyses, the Wald statistics show that military experience is a stronger predictor than combat experience, education, and the interaction term. Adding the dummy variable for service in the Army or Marine Corps did not change the effects of the other variables, and service in either branch had no significant effect on the victimization of a child or step-child (b=0.105; p=.741).

DISCUSSION AND DIRECTIONS FOR FUTURE RESEARCH

Overall, the results of this study suggest that military experience may have some effect on later criminal behavior, including domestic violence. However, because this dataset only includes individuals who have been incarcerated, it is not optimal for addressing the hypotheses presented in this study. The best method of testing these hypotheses would involve a sample which also includes nonincarcerated individuals. Although the results and interpretations from this study only apply to those who have committed a crime and have been incarcerated, the data provide some preliminary answers to guide future research, including addressing problems with the data.

An analysis measuring violent offending indicates that, for those who are incarcerated, men with military experience are more likely to have committed a violent crime. This relationship is strong, even when controlling for significant predictors such as age, education, race, and a predisposition to criminal behavior. The same is true for a measure of the length of military service. However, the effect of this measure is not significant in a sample of only those with military experience, suggesting that the presence of military experience is a more accurate predictor of violence than the length of military service.

Analyses of this hypothesis also found an interaction between military experience and age at first arrest. Individuals who are older at their first arrest (presumably less predisposed to criminal behavior) and who enter the military are more likely to have been incarcerated for a violent offense. These results provide support for the hypothesis that individuals who were not predisposed to violent behavior may learn violence from military or combat training.

This study also provides support for the hypothesis that domestic violence may be more prevalent in the military. In particular, though the numbers are very small, those with military experience have a greater tendency to victimize an intimate partner or their own child or a step-child. This finding suggests that the violent conflict-resolution tactics learned in military training may translate to the treatment of a spouse or a child, increasing the likelihood of domestic violence in a military population or among veterans.

Some evidence, however, refutes the suggestion that individuals with military experience have learned violent behavior from military training. This study hypothesized that, in addition to military training, combat experience provides an environment in which to learn violence. Combat experience, however, consistently had no effect on any of the measures used in these analyses. Also, as seen in the analysis of violent offending, the relationship between military experience and violent offending does not translate into an increased likelihood of using a weapon or injuring the victim during the offense. Though individuals with military experience are more likely to commit violent offenses, their level of violence appears to be no greater than those without military experience.

Though service in the Army or Marine Corps was predicted to have an important effect on both violent offending and victim characteristics, the effect of this variable was consistently insignificant. If this study was correct in assuming that individuals in these branches receive more hand-to-hand combat training, this finding seems to contradict the suggestion that individuals in the military learn violence from their training. Other findings, however, provide evidence that, though it may not be the combat training, military service does have some influence on violent offending. It may be that individuals learn aggressive or violent attitudes from the military environment, though not specifically from training.

Another important finding is the difference in the effect of the interaction between age at first arrest and military experience between the violent offending model and the family victimization models. Contrary to the estimation of violent offending, the effect of this interaction was negative when looking at domestic violence. In these models, those who were predisposed to criminal behavior (offending at an earlier age) and who later entered the military had a greater likelihood of domestic violence, suggesting that predisposition to criminal behavior has a greater influence on domestic violence than on violent offending. The effect of military experience alone, however, was consistently stronger than the effect of the interaction, indicating that military experience is a better predictor of the victimization of family members.

Due to the limitations of the samples mentioned above, definitive conclusions are difficult to make. Despite this, there are some strong preliminary indications that military experience has a significant effect on offending, and additional research is needed to answer these questions more conclusively. In particular, it is important to determine whether the military attracts individuals who are predisposed to violence as suggested by the significance of the interaction term. To provide a clearer answer to this question, future research should use a longitudinal design, following both those who enter the military and those who do not, as well as both criminal and noncriminal individuals. This will also eliminate the selection bias inherent in a sample of incarcerated individuals. Future studies should also include self-report measures of criminal behavior instead of relying on official arrest or sentencing information. This will allow a better examination of whether those who serve in the military are more involved in offending before they enter the military. Additionally, a self-report might provide a more accurate measure of criminal involvement than the official measure of arrest and incarceration. This type of dataset would probably provide the most accurate answers to the questions posed.

Additional factors which may be important to the question of whether individuals learn to behave violently in the military include additional measures of exposure to training, such as military specialty and rank. For these measures, some groups within the military may be exposed to more training and may more readily learn violence. With military specialty, those who serve in medical, law, or other support divisions may receive less combat training than those in the infantry and other combat units. Also, enlisted individuals may receive more combat training while officers receive more leadership training. Some units, such as special forces, rangers, or airborne units, may also have a more masculine, aggressive image, increasing the likelihood of attracting aggressive or violent individuals.

In general, because of the sample and measurement limitations, these conclusions can only be considered preliminary. However, this study has provided support for the proposed hypotheses, finding a significant influence of military experience on some characteristics of violence and victimization. Since it appears that violence, particularly domestic violence, may be strongly related to experience in the military, there exists the need for additional research to begin providing more conclusive answers to the questions posed by this study.

REFERENCES

Archer, D., & Gartner, R. (1976). Violent acts and violent times: A comparative approach to postwar homicide rates. *American Sociological Review, 41*, 937-963.

Bebber, C. C. (1994). Increases in U.S. violent crime during the 1980s following four American military actions. *Journal of Interpersonal Violence, 9*, 109-116.

Beckerman, A., & Fontana, L. (1989). Vietnam veterans and the criminal justice system: A selected review. *Criminal Justice and Behavior, 16*, 412-428.

Bohannon, J. R., Dosser, Jr., D. A., & Lindley, S. E. (1995). Using couple data to determine domestic violence rates: An attempt to replicate previous work. *Violence and Victims, 10*, 133-141.

Borus, J. R. (1973). Adjustment issues facing the Vietnam returnee. *Archives of General Psychiatry, 28*, 501-506.

Boulanger, G. (1986). Violence and Vietnam veterans. In G. Boulanger & C. Kadushin (Eds.). *The Vietnam Veteran Redefined: Fact and Fiction* (pp. 79-90). Hillsdale, NJ: Lawrence Erlbaum Associates.

Bryant, C. D. (1979). *Khaki-Collar Crime: Deviant Behavior in the Military Context.* New York: The Free Press.

Bureau of Justice Statistics. (1981). *Veterans in prison.* Washington, DC: U.S. Government Printing Office.

Bureau of Justice Statistics. (1991). *Survey of Inmates of State Correctional Facilities, 1991: United States.* Conducted by U.S. Department of Commerce, Bureau of the Census. ICPSR ed. Ann Arbor, MI: Inter-university Consortium for Political and Social Research [producer and distributor].

Cronin, C. (1995). Adolescent reports of parental spousal violence in military and civilian families. *Journal of Interpersonal Violence, 10*, 117-123.

Dubanoski, R. A., & McIntosh, S. R. (1984). Child abuse and neglect in military and civilian families. *Child Abuse & Neglect, 8*, 55-67.

Galvin, R. P. (1995). Army seeks answers after Bragg murders. *Navy Times, 45,* 10.

Griffin, W. A., & Morgan, A. R. (1988). Conflict in maritally distressed military couples. *American Journal of Family Therapy, 16,* 14-22.

Grinker, R. R., & Spiegel, J. P. (1963). *Men Under Stress.* Philadelphia: Blakiston.

Hackworth, D. H. (1995). Talking 'soldier to soldier' behind bars. *Newsweek, 126,* 27-28.

Hakeem, M. (1946). Service in the armed forces and criminality. *Journal of Criminal Law and Criminology, 37,* 120-137.

Jensen, P. S., Lewis, R. L., & Xenakis, S. N. (1986). The military family in review: Context, risk, and prevention. *Journal of the American Academy of Child Psychiatry, 25,* 225-234.

Jordan, B. K., Marmar, C. R., Fairbank, J. A., Schlenger, W. E., Kulka, R. A., Hough, R. L., & Weiss, D. S. (1992). Problems in families of male Vietnam veterans with posttraumatic stress disorder. *Journal of Consulting and Clinical Psychology, 60,* 916-926.

MacKenzie, D. L., & Souryal, C. (1995). Inmates' attitude change during incarceration: A comparison of boot camp with traditional prison. *Justice Quarterly, 12,* 325-354.

Martin, D. (1976). *Battered Wives.* San Francisco, CA: Glide.

Morash, M., & Rucker, L. (1990). A critical look at the idea of boot camp as a correctional reform. *Crime & Delinquency, 36,* 204-222.

Petrik, N., Rosenberg, A. M., & Watson, C. G. (1983). Combat experience and youth: Influences on reported violence against women. *Professional psychology: Research and Practice, 14,* 895-899.

Resnick, H. S., Foy, D. W., Donahoe, C. P., & Miller, E. N. (1989). Antisocial behavior and post-traumatic stress disorder in Vietnam veterans. *Journal of Clinical Psychology, 45,* 860-866.

Schneider, A. J. N., & LaGrone, C. W. (1945). Delinquents in the army: A statistical study of 500 rehabilitation center prisoners. *American Journal of Psychiatry, 102,* 82-91.

Sterngold, J. (1993). Sailor admits he killed shipmate in case that reflects gay debate. *New York Times,* 4 May, sec A, p. 1.

World Almanac Books. (1996). *World Almanac and Book of Facts.* Mahwah, NJ: Author.

Worthington, E. R. (1978). Demographic and pre-service variables as predictors of post-military service adjustment. In C. R. Figley (Ed.), *Stress Disorders Among Vietnam Veterans: Theory, Research and Treatment* (pp. 173-182). New York: Brunner/Mazel.

Yager, J. (1976). Postcombat violent behavior in psychiatrically maladjusting soldiers. *Archives of General Psychiatry, 33,* 1332-1335.

Yager, T., Laufer, R., & Gallops, M. (1984). Some problems associated with war experience in men of the Vietnam generation. *Archives of General Psychiatry, 41,* 327-333.

Yesavage, J. A. (1983a). Dangerous behavior by Vietnam veterans with schizophrenia. *American Journal of Psychiatry, 140,* 1180-1183.

Yesavage, J. A. (1983b). Differential effects of Vietnam combat experiences vs. criminality on dangerous behavior by Vietnam veterans with schizophrenia. The *Journal of Nervous and Mental Disease, 171*, 382-384.

Section II

CHILD ABUSE IN THE MILITARY FAMILY

The chapters that follow in this section address the problem of child abuse in the military, including its prevalence and the dynamics involved in detecting abusive behavior. In Chapter 7, David Soma reports the results of an analysis of child maltreatment in the U.S. Army by rank of sponsor and age of child. Using precollected survey data from the Army Family Advocacy Central Registry for the years 1983 through 1985, he finds what appears to be a significant rank and age effect in the Army population. Soma argues that these results suggest that younger children of parents in lower ranks are at an increased risk for maltreatment, which lends support to the wealth of sociological literature suggesting young children with young parents are at greater risk of abuse.

Willard Mollerstrom and his colleagues, in Chapter 8, report on the incidence of child maltreatment in the United States Air Force by presenting descriptive data on over 19,587 substantiated cases of child abuse and neglect which occurred over a six-year period. They discuss the annual percentage increases in child maltreatment, as well as the substantiation rates for child abuse and neglect. Mollerstrom, Patchner, and Milner also describe various types of programs the Air Force offers to military personnel and their families.

In Chapter 9, Nancy Raiha and David Soma investigate child abuse and neglect in the Army, drawing on 1992 to 1994 records from 8,422 cases. Their analyses reveal lower maltreatment and markedly lower neglect rates for Army children as compared to children in the general population. Their results suggest that low neglect rates reflect the Army's exclusion of persons who are serious substance abusers, chronically unemployed, or mentally ill. Raiha and Soma conclude that infants and toddlers with low-ranking parents are at the greatest risk for physical abuse and neglect, that boys are neglected more frequently than girls, that younger boys are at higher risk for physical abuse and neglect than girls, and that teenage girls are the highest risk group for minor physical, sexual, and emotional abuse.

Chapter 7

AN ANALYSIS OF RANK EFFECTS ON CHILD MALTREATMENT IN THE UNITED STATES ARMY: 1983 - 1985

DAVID J. SOMA

To date, a comprehensive analysis of the child maltreatment data collected by the Army has been limited. While a number of preliminary analyses have been conducted (Lanier, 1977; Mangelsdorff, Furukawa & James, 1982; Miller, 1972, 1976), these studies have largely reported frequency distributions and have not answered more discriminating questions, such as which children are more likely to be maltreated and which persons in the Army are most likely to be maltreators. Therefore, this study, then, tests the following hypotheses: that neglect will be found in proportionally greater number in the junior enlisted grades; that the ratio of serious to minor injuries will also be higher in the junior enlisted grades.

Generally, the emphasis in child-maltreatment research has been on children from birth to 17 years. This analysis, however, will use birth to 11 years because the availability of comparison data was only compatible from birth through 11 years old.

Although this appears to leave out a segment of the population of interest, there are those who see this as a logical cut-off point. Research has shown that there are important differences between types of abuse (Pagelow, 1984), and adolescent maltreatment has been recognized as a specialized problem area within the overall field of child maltreatment since the late seventies (Fisher & Berdie, 1978; Garbarino & Jacobson, 1978; Libby & Bybee, 1979; Morgan, 1978). Studies by Daley and Pilliavin (1982), Garbarino and Carson (1979), Garbarino and Gilliam (1980), and Lourie (1977, 1979) found that maltreatment of adolescents is different from the maltreatment of younger children. Trainor (1984) also suggests that adolescent maltreatment has certain dissimilar dynamics when compared to the maltreatment of younger children. Table 7-1 reflects the overall child maltreatment rates by rank of sponsor and age of the maltreated child. The rates are extremely interesting in that they show a rather definite rank effect. This rank effect suggests some relationship between the sponsor's rank and the child maltreatment rate.

Table 7-1
CHILD MALTREATMENT RATES FOR ALL CHILDREN BY RANK OF SPONSOR

| Rank of Sponsor | AGE OF CHILD | | | | | | | | | Age Adjusted Rate | |
| | 0 – 2 | | | 3 - 5 | | | 6 - 11 | | | | |
	A	B	C	A	B	C	A	B	C	A	C
E1*	24	3,705	3.2	8	1,802	2.2	2	1,017	1.0	34	1.8
E2*	80	2,041	19.6	37	1,271	4.6	24	687	17.5	141	17.1
E3	217	5,451	19.9	76	3,716	10.2	50	2,277	11.0	343	12.7
E4	486	20,088	12.1	316	18,711	8.4	258	13,616	9.5	1,060	9.7
E5	324	18,914	8.6	360	27,546	6.5	388	32,218	6.2	1,072	6.8
E6	129	12,753	5.1	196	25,080	3.9	422	53,982	3.9	474	4.2
E7	25	4,840	2.6	43	10,736	2.0	138	38,658	1.8	206	2.0
E8-E9	3	823	1.8	3	1,973	0.8	24	8,607		30	1.3
WO1-CW4	9	1,462	3.1	10	2,841	1.8	16	8,681	0.9	35	1.6
01	5	786	3.2	6	603	5.0	4	554	3.6	15	3.9
02	3	1,559	1.0	2	1,265	0.8	3	1,421	1.1	8	1.0
03	9	7,161	0.6	15	9,065	0.8	13	11,217	0.6	37	0.7
04-06	4	2,505	0.8	8	5,039	0.8	14	17,429	0.4	26	0.6
Total	1,318	82,088	8.0	1,080	109,648	4.9	1,367	190,364	3.6		
Rank Adjusted Rate/1000			6.1			4.5			4.5		
Error Rate per 1,000			± .4			± .3			± .2		

A: Number of children maltreated over a 2-year period.
B: Number of children at risk
C: Rate per 1,000 per year.
*Note: These are in training - so be cautious in interpreting.

METHODOLOGY

The data analyzed were preexisting survey data. These data were taken from the Army's completed survey forms (DA Form 4461-R) devised as a straightforward method of determining the incidence of child maltreatment and neglect among military dependents. As Kerlinger (1964) notes, systematic reporting of this kind is typically done in order to assess the relative incidence, distribution, and interrelations of natural occurring phenomena.

The totals for the "physical maltreatment" tables and the "neglect" tables will not match the totals on the "physical maltreatment/neglect" tables, because both physical maltreatment and neglect cases were included in the tables. This was done in order to be as accurate and as fair as possible, using the assumption that the physical maltreatment and neglect category includes cases in which both physical maltreatment and neglect exist. In addition, the rank groupings were collapsed in order to make them as meaningful as possible. The groups that were collapsed were chosen because they did not have enough maltreated children in the subgroups (a minimum of five in either collapsed group was the normal cut-off) for valid analysis.

RESULTS

Army-wide figures show a child maltreatment rate of 7.5 per 1,000 per year including physical maltreatment, neglect, physical maltreatment and neglect, sexual abuse, and emotional maltreatment for children between birth and 17 years old. (This rate does not appear on Table 7-1, but comes from the original data prior to the deletion of sexual abuse and emotional maltreatment.) This rate, more than 4 points less than the national rate of 11.7 for 0 to 17 year olds, seems to contradict the widely held belief that Army children are at greater risk for abuse (American Association for Protecting Children, 1985; Miller, 1976; U. S. Department of Health and Human Services, 1980). On the other hand, the data in Table 7-1 are quite consistent with national data patterns showing that younger children are maltreated more frequently than older children. In addition, Table 7-1 shows a rather definite rank effect. This rank effect suggests some relationship between the spouse's rank and the child maltreatment rate. Army-wide rates comparing children from birth to 2 years old to those from 3 to 5-years-old are consistent with this pattern. For the children of enlisted members, the risk increases from between 1.3 and 2.3 times from birth to 2-year-olds as for 3–5 year olds. For children of warrant officers, the risk is one and three-quarters greater for the younger group. For officers, however, the rate is remarkably different. The same risk for the officer pay grades of O–4 to O–6 is two-thirds of the risk for the children of O-1s in the birth to 2-year-old group compared to those in the 3–5 year old group. However, this difference may be explained by the fact that the numbers are quite small and slight movement in cases of maltreatment could easily change the results, especially noting that the rates are essentially equal across these ranks and ages.

The total rates by age also prove interesting in that there is a noticeable decrease in the rates of child maltreatment as the child's age increases. Children from birth to 2 years old have 1.6 times greater risk of maltreatment than children from 3–5 years old. The 3–5 year old children, in turn, had a 1.4 times greater risk of maltreatment than children from 6–11 years old. And children from birth to 2 years old had over twice the risk of maltreatment as children from 6 to 11.

The most startling results, however, come from the rates of maltreatment across ranks and ages. A definite effect is seen, the higher rate essentially associated with lower rank and younger children (see Table 7-1). For this analysis, E-1s and E-2s are excluded because by majority, E-1s and E-2s are considered to be in training status, and therefore, are not representative of the overall group (U. S. Army Soldier Support Center, 1985). Though the families of those in training are eligible for all military benefits, including medical care, a great many of these families do not constitute part of the military community until after the sponsor has completed his/her initial training. Because they do not utilize the medical or other military programs available to them, they do not have the same chance of being included in these data.

Table 7-1 demonstrates the inverse relationship between rates of child maltreatment and service members' pay grade: between birth and 2 years, the incidence rate of maltreatment decreases steadily for the children of E-3s through E-7s (from 19.9 per 1000 for E-3s to 2.6 per 1,000 for E-7s). For children between the ages of three and five, the results are basically the same, in that they decline as the members' pay grade increases from E-3 to E-7. Incidence rates are generally lower in this age range. For children between the ages of six and eleven, the results are similar, though actual rates differ. Of particular note in this age range is the difference in maltreatment rates for the children of E-3s, as compared with those of E-7 through E-9. The risk is six times as great for children of E-3s as compared to those of E-7 in this category, and almost eight times greater than those of E-8 and E-9.

For warrant officers, the decrease in maltreatment rates is related to an increase in the child's age, and all rates are well below both national and Army-wide rates. Of note also is that children in the birth to 2-year-old group are one and three-quarters times as likely to be maltreated as those in the 3–5 year old group and 3.3 times as likely as those in the 6–11 year old group. This appears to give additional support to the young child at risk theory. It must be noted that the warrant officer category (CWO-1 through CWO-4) was collapsed across all ranks due to insufficient numbers. This collapsing confounds the age, income, and status variables making it difficult to conclude much about them. The category was included for completeness.

The numbers in the officer categories are quite small, making meaningful interpretation difficult. However, the second lieutenants (O-1) are interesting in that their rates appear to be higher than the other officer categories. A child whose sponsor is a second lieutenant and is newborn to 2 years old is three times more likely to be maltreated than one whose sponsor is a first lieutenant (O-2), five times more likely than one whose sponsor is a captain (O-3), and four times as likely as one whose sponsor is a major (O-4) or above. The difference is even more dramatic for the 3–5 year olds. The child of a second lieutenant has more than six times the risk of a first lieutenant or above. For 6–11 year olds, maltreatment rates indicate that the children of second lieutenants are at somewhat greater risk than those of first lieutenants and considerably greater risk than those of majors and above.

The fact that the newest, youngest, and least paid officer group has the highest risk ratio appears to reinforce the results derived from the enlisted data. Overall, the officer rates appear to be consistently low, except for second lieutenants' children; this difference is possibly related to the age of the sponsor.

Tables 7-2 and 7-3 show the numbers and maltreatment rates for male and female children respectively. Table 7-2 shows a child maltreatment rate of 5.4 per 1,000 male children between birth and 11 years old, while Table 7-3 shows a child maltreatment rate of 4.5 per 1,000 female children, making a risk of child maltreatment approximately 1.2 times greater for male than for female children. Compared to the national rates of 9.5 for males and 10.4 for females from birth to 17 years old (American Association for Protecting Children, 1985; U.S. Bureau of the Census, 1984), it appears that the army's rates of child maltreatment are notably lower. It should be noted that the rates used in this section of the study are for children from birth to 11 years old, which may have an impact on the rates. However, since the rate of child maltreatment normally decreases with age, the results of adding the 12–17 year old group to the army data would almost certainly lower the army rate and therefore increase the disparity. In the future, it is hoped that compatible age groupings through 17 years old will be available and will correct this particular problem.

According to Tables 7-2 and 7-3, the overall rate of child maltreatment, both unadjusted and rank adjusted, are higher for all age groups of male children compared to female children. Tables 7-5 and 7-6, which show the rate of physical maltreatment for male children and for female children, support this phenomenon. The risk for birth to 2 years old is relatively equal while the risk for 3–5 year olds is 1.3 times greater for male children, and the risk is 1.6 times as great for male children in the 6–11 year old group. Rank adjusted rates show basically the same risk ratios as the unadjusted rates. Otherwise, these two tables seem to reinforce the aforementioned rank effect and suggest possible contributing factors of income, status, stability, and age.

Table 7-2
CHILD MALTREATMENT RATES FOR MALE CHILDREN
BY RANK OF SPONSOR

| Rank of Sponsor | AGE OF CHILD | | | | | | | | | Age Adjusted Rate | |
| | 0 – 2 | | | 3 - 5 | | | 6 – 11 | | | | |
	A	B	C	A	B	C	A	B	C	A	C
E1*	12	1,917	3.1	5	939	2.7	2	513	1.9	19	2.4
E2*	58	1,095	26.5	19	603	15.8	15	355	21.1	92	20.8
E3	112	2,818	19.9	32	1,901	8.4	25	1,187	10.5	169	11.9
E4	245	10,313	11.9	172	9,434	9.1	148	6,921	10.7	565	10.5
E5	171	9,650	8.9	192	13,908	6.9	225	16,417	6.9	588	7.3
E6	67	6,473	5.2	123	12,794	4.8	257	27,437	4.7	447	4.8
E7	14	2,448	2.9	25	5,502	2.3	87	19,641	2.2	126	2.4
E8-E9	3	438	3.4	2	968	1.0	17	4,386		22	2.0
WO1-CW4	6	734	4.1	6	1,455	2.1	9	4,464	1.0	21	2.0
01	2	391	2.6	3	303	5.0	2	275	3.6	7	3.8
02	2	809	1.2	1	654	0.8	2	741	1.3	5	1.1
03	5	3,654	0.7	7	4,636	0.8	8	5,746	0.6	20	0.7
04-06	2	1,265	0.8	4	2,542	0.8	6	8,956	0.3	12	0.6
Total	699	42,005	8.3	591	55,645	5.3	803	97,039	4.1		
Rank Adjusted Rate/1000			6.4			4.8			5.1		
Error Rate per 1,000			± .6			± .4			± .3		

A: Number of children maltreated over a 2-year period.

B: Number of children at risk.

C: Rate per 1.000 per year.

*Note: These are in training - so be cautious in interpreting.

Table 7-3
CHILD MALTREATMENT RATES FOR FEMALE CHILDREN
BY RANK OF SPONSOR

Rank of Sponsor	AGE OF CHILD									Age Adjusted Rate	
	0 - 2			3 - 5			6 - 11				
	A	B	C	A	B	C	A	B	C	A	C
E1*	12	1,788	3.4	3	863	1.7	0	504	0.0	15	1.2
E2*	22	946	11.6	18	668	13.5	9	332	13.6	49	13.1
E3	105	2,633	19.9	44	1,815	12.1	25	1,090	11.5	174	13.5
E4	241	9,775	12.3	144	9,277	7.8	110	6,695	8.2	495	9.0
E5	153	9,264	8.3	168	13,638	6.2	174	15,801	5.5	495	6.3
E6	62	6,280	4.9	73	12,286	3.0	165	26,545	3.1	300	3.5
E7	11	2,392	2.3	18	5,234	1.7	51	19,017	1.3	80	1.6
E8-E9	0	385	0.0	1	1,005	0.5	7	4,221		8	0.5
WO1-CW4	3	728	2.1	4	1,380	1.4	7	4,217	0.8	14	1.3
01	3	395	3.8	3	300	5.0	2	279	3.6	8	4.0
02	1	750	0.7	1	611	0.8	1	680	0.7	3	0.7
03	4	3,507	0.6	8	4,429	0.9	5	5,471	0.5	17	0.6
04-06	2	1,240	0.8	4	2,497	0.8	8	8,473	0.5	14	0.7
Total	619	40,083	7.8	489	54,003	4.5	564	93,325	3.0		
Rank Adjusted Rate/1000			5.9			4.0			3.8		
Error Rate per 1,000			± .6			± .4			± .2		

A: Number of children maltreated over a 2-year period.
B: Number of children at risk.
C: Rate per 1,000 per year.
*Note: These are in training - so be cautious in interpreting.

Tables 7-4 and 7-7 reflect the overall child maltreatment rates for physically maltreated and for neglected children respectively. Although the rates are not the same, a similar pattern of rank effect remains quite strong on both tables. With only a few exceptions, the incidence rates are all higher for neglect than for physical maltreatment. This can be seen by looking at the incidence rates for E-3s through E-7s across age groups for the two tables. From birth to 2 years old, there is a six and one-half times greater risk of physical maltreatment for the children of E-3s than for those of E-7s, while there is a nine and three-fifths times greater risk of neglect for the same group. For 3–5 year olds, the risk of physical maltreatment is slightly over 3 times greater for the children of E-3s than for those of E-7s, while for neglect the risk is almost 9 times greater for E-3s' children. A similar relationship exists for 6–11 year olds, with 4 times the risk of physical maltreatment for the children of E-3s as compared to those of E-7s and nine and one-quarter times the risk for neglect for E-3s' children.

Table 7-4

PHYSICAL MALTREATMENT RATES FOR ALL CHILDREN
BY RANK OF SPONSOR

Rank of Sponsor	AGE OF CHILD									Age Adjusted Rate	
	0 - 2			3 - 5			6 – 11				
	A	B	C	A	B	C	A	B	C	A	C
E1*	11	3,705	1.5	4	1,802	1.1	2	1,017	0.5	16	0.9
E2*	35	2,041	8.6	12	1,271	4.7	9	687	6.6	56	6.5
E3	88	5,451	8.1	30	3,716	4.0	18	2,277	4.0	136	4.9
E4	194	20,088	4.8	136	18,711	3.6	132	13,616	4.8	462	4.5
E5	125	18,914	3.3	129	27,546	2.3	216	32,218	3.4	470	3.1
E6	47	12,753	1.8	78	25,080	1.6	231	53,982	2.1	356	1.9
E7	12	4,840	1.2	27	10,736	1.3	75	38,658	1.0	114	1.1
E8-E9	3	823	1.8	2	1,973	0.5	20	8,607	1.2	25	1.1
WO1-CW4	7	1,462	2.4	7	2,841	1.2	9	8,681	0.5	23	1.1
01	1	786	0.6	1	603	0.8	1	554	0.9	3	0.8
02	3	1,559	1.0	1	1,265	0.4	2	1,421	0.7	6	0.7
03	2	7,161	0.1	6	9,065	0.3	6	11,217	0.3	14	0.3
04-06	2	2,505	0.4	5	5,039	0.5	11	17,429	0.3	18	0.4
Total	530	82,088	3.2	438	109,648	2.0	732	190,364	1.9		
Rank Adjusted Rate/1000			2.5			1.8			2.3		
Error Rate per 1,000			± .3			± .2			± .1		

A: Number of children maltreated over a 2-year period.
B: Number of children at risk.
C: Rate per 1,000 per year.
*Note: These are in training - so be cautious in interpreting.

Table 7-5
PHYSICAL MALTREATMENT RATES FOR MALE CHILDREN
BY RANK OF SPONSOR

| Rank of Sponsor | AGE OF CHILD | | | | | | | | | | |
| | 0 - 2 | | | 3 - 5 | | | 6 – 11 | | | Age Adjusted Rate | |
	A	B	C	A	B	C	A	B	C	A	C
E1*	3	1,917	0.8	3	939	1.6	1	513	1.0	7	1.1
E2*	23	1,095	10.5	7	603	5.8	8	355	11.3	38	9.6
E3	42	2,818	7.5	18	1,901	4.7	10	1,187	4.2	70	5.1
E4	95	10,313	4.6	78	9,434	4.1	80	6,921	5.8	253	5.1
E5	70	9,650	3.6	69	13,908	2.5	129	16,417	3.9	268	3.4
E6	26	6,473	2.1	50	12,794	2.0	141	27,437	2.6	217	2.3
E7	7	2,448	1.4	14	5,502	1.3	50	19,641	1.3	71	1.3
E8-E9	3	438	3.4	1	968	0.5	15	4,386	1.7	19	1.7
WO1-CW4	15	734	3.4	4	1,455	1.4	6	4,464	0.7	15	1.5
01	0	391	0.0	0	303	0.0	1	275	1.8	1	0.9
02	2	809	1.2	0	654	0.0	2	741	1.3	4	0.9
03	2	3,654	0.3	5	4,636	0.5	3	5,746	0.3	10	0.4
04-06	1	1,265	0.4	4	2,542	1.8	5	8,956	0.3	10	0.5
Total	289	42,005	3.3	253	55,639	2.3	451	97,039	2.3		
Rank Adjusted Rate/1000			2.5			2.1			2.8		
Error Rate per 1,000			± .4			± .3			± .2		

A: Number of children maltreated over a 2-year period.
B: Number of children at risk.
C: Rate per 1,000 per year.
*Note: These are in training - so be cautious in interpreting.

Battle Cries on the Home Front

Table 7-6
PHYSICAL MALTREATMENT RATES FOR FEMALE CHILDREN
BY RANK OF SPONSOR

Rank of Sponsor	AGE OF CHILD										
	0 - 2			3 - 5			6 – 11			Age Adjusted Rate	
	A	B	C	A	B	C	A	B	C	A	C
E1*	8	1,788	2.2	1	863	0.6	0	504	0.0	9	0.6
E2*	12	946	6.3	5	668	3.7	1	332	1.5	18	3.2
E3	46	2,633	8.7	12	1,815	3.3	8	1,090	3.7	66	4.7
E4	99	9,775	5.1	58	9,277	3.1	52	6,695	3.9	209	3.9
E5	55	9,264	3.0	60	13,638	2.2	87	15,801	2.8	202	2.7
E6	21	6,280	1.7	28	12,286	1.1	90	26,545	1.9	139	1.5
E7	5	2,392	1.0	13	5,234	1.2	25	19,017	0.7	43	0.9
E8-E9	0	385	0.0	1	1,005	0.5	5	4,221	0.6	6	0.4
WO1-CW4	2	728	1.4	3	1,380	1.1	3	4,217	0.4	8	0.8
01	1	395	1.3	1	300	1.7	0	279	0.0	2	0.8
02	1	750	0.7	1	611	0.8	0	680	0.0	2	0.4
03	0	3,507	0.0	1	4,429	0.1	3	5,471	0.3	4	0.2
04-06	1	1,240	0.4	1	2,497	0.2	6	8,473	0.4	8	0.3
Total	251	40,083	3.1	185	54,003	1.7	280	93,325	1.5		
Rank Adjusted Rate/1000			2.3			1.6			1.8		
Error Rate per 1,000			± .4			± .2			± .2		

A: Number of children maltreated over a 2-year period.
B: Number of children at risk.
C: Rate per 1,000 per year.
*Note: These are in training - so be cautious in interpreting.

Table 7-7
NEGLECT RATES FOR ALL CHILDREN BY RANK OF SPONSOR

Rank of Sponsor	AGE OF CHILD									Age Adjusted Rate	
	0 - 2			3 - 5			6 – 11				
	A	B	C	A	B	C	A	B	C	A	C
E1*	16	3,705	2.2	6	1,802	1.7	1	1,017	0.5	23	1.2
E2*	51	2,041	12.5	25	1,271	9.8	16	687	11.6	92	11.3
E3	141	5,451	12.9	49	3,716	6.6	36	2,277	7.9	226	8.6
E4	313	20,088	7.8	194	18,711	5.2	132	13,616	4.8	639	5.6
E5	211	18,914	5.6	246	27,546	4.5	199	32,218	3.1	656	4.0
E6	94	12,753	3.7	128	25,080	2.6	204	53,982	1.9	426	2.5
E7	13	4,840	1.3	16	10,736	0.7	66	38,658	0.9	95	0.9
E8-E9	0	823	0.0	1	1,973	0.3	5	8,607	0.3	6	0.2
WO1-CW4	2	1,462	0.7	4	2,841	0.7	7	8,681	0.4	13	0.6
01	4	786	2.5	5	603	4.1	3	554	2.7	12	3.1
02	1	1,559	0.3	1	1,265	0.4	1	1,421	0.4	3	0.4
03	7	7,161	0.5	9	9,065	0.5	7	11,217	0.3	23	0.4
04-06	2	2,505	0.4	3	5,039	0.3	3	17,429	0.1	8	0.2
Total	855	82,088	5.2	687	109,648	3.1	680	190,364	1.8		
Rank Adjusted Rate/1000			4.0			2.8			2.3		
Error Rate per 1,000			± .3			± .2			± .1		

A: Number of children maltreated over a 2-year period.
B: Number of children at risk.
C: Rate per 1,000 per year.
*Note: These are in training - so be cautious in interpreting.

Table 7-8

NEGLECT RATES FOR MALE CHILDREN BY RANK OF SPONSOR

| Rank of Sponsor | AGE OF CHILD | | | | | | | | | Age Adjusted Rate | |
| | 0 - 2 | | | 3 - 5 | | | 6 – 11 | | | | |
	A	B	C	A	B	C	A	B	C	A	C
E1*	9	1,917	2.3	4	939	2.1	1	513	1.0	14	1.6
E2*	38	1,095	17.4	12	603	10.0	8	355	11.3	58	12.2
E3	73	2,818	13.0	15	1,901	3.9	17	1,187	7.2	105	7.5
E4	156	10,313	7.6	101	9,434	5.4	70	6,921	5.1	327	5.7
E5	107	9,650	5.5	129	13,908	4.6	106	16,417	3.2	342	4.1
E6	48	6,473	3.7	78	12,974	3.0	123	27,437	2.2	249	2.8
E7	7	2,448	1.4	11	5,502	1.0	38	19,641	1.0	56	1.1
E8-E9	0	438	0.0	1	968	0.5	3	4,386	0.3	4	0.3
WO1-CW4	1	734	0.7	3	1,461	1.0	3	4,464	0.3	7	0.6
01	2	391	2.6	3	303	5.0	1	275	1.8	6	2.9
02	1	809	0.6	1	654	0.8	0	741	0.0	2	0.4
03	3	3,654	0.4	2	4,636	0.2	5	5,746	0.4	10	0.3
04-06	1	1,265	0.4	0	2,542	0.0	1	8,956	0.1	2	0.1
Total	446	42,005	5.3	360	55,845	3.2	376	97,039	1.9		
Rank Adjusted Rate/1000			4.0			2.9			2.4		
Error Rate per 1,000			± .5			± .3			± .2		

A: Number of children maltreated over a 2-year period.
B: Number of children at risk.
C: Rate per 1,000 per year.
*Note: These are in training - so be cautious in interpreting.

Table 7-9

NEGLECT RATES FOR FEMALE CHILDREN BY RANK OF SPONSOR

Rank of Sponsor	AGE OF CHILD									Age Adjusted Rate	
	0 - 2			3 - 5			6 – 11				
	A	B	C	A	B	C	A	B	C	A	C
E1*	7	1,788	2.0	2	863	1.2	0	504	0.0	9	0.8
E2*	13	946	6.9	13	668	9.7	8	332	12.0	34	10.2
E3	68	2,633	12.9	34	1,815	9.4	19	1,090	8.7	121	9.8
E4	157	9,775	8.0	93	9,277	5.0	62	6,695	4.6	312	5.5
E5	104	9,264	5.6	117	13,638	4.3	93	15,801	2.9	314	3.9
E6	46	6,280	3.7	50	12,286	2.0	81	26,545	1.5	177	2.1
E7	6	2,392	1.3	5	5,234	0.5	28	19,017	0.7	39	0.8
E8-E9	0	385	0.0	0	1,005	0.0	2	4,221	0.2	2	0.1
WO1-CW4	1	728	0.7	1	1,380	0.4	4	4,217	0.5	6	0.5
01	2	395	2.5	2	300	3.3	2	279	3.6	6	3.3
02	1	750	0.0	0	611	0.0	1	680	0.7	1	0.3
03	4	3,507	0.6	7	4,429	0.8	2	5,471	0.2	13	0.4
04-06	1	1,240	0.4	3	2,497	0.6	2	8,473	0.1	6	0.3
Total	409	40,083	5.1	327	54,003	3.0	304	93,325	1.6		
Rank Adjusted Rate/1000			3.9			2.7			2.2		
Error Rate per 1,000			± .5			± .3			± .2		

A: Number of children maltreated over a 2-year period.
B: Number of children at risk.
C: Rate per 1,000 per year.
*Note: These are in training - so be cautious in interpreting.

A pattern, higher rates of neglect than physical maltreatment, is also seen in the overall rates for each age group, but an interesting phenomenon occurs in the 6–11 year old group on both tables. The unadjusted rates of physical maltreatment and neglect for the 6–11 year old group are almost equal, though disparate for the two younger age groups. The rank adjusted rates, being identical, reinforce this pattern.

It appears, then, that younger children are both maltreated and neglected more frequently than older children. Yet as children become older, though less likely to be neglected, they are more likely to be physically maltreated. The literature and previous studies would support the same phenomenon.

Additionally, these data suggest that younger parents are more likely to neglect their younger children than physically maltreat them. For example, an E-3 with a child between birth and 2 years is over one and one-half times as likely to neglect as physically maltreat his/her child. Comparatively, an E-7 is as equally likely to neglect or physically maltreat his/her child of the same age. For children between 6 and 11 years old, the E-3 is twice as likely to neglect or physically maltreat his/her child while the E-7 is slightly more likely to physically maltreat his/her child.

The warrant officer rates, as well as the officer rates, essentially reflect those rates previously analyzed. However, the same limitations on interpretation apply with an additional decrease in raw numbers compounding the difficulty of interpretation. Again, warrant officer rates are included for completeness.

Tables 7-5 and 7-8 show the maltreatment rates for male children who were physically maltreated (Table 7-5) and neglected (Table 7-8). As in the combined tables, the data suggest that younger children with younger parents are more likely to be neglected than physically maltreated. Also, male children are 1.2 times more likely to be neglected than physically maltreated, compared to female children who are one and one-half times more likely to be neglected than physically maltreated (see Tables 7-6 and 7-9). It appears that these rates reinforce the theory that it is more acceptable to physically maltreat male children, and/or that males may be more likely to engage in socially unacceptable behavior, challenging the parents and the system at an earlier age. The data appear to support both possibilities in that the rates convert in the 6–11 year old group and become higher for physical maltreatment than for neglect for E-4 through E-9. In addition, it is seven and one-half times as likely that an E-3 parent with a 6–11 year old will neglect his/her child as compared with an E-7 parent, while it is only three and one-half times as likely that an E-3 with 6–11 year old will physically maltreat his/her child. Lastly, the overall rates, both adjusted and unadjusted, for physical maltreatment are higher only for the 6–11 year old group.

Tables 7-6 and 7-9, on the other hand, suggest a different process for female children. Again, the overall rank effect is present and the neglect rates are basically higher than the physical maltreatment rates. However, the only category between E-3 and E-9 in which the physical maltreatment rate for female children is higher than the neglect rate is the 6–11 year old group for E-6s. This is tempered by the slight difference in rate and the fact that a birth to 2 year old is more than twice as likely to be neglected than physically maltreated in this rank group, while equally likely to be physically maltreated in either the birth to 2 year old group or the 6–11 year old group. Additionally, in contrast to the male child tables, both the adjusted and unadjusted rates for the 6–11 year old group remain higher for neglect than for physical maltreatment for female children.

Comparing the overall rates for Tables 7-5 and 7-8 and Tables 7-6 and 7-9 supports some distinction between male and female children. Tables 7-8 and 7-9 show that overall rates, both adjusted and unadjusted, are basically equal across the age groups. On the other hand, Tables 7-5 and 7-6 show that, although the overall rates for the birth to 2-year-old groups are essentially the same, males between 3 and 5 years of age are at a one and one-third greater risk of physical maltreatment than their female counterparts. Likewise, males between 6 and 11 are over one and one-half times as likely as same-age females to experience physical maltreatment.

DISCUSSION

The data contained in Tables 7-1 through 7-9 appear to strongly support a significant rank effect as well as a significant age effect on child maltreatment in this setting.

These data also suggest some sex differentiation between physically maltreated and neglected children. It appears that in the earliest years there is little if any differentiation, but as the child ages, the rates of maltreatment become increasingly disparate.

This difference might be the result of basic behavioral differences between male and female children. The literature is quite consistent in suggesting that female children, in this age range, exhibit less socially unacceptable and more socially compliant behavior than male children, who challenge the societal and parental systems more (Bandura, 1973 ; Grossman, 1977) . Therefore, if physical maltreatment is the result of parental stress coupled with inappropriate parenting skills directed at a perceived "Problem Child" (Helfer, 1973), it seems reasonable that male children are physically maltreated more than female children as they age.

Another possibility is that both individual parents and society see it as more acceptable and sometimes even desirable to physically discipline male children as opposed to female children (Pagelow, 1984). The societally "expected," or at least socially acceptable behavior, would certainly offer some explanation for the difference in physical maltreatment rates as male and female children increase in age.

However, a more dramatic rank effect appears to be present suggesting several possible contributing factors. The first factor is income. Since the highest rates are in the lowest ranks of both officer and enlisted, it appears possible that income may be affecting maltreatment. This can be postulated as either directly contributing to physical neglect due to insufficient resources or indirectly contributing by encouraging social isolation, anxiety over financial matters, and/or less than adequate living conditions. Since unemployment is normally seen as a contributing factor in child maltreatment, underemployment might too be evaluated as a factor.

A closely linked factor may be the phenomenon of family instability. The army family is a mobile family, and mobility encourages instability, especially in regard to relationships with family, friends, and community support. This phenomenon may be compounded for the lower enlisted and junior officer groups because for most of these families this is their first time being separated from their prior support group(s). It seems possible that the increased stress combined with the lack of support groups to whom one normally looks for guidance and support might result in an increased amount of inappropriate parenting. Also, somewhat linked to both the stability and income issues is the issue of status or how a person perceives him/herself and his/her ability to influence his/her life and/or environment. It is quite commonly accepted that the military rank structure impacts specifically on the issues of status and control. Initially, a service member is accorded virtually no status and little if any control over his/her military environment. The necessity of this process in order to inculcate the necessary group values and goals is well recognized; however, such lack of status and potential feelings of impotency may "encourage" a negative self-image leading to destructive behavior in the soldier's "other" environment, the family.

Finally, the somewhat obvious variable of parental age must be evaluated. There is a strong correlation between low rank and young age, suggesting that the higher rates of maltreatment are found in young families. This is not at all startling as the literature has supported the young parent variable in maltreatment almost from the beginning (Kempe & Helfer, 1972). What is interesting is how age seems to relate to the other variables such as status (e.g., low rank), income (e.g., low rank), and stability (e.g., removal from extended family and community), as well as the fact that this is the group most likely to have young children, less education, and limited experience in life (Miller, 1976). It appears, then, that age of sponsor, as it relates to these other variables, is an important variable in the child maltreatment process.

RECOMMENDATIONS

From this analysis it would appear that the army should concentrate on the families of E-3s through E-5s and focus additional resources on those families that have children who are either five and under or 11 and under.

The appearance of a fairly strong rank effect in all of the tables using the sponsor's rank and the child's age suggests not only potential indicators of maltreatment but also possible areas for prevention.

The import for the Army of the strong rank effect is that this phenomenon suggests a bifurcated approach to intervention. It appears reasonable that, if the previously mentioned factors are found to be contributory, then the emphasis of prevention should be to increase the physical resources and community support for those with younger children, with emphasis on those who are new to the Army and of lower rank. In addition, quality day care at affordable prices should be provided. Conversely, it would appear that for those high risk families with older children, the emphasis would be on teaching parenting skills, including alternative discipline techniques and parent-child communication skills.

REFERENCES

American Association for Protecting Children. (1985). *Highlights of Official Child Neglect and Abuse Reporting.* Denver, CO: American Humane Association.

Bandura, A. (1973). *Aggression: A Social Learning Analysis.* Englewood Cliffs, NJ: Prentice-Hall.

Daley, M. R., & Pilliavin, I. (1982). Violence against children revisited: Some necessary clarification of findings from a major national study. *Journal of Social Service Research, 5*(1/2), 61-81.

Fisher, B., & Berdie, J. (1978). Adolescent abuse and neglect: Issues of incidents, intervention, and service delivery. *Child Abuse and Neglect, 2*(3), 173-192.

Garbarino, J., & Carson, B. (1979). Mistreated youth vs. abused children: Issues for protective services. Unpublished manuscript.

Garbarino, J., & Gilliam, G. (1980). *Understanding Abusive Families.* Lexington, MA: Lexington Books.

Garbarino, J., & Jacobsen, N. (1978). Youth helping youth in cases of maltreatment of adolescents. *Child Welfare, 57*(8), 505-510.

Gil, D. (1974). *Violence Against Children.* Cambridge, MA: Harvard University Press.

Grossman, B. (1977). Children's ideal self–which sex? Paper presented at the annual meeting of the American Psychological Association, San Francisco, CA.

Helfer, R. (1973). The etiology of child abuse. *Pediatrics, 51*(4), 777-779.

Kempe, C. H., & Helfer, R. (1972). *Helping the Battered Child.* Philadelphia, PA: J. B. Lippincott.

Kempe, C. H., & Helfer, R. (1980). *The Battered Child.* Chicago, IL: University of Chicago Press.

Kempe, R., & Kempe, C. (1978). *Child Abuse.* Cambridge, MA: Harvard University Press.

Kerlinger, F. (1964). *Foundations in Behavioral Research.* New York: Holt, Rinehart and Winston.

Lanier, D. (1977). A retrospective analysis of child abuse and neglect among military families. Paper presented at the Military Family Research conference, San Diego, CA.

Libbey, P., & Bybee, R. (1979). The physical abuse of adolescents. *Journal of Social Issues, 35*(2), 101-126.

Lourie, I. S. (1977). The phenomenon of the abused adolescent: A clinical study. *Victimology, 2*(2), 268-276.

Lourie, I. S. (1979). Family dynamics and the abuse of adolescents: A case for a developmental phase specific model of child abuse. *Child Abuse and Neglect, 3,* 967-974.

Mangelsdorff, A. D., Furukawa, T. P., & James, J. (1982). An Analysis of a Sample From the Case Management Incident Reports of the U. S. Army Child Protection Case Management Files. Ft. Sam Houston, TX: Health Care Studies Division.

Miller, J. K. (1972). The maltreatment syndrome in the military community. Paper presented at the Current Trends in Army Social Work conference, El Paso, TX.

Miller, J. K. (1976). Perspectives on Child Maltreatment in the Military. In R. E. Helfer & C. H. Kempe (Eds.), *Child Abuse and Neglect: The Family and the Community* (pp. 267-291). Cambridge, MA: Ballinger Publishing.

Morgan, R. (1978). The battered adolescent: A developmental approach to identification and intervention. In M. L. Lauderdale, R. N. Anderson, & S. E. Cramer (Eds.), *Child Abuse and Neglect: Issues in Innovation and Implementation* (pp. 343-348). Austin, TX: Region VI Resource Center on Child Abuse and Neglect.

Pagelow, M. D. (1984). *Family Violence.* New York: Praeger Publishing.

Straus, M. A., Gelles, R.J., & Steinmetz, S. K. (1980). *Behind Closed Doors: Violence in the American Family.* New York: Doubleday.

Trainor, C. (1984). *A Description of Officially Reported Adolescent Maltreatment and its Implications for Policy and Practice.* Denver, CO: American Humane Association.

U. S. Army Soldier Support Center. (1985). *I Am The American Soldier.* Ft. Benjamin Harrison, IN: Author.

U. S. Bureau of the Census. (1984). *Current Population Reports.* Washington, DC: U. S. Government Printing Office.

U. S. Department of Health and Human Services. (1980). *Child Abuse and Neglect Among the Military.* Washington, DC: U. S. Government Printing Office.

Chapter 8

CHILD MALTREATMENT: THE UNITED STATES AIR FORCE'S RESPONSE

WILLARD W. MOLLERSTROM
MICHAEL A. PATCHNER
JOEL S. MILNER

INTRODUCTION

Child abuse and neglect are prevalent in American society. According to the American Association for Protecting Children (AAPC), nationwide, child abuse reports increased 31 percent between 1985 and 1990 (American Humane Association, 1990), and for the latest period for which data are available (1992), almost three million children were reported to child protective service agencies as victims of child maltreatment (McCurdy & Daro, 1993). In 1989, over 1,237 fatalities were officially confirmed by child welfare agencies (Daro & Mitchel, 1990). Child maltreatment deprives children of a family environment where they should feel safe, secure, and loved, and such maltreatment can produce both short- and long-term psychological problems for the abused child (Augoustinos, 1987; Beitchman, Zucker, Hood, deCosta, & Akman, 1991; Beitchman, et al., 1991, 1992; Browne & Finkelhor, 1986; Crouch & Milner, 1993; Lamphier, 1985).

Families in the military are not unique to the problems of family violence. Over 15 years ago, the Air Force recognized a need to respond on behalf of its families and developed treatment programs and services to address child maltreatment and other forms of family violence. The Air Force Family Advocacy Program (FAP) was developed in 1985 to prevent and treat family violence. To date, however, very few data have been published that describe child abuse and neglect in the military. This article reports on the

Reprinted from Child Abuse and Neglect, 19, Mollerstrom, Willard W., Patchner, Michael A., & Milner, Joel S., (1995), with permission from Elsevier Science. Augoustinos, 1987; Beitchman, Zucker, Hood, deCosta, & Akman, 1991; Beitchman, et al., 1991, 1992; Brocone, 1986; Crouch & Milner, 1993; Lampher, 1985.

incidence of child maltreatment in the Air Force and describes the programs serving Air Force personnel and their families throughout the world. More specifically, this article reports on the incidence of specific types of child maltreatment in the Air Force, and describes the Air Force's services interventions. Additionally, perpetrators' and spouses' perceptions of the services received and the benefits derived are reported.

EXTENT OF CHILD MALTREATMENT IN THE AIR FORCE

Definitions

The following are definitions of terms used by the Air Force in addressing child maltreatment [Department of Defense (DOD), 1987] and, consequently, are the definitions used in this article. Physical child abuse is the maltreatment of a child under the age of 18 that results in major or minor physical injuries. A major physical injury "includes brain damage, skull fracture, subdural hemorrhage or hematoma, bone fracture, dislocations, sprain (sic), internal injury, poisoning, burn, scald, severe cut, laceration, bruise, welt, or any combination thereof, which constitutes a substantial risk to the life or well-being of the victim." A minor physical injury "includes twisting, shaking, minor cut, bruise, welt, or any combination thereof, which do not constitute a substantial risk to the life or well-being of the victim."

Child neglect (deprivation of necessities) "includes neglecting to provide [a] victim with nourishment, clothing, shelter, health care, education, supervision, or contributing to a failure to thrive, when able and responsible to do so."

Child sexual abuse (maltreatment) "includes the employment, use, persuasion, inducement, enticement, or coercion of any child to engage in, or having a child assist any other person to engage in, any sexually explicit conduct (or any simulation of such conduct) or the rape, molestation, prostitution, or other such form of sexual exploitation of children, or incest with children. All sexual activity between an offender and a child, when the offender is in a position of power over the child, is considered sexual maltreatment."

Emotional abuse (maltreatment) "includes behavior on the part of the offender that contributes to low-self esteem, undue fear or anxiety, or other damage to the victim's psychological well-being." Included are "active, intentional berating, disparaging (remarks), or other abusive behavior toward the victim that affects adversely the psychological well-being of the victim" as well as the "passive or passive-aggressive inattention to the victim's emotional needs, nurturing (needs), or psychological well-being."

Multiple abuse occurs when two or more categories of child maltreatment (physical abuse, neglect, sexual abuse, or emotional abuse) are present. Death is defined as a fatality of a child due to maltreatment.

A substantiated case is "a case that has been investigated and the preponderance of available information (indicated) that abuse (had) occurred. This means that the information that (supported) the occurrence of abuse (was) of greater weight or more convincing than the information that (indicated) that the abuse did not occur." An unsubstantiated case is "an alleged case that (had) been investigated and the available information (was) insufficient to support the claim that child abuse and/or neglect did occur."

When an event occurs involving possible child abuse or neglect, the family is referred to a Family Advocacy Officer (FAO) for an initial evaluation. Referrals come from a variety of sources, most often from commanders, medical providers, and school and child-care personnel. The FAO reviews family medical records, contacts the family, and arranges for appropriate medical appointments. Individual and family interviews are conducted by the FAO. An interdisciplinary case management team meeting takes place, which determines whether or not the "case" is substantiated, and if so, recommends specific treatment strategies and program interventions to be offered to the family and individuals involved.

Case Review Procedures

The DOD (1986, 1987, 1992) requires all military branches to collect information on child abuse reports. Consequently, all suspected cases of child maltreatment in the Air Force are reported to the Air Force Central Registry, located at Brooks Air Force Base in San Antonio, Texas. All data are reported on a standard form which identifies the type of maltreatment (i.e., physical, sexual, or emotional abuse or neglect), source of initial referral, and other demographic and descriptive data relevant to the case. When a case has been substantiated by a FAP case review committee, which consists of a multidisciplinary professional team at a medical treatment facility, more detailed information is obtained including the name and other identifying information about the victim and the circumstances related to the abuse or neglect.

Child Maltreatment Reports (FY 87 to FY 92)

Since the registry was initiated in 1987, U.S. Air Force Central Registry data show that during the period from FY 87 through FY 92, 40,178 maltreatment cases were reported and 19,587 were substantiated for child abuse and neglect. The number of cases reported and substantiated by type of maltreatment are reported by year for FY 87 through FY 92 (see Table 8-1).

Table 8-1
SUBSTANTIATED AND UNSUBSTANTIATED CHILD MALTREATMENT CASES
IN THE AIR FORCE REPORTED BY TYPE AND FISCAL YEAR

	FY87	FY88	FY89	FY90	FY91	FY92
Substantiated Cases						
Physical abuse	1,348	1,236	1,215	1,360	1,388	1,306
Neglect	1,019	1,039	1,150	1,117	1,306	1,113
Sexual abuse	521	460	488	487	409	497
Emotional abuse	199	373	275	323	255	385
Multiple	87	80	59	25	13	4
Total	3,174	3,188	3,187	3,312	3,371	3,305
Deaths	2	9	7	11	12	9
Unsubstantiated Cases	2,998	3,275	3,314	3,565	3,617	3,872
Total (all cases)	6,172	6,463	6,501	6,877	6,988	7,177
Substantiation Rate	51%	49%	49%	48%	48%	46%

There were 7,177 cases of reported child abuse and neglect during the 1992 fiscal year (October 1, 1991 through September 30, 1992), which represents an increase of 189 over the previous fiscal year. Overall, 3,305 or 46 percent of the reports were substantiated cases, meaning that these cases were evaluated by a multidisciplinary case management team and found to be valid. While this substantiation rate is slightly lower than the previous fiscal year's rates, it appears to have remained relatively constant over the 6 fiscal years, ranging from 46 to 51 percent (see Table 8-1). This compares to the reported civilian substantiation rate of 39 percent, which was found by averaging the substantiation rates of 44 states that ranged from 15 to 63 percent (Daro & McCurdy, 1991).

Data in Table 8-1 indicate that there has been a slight increase in the absolute numbers of substantiated child maltreatment cases from fiscal years 1987 through 1992. Overall, during this 6-year period the total number of substantiated child maltreatment cases increased 3.96 percent. Regarding specific types of maltreatment, emotional abuse increased 93.5 percent and child neglect increased 8.4 percent; however, the cases of substantiated sexual abuse decreased 4.6 percent and physical abuse declined 3.1 percent. Over the 6-year period from FY 87 through FY 92, physical abuse had an increase rate ranging from 2.53 to 2.85 per 1,000 Air Force children, neglect 2.05 to 2.66, sexual abuse .83 to 1.06, and emotional abuse .40 to .82 (see Table 8-2). Multiple abuse ranged from .01 to .17, but these figures may not be reliable, since such cases are often classified according to the primary type of abuse.

Table 8-2
RATES OF SUBSTANTIATED VICTIM MALTREATMENT PER 1000
AIR FORCE CHILDREN BY TYPE AND FISCAL YEAR

	FY87	FY88	FY89	FY90	FY91	FY92
Type of Maltreatment						
Physical abuse	2.71	2.54	2.53	2.85	2.83	2.78
Neglect	2.05	2.14	2.39	2.34	2.66	2.37
Sexual abuse	1.05	.95	1.01	1.02	.83	1.06
Emotional abuse	.40	.77	.57	.68	.52	.82
Multiple	.17	.16	.12	.05	.03	.01

The Air Force's Central Registry shows that of the substantiated cases of child maltreatment during the 1992 fiscal year, 52 percent of the victims were female and 48 percent male, with the average age of the victims being 7.6 years. The victims' racial backgrounds were 74 percent White, 15 percent Black, 5.5 percent Hispanic, 5 percent Asian or Pacific Islander, and .5 percent American Indian or Alaskan Native. By comparison, ethnic categories for the Air Force at large are 78.8 percent White, 15.4 percent Black, 3.5 percent Hispanic, 1.7 percent Asian or Pacific Islander, and .6 percent American Indian or Alaskan Native (Mollerstrom, Patchner, & Milner, 1992a). Table 8-3 shows the gender of offenders of maltreatment by type of maltreatment over a 6-year period and Table 8-4 shows the race.

Table 8-3
SUBSTANTIATED MALTREATMENT CASES AND DEATHS BY
GENDER OF THE OFFENDERS

	FY87	FY88	FY89	FY90	FY91	FY92
Physical abuse						
Male	65%	66%	65%	65%	62%	67%
Female	35%	34%	35%	35%	38%	33%
Neglect						
Male	52%	51%	49%	55%	48%	47%
Female	48%	49%	51%	45%	52%	53%
Sexual abuse						
Male	95%	93%	93%	93%	95%	95%
Female	5%	7%	7%	7%	5%	5%
Emotional abuse						
Male	56%	58%	54%	62%	58%	65%
Female	44%	42%	46%	37%	42%	35%
Deaths						
Male	50%	89%	57%	82%	67%	89%
Female	50%	11%	43%	18%	33%	11%

Note. Data are not available for multiple abuse cases.

Table 8-4

PERCENT OF SUBSTANTIATED MALTREATMENT CASES AND DEATHS BY
RACE/ETHNICITY OF THE OFFENDERS

	FY87	FY88	FY89	FY90	FY91	FY92
Physical abuse						
White	73.6	68.3	66.9	69.0	70.1	71.8
Black	18.3	20.4	21.3	19.2	17.1	17.1
Hispanic	3.8	5.0	5.9	5.3	6.0	6.5
Asian	3.8	5.9	5.8	6.4	6.8	4.4
Native American	.5	.4	.1	.1	<.1	.2
Neglect						
White	77.9	71.3	68.6	72.6	74.4	76.2
Black	16.7	17.3	20.9	17.7	16.9	14.8
Hispanic	1.7	5.0	3.5	4.4	3.7	2.3
Asian	3.7	6.0	6.8	5.0	4.6	5.7
Native American	0	.4	.2	.3	.4	1.0
Sexual abuse						
White	84.0	78.4	78.9	81.6	83.2	79.3
Black	9.2	11.7	17.2	10.5	10.1	10.7
Hispanic	3.9	7.7	2.4	5.9	5.0	8.3
Asian	1.8	2.2	1.1	2.0	1.7	1.7
Native American	1.1	0	.4	0	0	0
Emotional abuse						
White	82.9	74.6	80.6	69.9	70.1	73.3
Black	7.9	10.3	10.4	15.7	16.3	14.6
Hispanic	1.3	4.7	3.0	4.1	3.9	6.3
Asian	5.3	9.9	6.0	9.7	9.3	5.5
Native American	2.6	.5	0	.6	.4	.3
Deaths						
White	50.0	66.7	85.7	45.5	66.7	77.8
Black	50.0	33.3	14.3	54.5	25.0	11.1
Hispanic	0	0	0	0	8.3	11.1
Other	0	0	0	0	0	0

In Fiscal Year 1992, the marital status of the perpetrators was 75 percent
married, 16 percent divorced/separated, and 9 percent single. The perpetrators' racial background was almost identical to that of the victims, while in
terms of gender, 63.6 percent of the perpetrators were male and 36.4 percent
female. The average number of children in the home was 2.5 (Mollerstrom,
1992). Table 8-5 shows the gender of the victims by type of maltreatment
from FY 87 through FY 92, and Table 8-6 shows the victims' race.

Table 8-5
SUBSTANTIATED MALTREATMENT CASES AND DEATHS BY
GENDER OF THE VICTIMS

	FY87	FY88	FY89	FY90	FY91	FY92
Physical abuse						
Male	55%	55%	54%	52%	54%	52%
Female	45%	45%	46%	48%	46%	48%
Neglect						
Male	53%	52%	54%	53%	54%	56%
Female	47%	48%	46%	47%	46%	44%
Sexual abuse						
Male	18%	17%	24%	23%	20%	21%
Female	82%	83%	76%	77%	80%	79%
Emotional abuse						
Male	48%	52%	49%	48%	52%	48%
Female	52%	48%	51%	52%	48%	52%
Deaths						
Male	0%	56%	71%	36%	50%	33%
Female	100%	44%	29%	64%	50%	67%

Note. Data are not available for multiple abuse cases.

Table 8-6

PERCENT OF SUBSTANTIATED MALTREATMENT CASES AND DEATHS
BY RACE/ETHNICITY OF THE VICTIMS

	FY87	FY88	FY89	FY90	FY91	FY92
Physical abuse						
White	73.4	68.0	66.9	69.9	72.5	71.4
Black	17.9	20.1	21.0	18.4	16.2	17.2
Hispanic	3.3	5.5	5.9	4.8	5.6	6.3
Asian	4.6	5.6	6.0	6.8	5.5	4.8
Native American	.7	.8	.2	.1	.2	.3
Neglect						
White	76.7	70.4	68.7	73.2	73.9	73.7
Black	16.7	17.5	21.7	17.6	17.5	16.1
Hispanic	3.0	6.0	3.8	4.4	3.7	3.9
Asian	3.5	5.5	5.6	4.5	4.3	5.2
Native American	.1	.6	.2	.3	.6	1.1
Sexual abuse						
White	81.0	78.1	77.8	79.5	83.2	79.8
Black	10.6	10.1	11.6	11.1	8.9	8.7
Hispanic	3.2	6.6	2.8	4.5	5.2	6.1
Asian	4.2	5.0	6.9	4.9	2.7	5.2
Native American	1.0	.2	.9	0	0	.2
Emotional abuse						
White	85.5	75.6	75.7	67.2	68.3	74.3
Black	7.9	15.0	12.4	16.9	20.9	13.8
Hispanic	1.3	4.7	3.5	3.4	2.7	8.6
Asian	5.3	4.2	8.4	11.6	7.7	3.3
Native American	0	.5	0	.9	.4	0
Deaths						
White	50.0	66.7	85.7	36.4	75.0	77.8
Black	50.0	33.3	14.3	63.6	16.7	11.1
Hispanic	0	0	0	0	8.3	11.1
Other	0	0	0	0	0	0

Child abuse and neglect occur in all segments of society, and the same is true for the Air Force population. As in the civilian population, the incidence of abuse and neglect tends to be associated with lower income and education (Gelles, 1989; Hampton, 1987; McCurdy & Daro, 1993; Pelton, 1978, 1989). The rates of child abuse and neglect per 1,000 active-duty Air Force personnel by pay grade for FY 92 include: 7.13 from grades E-1 to E-3 ($1,363 to $1,516 per month), 7.64 for E-4 to E-6 ($1,659 to $2,161 per month), and 5.01 for E-7 to E-9 ($2,261 to $3,347 per month). For the officer corps, the rates were 1.80 per 1,000 for grades O-1 to O-3 ($2,172 to $3,230) and 1.10 for O-4 to O-7 ($3,829 to $6,765). Monthly income calculations included basic pay, housing, and subsistence allowances as of January 1, 1994. While other factors may account for the differences found, these data indicate that the lower grades with less income had the higher rates of abuse.

In April, 1991, the National Center on Child Abuse Prevention Research, through a program of the National Committee for Prevention of Child Abuse (NCPCA), published results of a 1990 Annual Fifty State Survey on the Current Trends in Child Abuse regarding rates of maltreatment including fatalities. NCPCA found overall child abuse reports nationally increased 31 percent between 1985 and 1990, with annual increases averaging 5 percent from the 45 states that were recorded; however, this growth rate is less than one-half the growth of reported cases from 1980 to 1985. Increases and decreases in reports varied from state to state. Reasons for decreased reporting in respective states varied, from computer systems differing and increased prescreening to fewer child residents in the state. Increased reporting was credited to increased public awareness and improved reporting systems, but also was assumed to reflect a real increase in maltreatment incidence. Social and economic stresses, as well as increased substance abuse, were also listed by the states as primary causes for increased reporting. Caution in interpreting NCPCA's figures is required, since each state uses unique reporting, screening, and assessment methods in determining child abuse/neglect incidence. No statistically significant relationship was found between the extent of pre-investigation screening and the substantiation rates (Daro & McCurdy, 1991). There seemed to be no consistent relationship between the scope of the state's child abuse reporting laws and the number of reports that were substantiated in each state; debate also centered on what "substantiation" means, with differences occurring from state to state (Daro & McCurdy, 1991). Despite the limitations, the annual 5 percent increase found in this report can be used as a basis for comparing civilian data with those of the Air Force.

The Family Advocacy Program

In response to passage by the U.S. Congress of the Child Abuse Prevention and Treatment Act of 1974, Public Law 98-457, the U.S. Air Force developed a Child Advocacy Program Regulation in 1975. It was the first military service to do so. DOD directives to implement national legislation followed in 1981. These directives assigned responsibility to the services for establishing and operating programs designed to address child abuse and neglect. The DOD directives defined specific categories and types of child and spouse abuse, mandated that each military service establish a central registry, and required the reporting of all such incidents to the respective service's central registry (DOD, 1986, 1992).

In 1985-86, the Air Force expanded the FAP and began to focus on preventing family maltreatment. With U.S. Congress designated funding, outreach workers were hired to implement prevention services, and education and outreach services began to be provided at selected Air Force bases. In performing their jobs, the outreach workers often identified family problems and made referrals to the treatment staff. Treatment staff, however, which usually consisted of a part-time person from mental health programs, began to be overwhelmed with the scope and magnitude of the problems, not to mention the service demands being made of them. Recognizing the growing need for additional personnel, the Department of the Air Force (DAF) in 1988 received Congressional support to augment FAP staff with treatment personnel trained in working with victims, offenders, and families experiencing violence. Continued support has allowed the hiring of FAP staff at all Air Force bases worldwide.

The overall goal of the FAP is to enhance the health and well-being of Air Force families so that military members can concentrate on their assigned duties and job performance. Air Force Regulation 160-38, entitled "Family Advocacy Program," assigns specific tasks for all FAPs throughout the world, including identifying, reporting, assessing and treating families with exceptional medical or educational needs, children who are at risk for injury, and families who are experiencing maltreatment (DAF, 1992). There are five broad elements included in the FAP: (a) prevention, (b) direct service, (c) administration, (d) training, and (e) program evaluation.

Primary and secondary prevention services for families are available at the majority of Air Force bases throughout the world and are overseen by the family advocacy outreach manager. The outreach manager collaborates with other base and civilian agencies to identify and address the needs of families on Air Force bases. Enhancing family strengths, providing services for high-stress events like family separations and reunions, and providing education to at-risk individuals and families are among the prevention services available.

Direct services usually include conducting assessments; substantiating referred cases; providing individual, family, and group counseling, making referrals to Air Force, state, and community agencies; and providing follow-up services. These services are primarily provided by staff at the Air Force bases' medical facility and are coordinated by the Family Advocacy Officer (FAO), who is a credentialed social worker assigned to the medical facility.

The overall administration of the FAP is provided by the office of the Air Force Surgeon General's staff. Policy guidance, standard setting, and day-to-day operations are managed from Brooks Air Force Base, located in San Antonio, Texas, as well as through FAP managers at the major command headquarters located throughout the world.

Training of family advocacy staff and other base personnel occurs through each agency's educational programs, by an individual's continuing education, and through centralized training sponsored by the Surgeon General's staff at Brooks Air Force Base. FAOs, therapists, outreach managers, lawyers, physicians, and family advocacy data support specialists receive administrative, program, and clinical training.

FAP evaluation is overseen by the Air Force Surgeon General's staff at Brooks Air Force Base. The FAP Director of Research has designed, developed, and implemented a 4-year research and treatment evaluation initiative that addresses intrafamilial child and spouse abuse within the Air Force (Mollerstrom, 1989). The ultimate goal of this initiative is to determine which maltreatment interventions work, with which people, and under what conditions. The evaluation protocol, which is administered at pretreatment, post-treatment, and six months following case closure, includes the Family Environment Scale (Moos & Moos, 1986), the Index of Marital Satisfaction (Hudson, 1982), and the Child Abuse Potential Inventory (Milner, 1986). Previous research in the FAP clinical population, using these scales, has indicated a significant relationship between presence of family conflict, lack of family cohesion, lack of marital satisfaction, and potential for abuse (Mollerstrom et al., 1992a).

Services Provided

A varying array of treatment services have been recommended for and completed by child maltreatment perpetrators, depending upon individual situations. The top four services recommended by Air Force FAP and completed by maltreating families were family therapy (35.5%), structured parenting training (34.5%), general parenting education (31.8%), and individual therapy (26.5%). Nineteen additional treatment modalities were recommended and completed, occurring .3% to 17.6% of the time. The number of services recommended per family averaged 2.62, and the number of services completed averaged 2.25 per family.

Air Force findings are in marked contrast to service levels reported nationally, which indicate that on average only 78 percent of substantiated child abuse cases receive some type of child protective services, and that when services are provided, they primarily involve case management and foster care with therapeutic services being limited (Daro & McCurdy, 1991). A 1988 review of child abuse cases in the State of New York found that over one-half of all indicated cases were closed the same day they were officially substantiated (Salovitz & Keys, 1988). Thus, to the extent that data are available, it appears that Air Force families receive more services than civilian families involved in child maltreatment.

Perceptions of Services Received

An earlier report described the initial phase of the 4-year evaluation and provided a profile of the offenders and victims of family violence (Mollerstrom et al., 1992b). Currently in the third year of the 4-year FAP evaluation initiative, preliminary data are available on offenders' and spouses' perceptions of the FAP services received and of the benefits derived as a result of receiving those services.

Preliminary data reported here on the FAP evaluation initiative represent a subset of those cases in the U.S. Air Force Central Registry. When substantiated cases were closed, offenders and spouses were asked to complete a client satisfaction questionnaire. Following removal of 154 subjects' incomplete or invalid protocols based on the validity indices (faking-good index, faking-bad index, random spouse index) taken from the Child Abuse Potential Inventory, 208 offenders and 69 of their spouses remained for analysis.

In this preliminary sample, subjects' responses revealed that 90.9 percent of the offenders and 87.5 percent of the spouses rated the FAP services as good or very good on a four-point Likert-type scale (i.e., very poor, poor, good, very good). When asked if the FAP services received were beneficial, 80.4 percent of the offenders and 86.4 percent of the spouses indicated that they were. Further, for the offenders, 78.8 percent reported that their family situation had improved overall; for the spouses, 82.6 percent reported overall improvement in their family situation.

The FAP also obtained clinician ratings of level of cooperation of the offender and perceived risk of future maltreatment. The ratings were determined by credentialed social work providers in Air Force medical treatment facilities utilizing a standard format. Social workers rated cooperation on a four-point scale from no cooperation (1) to high cooperation (4), and risk on a four-point scale from no risk (1) to high risk (4). Interrater reliabilities for this scale were determined by presenting clinical case vignettes describing six different maltreatment types to one or more workers from 120 Air Force Bases worldwide. Based on these evaluations, the percents of agreement were 77 percent for cooperation and 73 percent for risk.

For these offenders, the level of cooperation significantly ($F=20.19$, $p<.0001$) improved from a mean of 2.88 (SD=.70) pretreatment to a mean of 3.10 (SD=.72) posttreatment. The perceived risk of future maltreatment significantly ($F=24.74$, $p<.0001$) decreased from a mean of 2.21 (SD=.62) pretreatment to a mean of 2.01 (SD=.56) posttreatment.

SUMMARY

Annual percentage changes in state child maltreatment reports indicate a steady growth in child abuse reports throughout the U.S. between 1985 and 1990. Information collected from 45 states further indicates that states averaged a 4 percent increase in reports between 1989 and 1990; annual civilian increases in child abuse reports have averaged approximately 5 percent over the five-year period 1985–1990 (Daro & McCurdy, 1991). During the 1987–1992 fiscal years, the Air Force has experienced a similar growth in child abuse reports. Specifically, Air Force data show an overall increase of 4.1 percent in reports of child maltreatment (see Table 8-1).

Although difficult to assess, national civilian substantiation rates have been estimated at 39 percent and have ranged from 15 to 63 percent. During the last six years, the Air Force's substantiation rates have remained consistently in the 46-51 percent range, which is higher than the states' estimated average but falls well within their range.

In conclusion, child maltreatment is a problem in the military as well as in the civilian population. Currently, the Air Force is actively and substantially involved in the assessment and treatment of child abuse and neglect, as well as in the evaluation of its services. Preliminary data indicated that families have evaluated the services positively and have reported significant benefits as a result of having received services. As quantitative data obtained at the pretreatment, posttreatment, and follow-up assessments become available, Family Advocacy in the Air Force will be able to more effectively evaluate the effects of its programs and better identify services that are associated with client change.

REFERENCES

American Humane Association. (1990). *Member Update*. Denver, CO: Author.

Augoustinos, M. (1987). Developmental effects of child abuse. *Child Abuse & Neglect, 2*, 15-27.

Beitchman, J. H., Zucker, K. J., Hood, J. E., deCosta, G.A., & Akman, D. (1991). A review of short-term effects of child sexual abuse. *Child Abuse & Neglect, 15*, 537-556.

Beitchman, J. H., Zucker, K. J., Hood, J. E., deCosta, G.A., Akman, D., & Cassavla, E. (1992). A review of the long-term effects of child sexual abuse. *Child Abuse & Neglect, 16*, 101-118.

Browne, A., & Finkelhor, D. (1986). Impact of child sexual abuse: A review of the research. *Psychological Bulletin, 99*, 66-77.

Crouch, J. L., & Milner, J. S. (1993). Effects of child neglect on children. *Criminal Justice and Behavior, 20*, 49-65.

Daro, D., & McCurdy, K. (1991). *Current Trends in Child Abuse Reporting and Fatalities: The Results of the 1990 Annual Fifty State Survey*. Chicago, IL: National Committee for Prevention of Child Abuse.

Daro, D., & Mitchel, L. (1990). *Current Trends in Child Abuse Reporting and Fatalities: The Results of the 1989 Annual Fifty State Survey*. Chicago, IL: National Committee for Prevention of Child Abuse.

Department of the Air Force. (1992). *Family Advocacy Program* (Regulation 160-38). Washington, DC: Author.

Department of Defense. (1986). *Family Advocacy Program* (Directive 6400.1). Washington, DC: Author.

Department of Defense. (1987). *Child and Spouse Abuse Report* (Instruction 6400.2). Washington, DC: Author.

Department of Defense. (1992). *Family Advocacy Program* (Directive 6400.1). Washington, DC: Author.

Gelles, R. J. (1989). Child abuse and violence in single-parent families: Parent absence and economic deprivation. *American Journal of Orthopsychiatry, 59*(4), 492-501.

Hampton, R. L. (1987). Race, class, and child maltreatment. *Journal of Comparative Family Studies, 18*(1), 113-126.

Hudson, W. W. (1982). *The Clinical Measurement Package: A Field Manual*. Homewood, IL: The Dorsey Press.

Lamphear, V. S. (1985). The impact of maltreatment on children's psychosocial adjustment: A review of the literature. *Child Abuse & Neglect, 9*, 251-263.

McCurdy, K., & Daro, D. (1993). *Current Trends in Child Abuse Reporting and Fatalities: The Results of the 1992 Annual Fifty State Survey*. Chicago, IL: National Committee for Prevention of Child Abuse.

Milner, J. S. (1986). *The Child Abuse Potential Inventory: Manual* (2nd ed.). Webster, NC: Psytec Corporation.

Mollerstrom, W. W. (1989). Program evaluation and family advocacy. In the Office of the Surgeon General, Family *Advocacy Program Manual*. Brooks Air Force Base, TX: Author.

Mollerstrom, W. W. (1992). *USAF Family Advocacy Central Registry Report.* Unpublished manuscript.

Mollerstrom, W. W., Patchner, M. A., & Milner, J. S. (1992a). Family violence in the Air Force: A look at offenders and the role of the family advocacy program. *Military Medicine, 157,* 371-374.

Mollerstrom, W. W., Patchner, M. A., & Milner, J. S. (1992b). Family functioning and child abuse potential. *Journal of Clinical Psychology, 48,* 445-454.

Moos, R. H., & Moos, R. S. (1986). *Family Environment Scale Manual* (2nd ed.). Palo Alto, CA: Consulting Psychologists Press.

Pelton, L. (1989). *For Reasons of Poverty: A Critical Analysis of the Public Child Welfare System in the United States.* New York: Praeger Press.

Pelton, L. H. (1978). Child abuse and neglect: The myth of classlessness. *American Journal of Orthopsychiatry, 48*(4), 608-617.

Salovitz, B., & Keys, D. (1988). Is child protective services still a service? *Protecting Children, 5*(2), 17-23.

Chapter 9

VICTIMS OF CHILD ABUSE AND NEGLECT IN THE U.S. ARMY

Nancy K. Raiha
David J. Soma

Domestic violence in the United States Armed Forces has provoked much interest in the national media in recent years. Articles and programs (Longley, 1995; Phelan, 1995; Schmitt, 1994; Thompson, 1994) point to "an alarming increase" in domestic violence on America's military bases and "a tendency for violent military training to spill over into domestic violence." Many of these articles and newscasts are based on anecdotal accounts of particularly grisly episodes and reports of overall increases in reporting rates. Although all branches of the service collect extensive information about reported cases of abuse, detailed analyses have not been abundant. Soma's 1987 analysis was not widely distributed. The Air Force has played a leadership role in disseminating data related to domestic violence. Published Air Force studies (Mollerstrom, Patchner, & Milner, 1992, 1994) include breakdowns of demographic variables by abuse type.

Military family violence data can be a rich source of information. Some of this information would be more difficult to obtain in civilian studies. For example, sponsor's rank provides a more valid representation of socioeconomic status than is generally available in civilian studies. The term "sponsor" refers to the active duty military member of a family, because other family members access military benefits through the active duty member's sponsorship. Army ranks increase from the enlisted grades (E1 to E9) through warrant officer (W1 through W4) and officer (O1 to O10). Sponsor's rank is highly correlated with family income, age, parental education level, and social standing. The Army's division of physical abuse cases into major and minor categories provides an opportunity to analyze the differences between profiles of the victims/offenders involved in major and minor abuse cases.

Reprinted from *Child Abuse and Neglect, 21*, Raiha, Nancy K., & Soma, David J. (1997), with permission from Elsevier Science.

Precise comparison of abusing groups to the larger population is possible because the military routinely maintains accurate counts of family members and their demographic characteristics.

Analysis of existing military child abuse data can inform prevention efforts by identifying those groups at greatest risk for child maltreatment.

METHOD

This study analyzes the 8,422 substantiated child maltreatment cases involving active duty Army families which were reported to the Army Family Advocacy Central Registry in 1992 and 1993. Each case of alleged child abuse or neglect reported to Army authorities is investigated and subsequently presented to the local military community's Family Advocacy Case Management Team. This multidisciplinary team determines whether the allegations of abuse or neglect are substantiated. Determination is based on the "preponderance of the available evidence" (Department of the Army, 1987). A detailed report of each substantiated case is sent to the Army's Central Registry. Cases in the Army Central Registry generally include all cases with Army family member victims, both on and off the military installation, as military officials work together with local child protection agencies.

Demographic profiles of the total Army population were obtained from the U.S. Army Family Demographics System (1994). The Army Family Demographics System data were obtained from the Defense Eligibility Enrollment System (DEERS) which collects demographic information about each enrolled military family member. Family members must enroll in this system to be eligible for any military benefits. This study utilized the Family Demographic System September 1992 historical data set. September 1992 was the closest compilation date to the midpoint in the study period. Comparison information about child abuse and neglect in the U.S. population was obtained from the National Center on Child Abuse and Neglect's summary of reports from the states (U.S. Department of Health and Human Services [DHHS], 1994, 1995).

Rates of abuse were estimated by dividing the number of reported cases by the person-years of exposure. All Army family member children under the age of 18 are considered the exposed population. This population was 570,531 children in September 1992. The study period was two years. Estimated rates are reported per 1,000 person-years. Confidence intervals (95%) for rate ratios were calculated using Taylor series methods as discussed in Kleinbaum, Kupper, and Morgenstern (1982). This study is exploratory in nature. Between group comparisons, which are reported using rate ratios, were chosen based on observed data trends rather than a *priori* hypotheses.

Reports to the Army's Central Registry divide incidents of child abuse or neglect into five main categories: minor physical abuse, major physical abuse, emotional abuse, neglect, and sexual maltreatment. A case may involve more than one type of substantiated abuse. Major physical abuse is differentiated from minor physical abuse as involving injuries which constitute a substantial risk to life or well-being. Such injuries include brain damage, skull fracture, subdural hemorrhage or hematoma, bone fracture, dislocation, sprain, internal injury, poisoning, burn, scald, or severe cut, laceration, or welt (Department of the Army, 1987).

Abuse rates for each type of maltreatment are analyzed by gender, age, and sponsor rank. Because children's age is correlated with sponsor rank within each major rank category (enlisted, warrant officer, and officer), age and rank may act as confounding variables. There is a possibility that an apparent relationship between age and maltreatment rate might be due to the influence of sponsor rank. An apparent relationship between sponsor rank and maltreatment rate might also be due to the influence of age. To rule out these possibilities in appropriate circumstances, analyses were repeated controlling for age or sponsor rank. When trends involving age and rank were both found, analyses were repeated to ensure that the age trends persisted within each sponsor rank, and that sponsor rank trends persisted at each victim age.

RESULTS

The 4,280 substantiated Army child maltreatment cases reported in 1992 and the 4,162 cases reported in 1993 did not differ substantially. In both years, 38 percent of all cases involved minor physical abuse, 39 percent involved neglect, 17 percent involved sexual maltreatment, and less than 4 percent major physical abuse. The percentage of reported cases involving emotional abuse increased from 8.9 percent to 10.2 percent. The percentages total to more than 100 percent because 7.1 percent of the cases involved more than one type of abuse. The proportion of cases involving another type of abuse was less than 13 percent in four of the five maltreatment groups, but nearly half (47%) of all emotional abuse cases were reported in conjunction with at least one other type of abuse or neglect.

Figure 9-1 shows the annual victim rates for both the Army and general U.S. population. The overall 1992/93 abuse/neglect rate in the Army population is 7.4 annual cases per thousand (an average of 422 annual cases in a population of 470,531 children). This 1992/1993 abuse rate does not differ significantly from Soma's (1987) finding of a 7.5 per thousand rate in 1984 and 1985. This rate is substantially lower than the general U.S. population rate of 14 cases per thousand in 1992 and 1993 (Department of Health and Human Services [DHHS], 1994, 1995). The difference between Army and general population rates is primarily due to a neglect rate less than half that found in the general population.

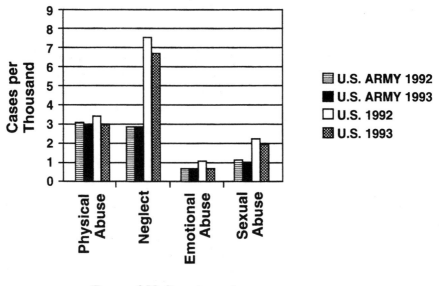

Type of Maltreatment

Figure 9-1. Child Maltreatment Rates for U.S. Army and U.S. Population

Tables 9-1, 9-2, and 9-3 show maltreatment rates by victim gender, victim age, and victim's sponsor's rank. When all maltreatment victims are considered together, it is clear that younger children with lower-ranking sponsors are at greatest risk for child maltreatment. The average age for all Army victims was 7.2 years. Females were slightly more often victims: 53.0 percent of victims were female, and 47 percent were male (Rate Ratio. = 1.15; C.I. = 1.10 - 1.20). Patterns of abuse become clearer as each type of abuse is considered separately.

Table 9-1
VICTIM RATES FOR CHILD MALTREATMENT BY VICTIM'S GENDER

Gender	Major Physical		Minor Physical		Neglect		Emotional		Sexual		All Types	
	Rate	n	Rate	n	Rate	n	Rate	n	Rate	n	Rate	n
Male	0.29	169	2.81	1632	3.05	1769	0.66	385	0.55	319	6.91	4004
Female	0.24	132	2.80	1569	2.74	1537	0.75	419	1.98	1109	7.91	4438
Total	0.26	301	2.81	3201	2.90	3306	0.70	804	1.25	1428	7.40	8442

Note. Rate = Annual rate per thousand.   n = number of cases in 1992 and 1993.

Table 9-2
VICTIMS RATES FOR CHILD MALTREATMENT BY VICTIM AGE

Age	Major Physical		Minor Physical		Neglect		Emotional		Sexual		All Types	
	Rate	n	Rate	n	Rate	n	Rate	n	Rate	n	Rate	n
<1	2.30	140	2.73	166	6.44	392	0.64	39	0.07	4	11.69	712
1	0.37	29	2.19	173	5.29	417	0.84	66	0.28	22	8.50	670
2	0.22	19	2.64	228	4.48	387	0.82	71	0.75	65	8.36	722
3	0.20	17	2.50	214	3.77	323	0.71	61	1.21	104	7.85	672
4	0.14	12	2.15	181	3.23	272	0.58	49	1.38	116	7.03	592
5	0.10	8	2.50	202	3.56	288	0.74	60	1.35	109	7.75	626
6	0.10	8	2.94	231	3.14	247	0.66	52	1.31	103	7.63	600
7	0.16	12	2.92	216	2.91	215	0.59	44	1.26	93	7.42	549
8	0.13	9	2.74	196	2.61	187	0.67	48	1.27	91	6.80	487
9	0.12	8	2.73	186	1.88	128	0.62	42	1.14	78	6.04	412
10	0.05	3	2.36	157	1.70	113	0.63	42	1.34	89	5.59	372
11	0.11	6	3.11	167	1.58	85	0.63	34	1.56	84	6.36	342
12	0.06	3	3.13	165	1.21	64	0.64	34	2.05	108	6.58	347
13	0.10	5	3.50	168	0.90	43	0.98	47	2.11	101	7.02	337
14	0.23	10	4.47	194	1.20	52	0.74	32	2.15	93	7.98	346
15	0.07	3	3.85	157	0.98	40	0.71	29	1.84	75	6.85	279
16	0.08	3	3.41	121	0.70	25	0.99	35	1.44	51	5.95	211
17	0.06	2	1.98	62	0.29	9	0.51	16	1.28	40	3.84	120

Note. Rate = Annual rate thousand.   *n* = number of cases in 1992 and 1993.
Missing cases = 46.

Table 9-3

VICTIM RATES FOR CHILD MALTREATMENT BY SPONSOR'S RANK

	Major Physical		Minor Physical		Neglect		Emotional		Sexual		All Types	
Rank	Rate	n	Rate	n	Rate	n	Rate	n	Rate	n	Rate	n
E1-E3	1.08	59	3.98	218	6.31	346	0.89	49	1.17	64	12.76	699
E4	0.68	124	4.25	772	6.36	1154	1.08	196	1.38	251	12.92	2345
E5	0.24	58	3.39	821	3.48	841	0.74	179	1.59	385	8.88	2148
E6	0.11	27	2.79	681	2.39	583	0.79	192	1.40	341	6.93	1693
E7	0.08	14	2.36	396	1.19	199	0.60	101	1.29	216	5.08	852
E8-E9	0.00	0	1.77	83	0.34	16	0.32	15	0.85	40	3.09	145
W1-W3	0.03	1	0.94	35	0.62	23	0.19	7	0.59	22	2.23	83
O1-O3	0.08	6	0.65	50	0.48	37	0.27	21	0.57	44	1.92	147
O4-O10	0.02	2	0.27	24	0.18	16	0.19	17	0.18	16	0.68	61

Note. Rate = Annual rate per thousand. n = number of cases in 1992 and 1993.
Missing cases = 269.

Major Physical Abuse

The victims of major physical abuse tended to be young children with low ranking parents (see Tables 9-2 and 9-3). Forty-seven percent of the major physical abuse victims were under one year of age. Children less than one were almost 16 times more likely to be seriously abused than older children (Rate Ratio=15.82 ; C.I.=12.60–19.86). Sixty-three percent of the sponsors of major physical abuse victims were privates (E1-E3) and specialists (E4). Only 21 percent of all Army children had private or specialist sponsors. Children of privates and specialists were more than six times as likely as children of higher ranking sponsors to be victims of major abuse (Rate Ratio=6.49; C.I.=5.12–8.23). Younger children were more often victims within each category of sponsor rank, and the trend for lower ranking sponsors persisted within all age ranges. Of the 297 child victims of major physical abuse in the two year study period with an identified sponsor rank, 127 were under the age of one with a private or specialist sponsor, an annual rate of 4.22 per thousand. This rate is more than 27 times the rate for all other children (Rate Ratio=27.59 ; C.I.=21.93–34.71). Although Table 9-1 shows male children were more often victims of major physical abuse than female children, the difference was not statistically significant (Rate Ratio.=1.24; C.I.=.99–1.56).

Minor Physical Abuse

As Table 9-2 illustrates, minor physical abuse rates peaked during the teen years. Children older than 11 were more likely to be abused than younger children (Rate Ratio=1.34; C.I.=1.24–1.45). Table 9-3 shows that rates of minor physical abuse generally decreased as sponsor's rank increased. Children of enlisted members were much more likely to be victims of minor physical abuse than children of officers and warrant officers (Rate Ratio=5.92 ; C.I.=4.89–7.17). Within the group of children with enlisted sponsors, the rate for lower grades (E1–E5) also exceeded that for higher graded (E6–E9) sponsors (Rate Ratio=1.54 ; C.I.=1.43–1.65). The trends for both age and sponsor rank persisted when the other variable was controlled. The relationship of gender to minor physical abuse was more complex, involving interactions with other variables. When the sponsor was enlisted, teenage girls (ages 12-17) were more often abused than teenage boys (Rate Ratio=1.77 ; C.I.=1.54–2.04). When the sponsor was an officer, more teenage boys than girls were victims, although numbers are very small and the relationship is not statistically significant. In the officer-sponsored group, 17 male teens were victims of minor physical abuse in the two year period ; 11 teenage girls were victims of minor physical abuse in the same period (Rate Ratio=1.48 ; C.I.=0.69–3.16). Among younger children, males were more frequently targets of minor physical abuse. In the 1–11 year old group, the annual rate per thousand for minor physical abuse was 2.88 for boys and 2.33 for girls (Rate Ratio=1.23 ; C.I.=1.14–1.34).

Neglect

Like the victims of major physical abuse, neglect victims tended to be younger children with lower-ranking sponsors (see Tables 9-2 and 9-3). Children less than one year of age were neglected at a rate more than twice that of all other children (Rate Ratio=2.40 ; C.I.=2.16–2.67). Children with sponsors in the lowest grades (private and specialist) were more than three times more likely to be neglected than children with higher ranking sponsors (Rate Ratio=3.35 ; C.I.=3.12–3.59). The trends for both age and sponsor rank persisted when the other variable was controlled. Table 9-1 shows that boys were more often neglected than girls (Rate Ratio=1.11; C.I.=1.04–1.19).

Emotional Maltreatment

Demographic trends for emotional abuse tended to be less clear cut than for other forms of abuse. Patterns were mainly confined to subgroups. Girls were more often emotional abuse victims than boys in the teen years. The annual emotional maltreatment rate was 1.03 per thousand for teenage girls (12–17) and 0.52 per thousand for teenage boys (Rate Ratio=1.99 ; C.I.=1.48 –2.68). Within the enlisted and officer rank groupings, there was no strong relationship between emotional abuse and individual sponsor rank. Rates for the majority of enlisted soldiers' children (E1–E7) were higher than for children of the most senior enlisted (E8–E9), warrant officers, and officers (Rate Ratio=3.37 ; C.I.=2.59–4.38). As Table 9-2 shows, the rates of emotional abuse were generally higher for teens and toddlers. However, the higher rate for teens than for children less than 12 was not statistically significant (Rate Ratio=1.12; C.I.=0.95–1.32). Children under three years of age were more likely to be victims than older children (Rate Ratio=1.27 ; C.I.=1.05 –1.54). When the relationship between age and emotional abuse rate is analyzed within each category of sponsor rank, few age-related trends are discernable within rank-groupings. The emotional abuse annual rate was higher for teens (0.90 per thousand) than other age groups (0.55 per thousand) when sponsors were in the senior enlisted (E6–E9) grades (Rate Ratio=1.66 ; C.I.=1.35–2.05).

Sexual Maltreatment

As shown in Table 9-1, female victims of sexual maltreatment outnumber male victims at every age (Rate Ratio=3.58 ; C.I.=3.16–4.06). Table 9-2 shows that sexual maltreatment rates for ages 12 to 15 are higher than for other ages (Rate Ratio=1.86 ; C.I.=1.64–2.09). For teens ages 12–15, the annual rate of sexual maltreatment is 3.70 girls and 0.45 boys per thousand (Rate Ratio=8.32; C.I.=6.04–11.47). The rate of abuse decreases with sponsor rank. The annual rate for children of lower and middle enlisted soldiers (E1–E7) was almost three times that for children of more senior enlisted, warrant officers, and officers (Rate Ratio=2.90; C.I.=2.41–3.50).

DISCUSSION/IMPLICATIONS

Limitations

In reviewing this study's results, the reader should note several limitations. Caution is required in drawing conclusions about the actual rate of child abuse from studies of substantiated reports of child abuse. The process by which any abusive incident may be reported and determined to be substantiated is complex. Reporting and substantiation rates may vary according to the nature of abuse and characteristics of the individuals involved (Zellman, 1992).

The data reported both through military and state channels are subject to human error. Reports to the Army's Central Registry are sent via computer disk from installations throughout the world. Although the instructions are widely distributed and there is an aggressive error detection program, some input errors may occur. The U.S. national child abuse statistics cited in this paper are limited by a lack of consistency in data collection and reporting procedures (Lewitt, 1994). All states do not report on all variables studied, and findings from those states reporting must be extrapolated to estimate U.S. population rates (DHHS, 1994, 1995).

Because this study is exploratory in nature, it involves multiple comparisons of child abuse rates between different demographic subgroups. A hypothesis-based study would generally involve fewer comparisons. The large number of comparisons decreases the statistical power of these comparisons, increasing the chances that one or more of the "significant differences" between groups is actually due to chance variations between the two groups rather than actual differences in the risk of child abuse.

Comparison to General Population

The substantially lower rate of child abuse and neglect in the military population appears to stem primarily from a neglect rate less than half of that reported in the general U.S. population. The lower neglect rate may reflect the presence in each military family of at least one parent who is employed, able to function effectively within a structured environment, and able to pass literacy and aptitude/intelligence tests, who is subject to elimination from the military population upon the discovery of major mental health problems, criminal conduct, or drug and alcohol abuse. Rates for other types of abuse tend to be slightly lower than U.S. population rates. The relative similarity of other maltreatment rates suggests that factors influencing physical, emotionals and sexual abuse may not differ markedly between military and civilian families.

Identified Groups/Risk Factors

Patterns of abuse found in this study identify a number of groups which are at greater risk for various types of maltreatment. Such groups could well be focal points for prevention, policy, and treatment. Infants and young children with low-ranking parents were at the greatest risk for major physical abuse and neglect. These findings match those of Soma's analysis of Army child abuse and neglect (1987) and civilian studies that link younger ages with increased severity of abuse (Hegar, Zuravin, & Orme, 1994; Pecora, Whittaker, & Maluccio, 1992; Rosenthal, 1988). Minor physical abuse, emotional abuse, and sexual abuse peaked in the teen years. Teenage girls with enlisted parents were at the highest risk. Boys were at greater risk than girls for physical abuse in the elementary school years. Rosenthal (1988) also found an interaction between age and gender, with preadolescent boys and adolescent girls at higher risk of physical injury. Hegar, Zuravin, & Orme's 1994 literature review found few studies to confirm Rosenthal's finding of an age-gender interaction, but commented that, "The adult caretaker's coping and disciplinary skills may be tried to the breaking point by boys and girls at different stages." As observed in civilian studies, girls of all ages were at greater risk for sexual abuse (DHHS, 1994 & 1995).

In general, lower rank was associated with higher rates of abuse. Lower rank can be associated with economic hardship, immaturity, lack of control over life, lower educational levels, and disadvantaged background. Impulsive behavior and poor judgment may contribute to lower likelihood of promotion to higher ranks as well as to increased risk for child abuse. The poorest performers will be removed from the Army and will never progress to higher ranks. Civilian studies have noted low family income, isolation from support systems, and young mothers as risk factors for child abuse (Garbarino, 1976; Pecora et al., 1992; Salzinger, Kaplan, & Artemyeff, 1983; Wahler, 1980). One factor contributing to these trends may be the greater likelihood that professionals will report incidents as abusive when a family has lower socioeconomic status (Zellman, 1992).

Prevention Services

The Army, like other U.S. military services, has a wide-ranging program of services to address child abuse and neglect. Prevention programs address all ages and risk groups. Specific program elements may vary from installation to installation, but standardization of basic program elements is becoming more common. The "Strong Families, Strong Soldiers Project," a collaborative effort of the Army, Department of Agriculture Extension Service, and Cornell University, is developing, testing, and marketing prevention resources and instructional material for use throughout the Army (U.S. Army Community and Family Support Center [USACFSC], 1995). The findings of the present study can be used to focus emphasis on existing program elements that address high risk groups.

Army leadership has recognized the need for services to the families of young children. This need is underscored by the current study. In 1995, the

New Parent Support Program was initiated on fourteen Army bases. This program provides visiting nurses, social workers, and primary prevention programs for young families. Newborns are a major focus of this program, but families with children as old as six may be served. Families identified as "at risk" of abuse or neglect receive more intensive services (Landsverk & Lindsay, 1995). More bases will begin New Parent Support Programs in 1996. Almost all Army bases have other support programs for young families. Such programs may include parenting training, mothers' groups, respite care, parent aides, "shaken baby" education programs, professional or volunteer home visitors, and food supplements in overseas areas where families are not eligible for WIC or food stamps. Child care providers receive mandatory training in identifying abuse and neglect.

School-based age specific prevention education is also provided to parents, caretakers, teachers, and children (USACFSC, 1995). Military community agencies also routinely offer parenting programs. This study supports the practice of offering specific parenting programs that target discipline problems in the elementary years and other programs dealing with teens, since the at-risk groups appear to differ.

The Army's Family Advocacy Program provides safety education targeted to parents, children, caretakers, and teachers. In a 6 month period in 1994, 406 presentations on the topic of Preventing Child Sexual Abuse at 56 installations reached 31,659 participants. A copy of "Preventing Child Sexual Abuse: A Parent's Guide" was distributed to every family within the U.S. Army Recruiting command, whose members are typically stationed away from the supports of the military community (USACFSC, 1995). This study supports the practice of providing sexual abuse prevention programs for all age ranges. More than half the victims of sexual maltreatment were under the age of ten.

Generally the most complex child abuse cases—those which involve felonies, removing children from the home, and court proceedings—include major physical abuse, sexual maltreatment, or very severe neglect. This study appears to reinforce the clinician's experience that the majority of complex cases involve sexual abuse. Only 3.6 percent of reported cases involved major physical abuse while 16.9 percent involved sexual maltreatment. The high incidence of sexual maltreatment cases supports the extra training made available for sexual abuse prevention and treatment. In addition to the general Family Advocacy Staff Training (FAST) Course, Army staff involved with child and spouse abuse teams can attend the Family Advocacy Staff Training Advanced (FASTA) course, which focuses on sexual abuse treatment and prevention. A number of military family advocacy staff members are offered Family Advocacy Command Assistance Team training, which prepares them to join an emergency response team for sexual abuse cases.

Prevention programs should, and often do, target lower ranking parents. Free child care, refreshments, transportation, and outreach to the mobile home parks and low rent apartments that often house lower-ranking families are effective. Educational programs may be linked to well-attended school and community events. The individual military unit plays a vital role in reaching the lower ranking soldier. Soldiers are often required to be at the workplace in the early morning and late evening and will often spend weeks or months away from home in "the field." Spouses may also be military members or have limited child care and transportation resources when the soldier is away. Young families are often not well-integrated into community organizations and support systems. Units can provide encouragement and time off to attend community and school-related prevention events. Many units sponsor parenting training, providing child care and strong encouragement for spouse participation. The key to unit support is the unit commander. All commanders receive a child and spouse abuse manual, "A Commander's Desk Guide." Commanders are briefed on the Army Family Advocacy Program upon taking command and receive annual updates.

SUMMARY

The preceding analysis of 1992 and 1993 Army child abuse reports contains a number of findings with implications for policy, practice, and prevention. Army child abuse rates were found to be lower than rates in the general U.S. population. This difference appears mainly attributable to lower Army neglect rates. The Army population does not include the chronically unemployed, mentally ill, and substance abusing groups who contribute to neglect rates in the civilian population.

The Army sponsors a wide-ranging child abuse prevention program. The results of this exploratory analysis help to define focus areas for prevention efforts. Infants and toddlers are at greatest risk for major physical abuse and neglect. Teen-age girls are at greatest risk for sexual, emotional, and minor physical maltreatment. At younger ages, boys are at greater risk for major and minor physical abuse and neglect than girls. Lower sponsor rank is generally associated with greater risk for all types of abuse.

REFERENCES

Department of the Army. (1987). *Army Regulation 608-18, The Army Family Advocacy Program.* Washington, DC: U.S. Government Printing Office.

Department of Defense, Personnel Support, Families and Education. (1995). *Child Abuse Prevention Month Resource Packet.* Washington, DC: U.S. Government Printing Office.

Department of Health and Human Services. (1994). *Child maltreatment 1992: Reports from the states to the National Center on Child Abuse and Neglect.* Washington, DC: U.S. Government Printing Office.

Department of Health and Human Services. (1995). *Child maltreatment 1993: Reports from the states to the National Center on Child Abuse and Neglect.* Washington, DC: U.S. Government Printing Office.

Garbarino, J. (1976). A preliminary study of some ecological correlates of child abuse: The impact of socioeconomic stress on mothers. *Child Development, 47,* 178-185.

Hegar, R. L., Zuravin, S. J., & Orme, J. G. (1994). Factors predicting severity of child abuse injury: A review of the literature. *Journal of Interpersonal Violence, 9*(2), 170-183.

Kleinbaum, D.B., Kupper, L.L., & Morgensternn, H. (1982). *Epidemiologic research: Principles and quantitative methods.* London, United Kingdom: Lifetime Learning Publications.

Landsverk, J., and Lindsay, S. (1995). *New Parent Support Program Semi-Annual Report.* San Diego: Children's Hospital.

Lewitt, E. M. (1994) Reported child abuse and neglect. *Sexual Abuse of Children, 4*(2), 233-247.

Longley, A. (1995, October 2). Out of bounds. *People,* 91-92.

Mollerstrom, W. W., Patchner, M. A., & Milner, J. S. (1995). Child Maltreatment: The United States Air Forces Response. *Child Abuse and Neglect, 19* (3), 325-334.

Mollerstrom, W. W., Patchner, M. A., & Milner, J. S. (1992). Family violence in the Air Force: A look at offenders and the role of the family advocacy program. *Military Medicine, 157,* 371-374.

Pecora, P.J., Whittaker, J.K., & Maluccio, A. N. (1992). *The child welfare challenge: Policy, practice and research.* New York: Aldine De Gruyter.

Phelan, K. (1995, June 1). Domestic violence in the military. In *ABC News Day One.* New York: American Broadcasting Company.

Rosenthal, J. (1988). Patterns of reported child abuse and neglect. *Child Abuse and Neglect, 12,* 263-271.

Salzinger, S., Kaplan, S., & Artemyeff, C. (1983). Mothers' personal social networks and child maltreatment. *Journal of Abnormal Psychology, 92*(1), 68-76.

Schmitt, E. (1994, May 23). Military struggling to stem an increase in family violence. *The New York Times, 143,* A1.

Soma, D. (1987). An Analysis of Child Maltreatment in the United States Army: 1983-1985. Unpublished doctoral dissertation, University of Washington, Seattle.

Thompson, M. (1994, May 23). The living room war. *Time,* 48-49.

U.S. Army Community & Family Support Center (1995). *Family advocacy program: Corporate report 1995.* Washington, DC: U.S. Government Printing Office.

U.S. Army Family Demographics System [Electronic database]. (1994). Alexandria, VA: U.S. Army Community and Family Support Center.

Wahler, R. G. (1980). The insular mother: Her problems in parent-child treatment. *Journal of Applied Behavioral Analysis, 13,* 207-219.

Zellman, G. L. (1992). The impact of case characteristics on child abuse reporting decisions. *Child Abuse and Neglect, 16,* 57-74.

Section III

PREVENTION AND TREATMENT OF DOMESTIC VIOLENCE IN THE MILITARY

Section III, Prevention and Treatment of Domestic Violence in the Military, has three chapters written by social science scholars, educators, and practitioners. The following chapters explore various issues relative to the treatment and prevention of domestic violence in the military. In Chapter 10, Laura Moriarty and Heath Graves identify strategies which may increase victims' reporting of spouse abuse and those measures which may decrease offender recidivism through treatment programs.

Mallary Tytel, in Chapter 11, describes a new Army model which addresses the prevention and reduction of 14 high-risk behaviors, including child and spouse abuse.

Finally, Chapter 12 concerns the work of Ronald Thompson and his colleagues, providing results of a study they conducted with 379 parents at 25 Air Force bases who participated in a collaborative child physical-abuse prevention project designed by the U.S. Air Force Family Advocacy Program and Father Flanagan's Boys Home.

Chapter 10

VICTIM REPORTS OF PARTNER VIOLENCE IN THE AIR FORCE: STRATEGIES FOR INCREASED REPORTING

LAURA J. MORIARTY
E. HEATH GRAVES

INTRODUCTION

In this chapter, we measure the likelihood of victims notifying an official agency of partner abuse. Studies have indicated that as many as 93 percent of domestic violence incidents involving physical assault may go unreported (Straus, 1993). While the focus of former studies is on a civilian population, the military should not be excluded, as nonreporting is potentially higher in the armed forces.

Left undetected, partner violence will continue, while reporting such violence may have a deterrent effect. What we believe to be true is that unreported incidents of partner violence without any intervention will result in the reoccurrence of such violence. Our goal then is to determine what strategies increase reporting while subsequently decreasing recidivism.

Before discussing reporting behaviors, four factors of the military legal system must be reviewed. First, in the military, an abused spouse has three main options for official reporting of abuse. He or she can report to the police; to the military spouse's unit through the member's supervisor, commander, or first sergeant; or to the base family-advocacy office. Any of these will result in an official investigation. Second, in most cases, the family advocacy office, not the criminal justice system, will be the primary agency to investigate an incident of abuse and make the determination as to whether the abuse is substantiated or not. Family advocacy workers are typically social workers or members of the health professions. Third, the commander of the military member's unit is usually the final authority as to what discipline the soldier will receive. Wide discretion is normally allowed, and spouses presumably are aware of this. Finally, forfeiture of pay and removal of rank (and consequently, income) are typical sanctions in the military justice system. Such sanctions may hurt the victims as well as the offender (Caliber Associates, 1996a; West, Turner, & Dunwoody, 1981).

In order to increase self-reporting of abuse, disincentives to victims' reports must be identified and interventions designed to minimize the disincentives and maximize the incentives. A recent study by Caliber Associates (1996a) used focus groups and reports from known victims of partner violence to identify the disincentives of reporting for military spouses. Although information on relative strengths could not be obtained and the groups and bases used in these focus groups were not picked to provide representativeness, this study offers an excellent overview of the general and military-specific reasons for not reporting abuse (see Figure 10-1).

General Reasons for Not Reporting	Military-Specific Reasons for not Reporting
• Lack of information on who to tell or how to get help	• Fear that the active duty member's career would be in trouble
• Fear of retaliation	• Poor image of family advocacy services
• Fear they would not be able to support themselves or their children	• Fear that the active duty member would be punished by the military
• Fear their family or friends would think badly of them	• Fear that it would be unpleasant for the active duty member at work
• Belief that they could handle the abuse by themselves	• Fear that the active duty member would be kicked out of the military
• Belief that the problem was not that serious	• Distrust of the military
• Embarrassment about the abuse	• Confusion over what the military sees as abuse
• Belief that it was a personal matter	
• Fear of a family break-up	• Perceived lack of services to help the victim
• Fear of being blamed	• Sense of Isolation

Figure 10-1. Disincentives to reporting identified by Caliber Associates.

In addition to identifying disincentives to reporting, the literature (Bachman & Saltzman, 1995a; Caliber Associates, 1996a; Edleson & Eisikovits, 1996; Frisch, 1992; Hilton, 1993) provides four broad areas of control which may increase reporting. They include (1) victim ability to chose between available policing and follow-up options; (2) victim education prior to, at, and after the incident; (3) safety measures to prevent retribution by the offender; and (4) provision for follow-up.

Keeping these in mind, we measured victim reporting on a scale ranging from 0 percent (would not report) to 100 percent (would definitely report) for nine hypothetical situations. Each reporting scenario falls into one of five categories: availability of educational material, victim control, protection from harmful effects, long term follow-up, and Caliber disincentive removal.

The overall research hypothesis is that victims will be more likely to report when education material is available, when they will have some control over the ensuing process, when they know they will be protected in a certain way in advance of reporting, when certain disincentives are removed (such as sanctions that may punish the victim as well), and when there is a provision for long term follow-up.

MEASUREMENT

The methodology for this study is explained in Chapter 3 of this text. In the present section, we explain the conceptualization and operationalization of the variables. Additionally, we examine the reliability and validity of the measures.

Items from the survey measuring reporting behaviors are found in Figure 10-2. The reliability and validity of the self-reported likelihood scores were assessed. A reliability analysis was run on the entire set of answers producing a Cronbach Alpha of .978. The lowest item-total correlation is .738. A separate reliability analysis was run to include only those questions designed to measure the effects of victim empowerment. These four questions yielded an alpha of .92.

Next, we examined the internal consistency of responses by comparing three questions that measured the effect of arrest on a respondent's likelihood to report ($X^2=21.8$; $P<.001$). Internal consistency was found, lending support for using these self-reported likelihoods to at least determine the presence of an effect on reporting and a direction of that effect.

Classification	Item from the Survey
Education	Educational material explaining what the victim can expect if he/she reports.
Victim Control	Ability to mandate time of separation (between 5 hours and 3 days) Ability to mandate counseling as part of the treatment Ability to suspend any sentence involving pay or rank reduction
Protection from Harm	Mandatory separation Orders against drinking alcohol for a certain period
Long Term Follow-up	Case worker will be assigned for a one year follow up period
Caliber Disincentive Removal	Loss of privacy Distrust of the military

Figure 10-2. Classification of Reporting Items

The validity of the responses was assessed by comparing the frequency of official reporting as self-reported to actual reporting behaviors found in this and other studies. A best guess from previous Air Force research is that about 8 percent of the incidents that occur are reported and substantiated. The report rate in the present research confirms this. Of the 59 couples having ever had an incident in which the USAF member had used a physical tactic, only five respondents said they had reported this first incident (8.5%).

To relate this figure to the measurement of reporting likelihood in this study, the "likelihood of reporting now" measure was tabulated for respondents who have never experienced violence. Since first event reporting is this study's primary focus, the group which had experienced violence was eliminated from the following analysis, as their answers would have reflected second or subsequent incident reporting likelihood. With this done, 45 percent of respondents reported a present likelihood of reporting at 60 percent or greater. Clearly, the respondents seem to overestimate the likelihood of their reporting (60 percent compared to 8 percent).

To handle this overestimation of reporting, several corrective methods were used. First, two "cut-offs" for reporting were considered in each case: anyone who reported 60 percent (Probably) or higher on the scale was considered to be a reporter and all those with 50 percent or lower scores considered non-reporters. A second criteria required a score of 90 percent (Very Likely) or 100 percent (Would Definitely) to be considered a report.

Table 10-1
TESTS FOR SIGNIFICANCE OF REPORTING ADJUSTMENT CRITERIA

	Significance Values for Adjustment			
	Prior Violence	Time as Partners	Violence & Time as Partners	Regression Probabilities
Likelihood to report now		.045	.001	.003
Educational Material		.020	.023	.006
Case worker for 1 year	.031	.029	.007	.002
Control over length of separation	.013	.013	.028	.001
Ability to mandate counseling	.014		.032	.000
Ability to "suspend" sentence	.014		.034	.061
No career affecting actions for first (minor) offense	.008	.002	.048	.034
All previous options together	.025			.056
Partner arrested, but no career actions		.025		.025
Partner arrested & all previous options		.007	.040	.000
Ability to make arrest decision		.040	.050	.001
Only commander and case-worker notififed	.015			.000
Partner given no-alcohol order	.015		.030	.002
Off-base agency/complete privacy	.050	.008	.001	.000

* Significance values for the first three categories are Eta values with likelihood as the dependent variable. The values for the fourth category are 2-tailed p-values based on Pearson product moment correlation coefficient calculations. 1-tailed values above .05 are omitted.

One possible explanation for this overestimation is that most of these respondents are in coupled relationships that would never present the necessity of a decision to report abuse. To correct for this effect and to create a better picture of reporting likelihood in couples who are at risk, two adjustments were made. First, the data from this study showed that over 96 percent of the couples that experienced violence in their relationship experience their first incident prior to 10 years of marriage. For this reason, all couples that had been violence-free for over 10 years were considered low risk and removed from consideration in the reporting analysis. Second, using the logistic regression model discussed in Chapter 3 for violence in the past year, probabilities of violence were computed for each couple. Members of the sample who remained after the two cuts were then weighted by these probabilities to give more emphasis to the answers of at-risk respondents. The weights were multiplied by a constant to create the same n-value as existed before weighting.

For each option discussed below, all four likelihoods will be reported. First, the raw responses from all couples (including couples with violence) in the study will be reported. Second, the results will be reported for all couples who had not experienced violence. Third, the scores for those without violence and with less than 10 years together will be reported. Finally, the results calculated using the adjusted and weighted sample will be shown.

We report all of the scores primarily because the elimination of all violent couples and couples that have been together over 10 years leaves only 81 couples. This allows smaller subgroups of scores within this group to possibly skew the overall score (especially in the weighted sample, in which some cases have several times the leverage of others). Also, because of the decreased sample size in these subgroup analyses, the power of tests for statistical significance is reduced. This lack of power may result in an increased incidence of Type II error. Thus, the larger groups' scores will put the smaller subgroups' results into perspective, preventing anomalies which could result from giving increased weight to such a few cases. Respondents who may have actually had violence in their relationship but who answered as if they did not would be of special concern here. The respondents, if they exist, would not have been eliminated by the violence cut and would hence be part of the smaller sample. If the logistic regression model is a good predictor of violence, it is likely that these couples would be very heavily weighted. Since these hypothetical respondents did not even report honestly on an anonymous survey, they are probably on the very extreme end of the official reporting spectrum when compared to those who answered honestly. Although there is no real way to assess this possibility, a scatterplot of the weights assigned to the smaller sample is helpful to get a picture of the overall result of the weighting scheme.

The plot revealed that five cases carry substantially more weight than other cases. To keep these cases from having an inordinate effect on this subgroup's scores, each of the weights above 4.5 were adjusted to equal 4.5.

Although it is less stable because of the weighting and the small sample size, reporting the adjusted subsample figures serves two purposes. First, it has been created to best predict the reporting of those who are most likely to experience domestic violence. Second, it tends to give the most conservative estimate of the change in reporting due to each intervention option. However, because of the loss of power and the instability involved in the weighted subsample and the unweighted, "established" non-violent subgroup, hypothesis testing will be done using the results from the entire sample and from the non-violent subgroup. A hypothesis will be confirmed if both of these groups report statistically significant differences both in (1) the percentage reporting at both 60 percent and 90 percent cut-off levels and (2) the respondents' reporting likelihood mean scores under the current option, as compared to the baseline introduced below. The results from the other two groups will be used to assess the strength of the effect and to temper the conclusions drawn from acceptance of the hypothesis.

The basis for comparison for each of these figures will be the baseline that was established at the beginning of the reporting section of the survey by asking respondents their likelihood of reporting with things as they are now. Since it was previously determined that respondents seem to have overestimated their likelihood of reporting based on official reporting statistics, a direct reliance on the additive difference in reporting percentages would clearly be misleading. Therefore, each analysis will measure the effect of the intervention as a multiplicative factor of the baseline score. Key reporting calculations will be figured for the baseline figure. The results of these are listed in Table 10-2.

Table 10-2
LIKELIHOOD OF REPORTING NOW

	Adjusted	Violent and "established" couples omitted	Violent Couples Omitted	Raw Data
Percent "Reporting" at 60% Cut-off	37.9%	44.4%	45.3%	42.9%
Percent "Reporting" at 90% Cut-off	22.8%	25.9%	28.4%	27.2%
		Mean Scores		
Mean Reporting Score	48.2	52.8	54.1	50.1
Standard Deviation	34.9	33.4	34.0	33.8

Whereas violent couples are less likely to report, "established" couples seem more likely. The sample weighted by the "at risk" factor, like those actually violent couples, seems less likely to report.

With this basis, the first reporting hypothesis is considered: Reporting will be greater if educational material is available detailing what the victim can expect if he or she reports. This was measured by asking for the likelihood of reporting if the respondent had this material. The results are shown in Tables 10-3 and 10-4.

Table 10-3
NET EFFECT OF EDUCATIONAL MATERIAL ON REPORTING LIKELIHOODS

| | **Net Effect of Intervention Option** | | |
| | Violent and "established" couples omitted | Violent Couples Omitted | Raw Data |
	Adjusted		
Percent "Reporting" at 60% Cut-off	50.1%	60.0%	61.7%	61.2%
Additive Increase from Baseline	12.2%	15.6%	16.5%	18.3%
Factor of Increase From Baseline	1.32	1.35	1.36	1.43
Significance of Change		.004	.000	.000
Percent "Reporting" at 90% Cut-off	26.3%	33.8%	34.2%	32.8%
Additive Increase from Baseline	3.5%	7.8%	5.8%	5.6%
Factor of Increase From Baseline	1.15	1.30	1.21	1.21
Significance of Change		.070	.021	.008

Table 10-4
REPORTING LIKELIHOODS WITH EDUCATIONAL MATERIAL

Differences in Self-Reported Likelihoods			
Mean Difference in Reporting Score from Baseline	10.7	10.9	9.2	10.8
Significance of Difference in Reporting Scores (paired T-Test)	.000	.000	.000	.000
Standard Deviation of the Differences	20.8	20.5	18.3	20.1
Lower Bound of Confidence Interval for Difference in Scores from Baseline	6.2	6.3	6.2	8.1

Table 10-3 shows the net effect of this intervention on the count of people whose likelihood score predicted reporting. The reporting rates and additive and multiplicative increases from the baseline are given for each group. A level of significance for the change in reporting is also given. This is a significance level from a McNemar test, which examines the number of people whose "decisions" (as defined by the cut-off) about reporting change between the current and baseline intervention. For higher numbers of changes, this test uses a chi-square type analysis. For low numbers of changes, it uses the binomial distribution.

The second half of the educational material is shown in Table 10-4. Here, the effects of the option on the respondents' actual self-reported likelihood scores are shown. The mean and standard deviation of the increase, the statistical significance of this difference from the baseline (produced from a paired T-test), and the lower bound of the confidence interval for this difference are all given. In subsequent analyses of other reporting interventions, these two result tables will often be combined.

As the results indicate, educational material has a small positive effect on the reporting scores and percentage of reporters for all groups, except that this change was not significant for the smaller, non-violent, established group at the 90 percent cut-off. The change in reporting likelihood score and in overall decisions to report (at 60% and 90% cut-off) were significant for the total sample and for the non-violent subgroup. Therefore, the stated criteria for confirming this hypothesis were met. However, the weakness of this effect is clear from the results in the two smaller groups.

One additional facet of this area was examined in this study. Since the reporting question above presumed the respondent had the material, another question addressed one possible means of getting that information to the respondent.

When asked how likely they were to pick up such information if it were available at a public, frequently traveled (e.g., Commissary, base exchange) area and at a private location (e.g., Family Advocacy, Family Support), just over 50 percent responded they would definitely or probably pick up the information, and 25.2 percent reported they would not.

The next hypothesis tested that the likelihood of reporting would be greater when the victim had some control over the ensuing process. This was addressed in four measures, each covering control over a different part of the intervention process. These areas were ability to decide the time of mandatory separation (between 5 hours and 3 days), the ability to mandate counseling as part of the treatment and sanction process, the ability to "suspend" any sentence involving pay or rank reduction (no such sanction applied unless a second offense occurs), and control over the arrest decision (in minor cases where probable cause existed).

The results for these four measures are reported in the Tables 10-5 and 10-6. The first measure examined is victim control over the period of mandatory separation.

Control over separation seemed to have a small positive effect on reporting likelihood scores. However, it did not have a significant effect on changing people's decisions to report. Thus, considered alone, this option does not produce a positive effect on reporting.

When the victim is given the ability to mandate counseling as part of the treatment or sanction, the results are meaningful, as can be seen in Table 10-6. This area of victim control has significant and strong effects across all groups with a multiplicative increase factor of around 1.7.

The next area of victim control is the victim's ability to make any rank or pay forfeiture into a suspended sentence. A victim exercising this ability would be able to block application of these sanctions unless a second violation occurred. This victim-control option had significant and moderately strong effects across all groups (see Table 10-7).

Table 10-5
REPORTING LIKELIHOOD RESULTS WITH VICTIM CONTROL OVER LENGTH OF SEPARATION (BETWEEN 5 HOURS AND 30 DAYS

| | **Net Effect of Intervention Option** | | | |
| | | Violent and "established" couples | Violent Couples | Raw |
	Adjusted	omitted	Omitted	Data
Percent "Reporting" at 60% Cut-off	43.8%	51.9%	55.1%	52.7%
Additive Increase from Baseline	5.9%	7.5%	9.8%	9.8%
Factor of Increase From Baseline	1.16	1.17	1.22	1.23
Significance of Change		.307	.074	.001
Percent "Reporting" at 90% Cut-off	20.4%	26.6%	29.9%	30.2%
Additive Increase from Baseline	-2.4%	0.7%	1.6%	3.0%
Factor of Increase From Baseline	0.89	1.03	1.05	1.11
Significance of Change		.999	.804	.170
Differences in Self-Reported Likelihoods				
Mean Difference in Reporting Score from Baseline	6.6	9.6	8.5	11.1
Significance of Difference in Reporting Scores (from paired T-Test)	.066	.004	.000	.000
Standard Deviation of the Differences	30.9	28.4	25.0	24.7
Lower Bound of Confidence Interval for Difference in Scores from Baseline (full confidence interval shown for adjusted group since it includes zero)	13.7 to -0.46	3.2	4.4	7.8

Table 10-6
REPORTING LIKELIHOOD RESULTS WITH VICTIM ABLE TO MANDATE COUNSELING AS PART OF TREATMENT OR SANCTION

| | **Net Effect of Intervention Option** | | | |
| | | Violent and "established" couples | Violent Couples | Raw |
	Adjusted	omitted	Omitted	Data
Percent "Reporting" at 60% Cut-off	74.1%	76.3%	76.5%	75.5%
Additive Increase from Baseline	36.2%	31.8%	31.2%	32.6%
Factor of Increase From Baseline	1.96	1.72	1.69	1.76
Significance of Change		.000	.000	.000
Percent "Reporting" at 90% Cut-off	39.5%	46.3%	45.0%	44.6%
Additive Increase from Baseline	16.7%	20.3%	16.6%	17.4%
Factor of Increase From Baseline	1.73	1.78	1.58	1.64
Significance of Change		.000	.000	.000
Differences in Self-Reported Likelihoods				
Mean Difference in Reporting Score from Baseline	22.6	21.5	18.8	19.6
Significance of Difference in Reporting Scores (from paired T-Test)	.000	.000	.000	.000
Standard Deviation of the Differences	30.12	27.4	26.4	27.4
Lower Bound of Confidence Interval for Difference in Scores from Baseline	15.6	15.4	14.4	15.9

Table 10-7
REPORTING LIKELIHOOD RESULTS WITH VICTIM ABLE TO "SUSPEND"
PAY AND RANK FORFEITURES

| | **Net Effect of Intervention Option** | | | |
	Adjusted	Violent and "established" couples omitted	Violent Couples Omitted	Raw Data
Percent "Reporting" at 60% Cut-off	56.7%	63.6%	62.8%	62.6%
Additive Increase from Baseline	18.8%	19.2%	17.5%	19.6%
Factor of Increase From Baseline	1.50	1.43	1.39	1.46
Significance of Change		.001	.000	.000
Percent "Reporting" at 90% Cut-off	38.0%	35.1%	34.5%	34.1%
Additive Increase from Baseline	15.2%	9.1%	6.1%	6.9%
Factor of Increase From Baseline	1.67	1.35	1.22	1.25
Significance of Change		.013	.031	.004
Differences in Self-Reported Likelihoods				
Mean Difference in Reporting Score from Baseline	22.0	17.9	13.6	15.3
Significance of Difference in Reporting Scores (from paired T-Test)	.000	.000	.000	.000
Standard Deviation of the Differences	30.86	29.7	32.5	31.0
Lower Bound of Confidence Interval for Difference in Scores from Baseline	14.9	11.1	8.2	11.1

The final area of victim empowerment was the ability to control the arrest decision for the first offense, provided there was no serious injury but that there was probable cause for a legal arrest.

Victim control over arrest had a weak effect on reporting likelihood scores and reporting decisions at the 60 percent cut-off across all of the groups (Table 10-8). However, the changes in reporting decisions at the 90 percent cut-off were not significant for any group.

Overall, victim control measures had a positive effect. However, the effect of control over arrest and control over the time of separation were not always significant. Overall, across these measures, the strength of this effect was inconsistent and varied depending on the part of the process over which the victim was given authority. The hypothesis that victim control would enhance reporting could only be confirmed when the victim was given control over mandating counseling or limiting the sanctions applied to the offender. No relationship was found in the case of control over arrest and time of separation.

The next reporting hypothesis was that victim likelihood of reporting would be greater when there was a provision for long-term follow-up. The option assessing this hypothesis called for caseworker follow-up for one year after the incident.

Table 10-8
REPORTING LIKELIHOOD RESULTS WITH VICTIM CONTROL OVER LENGTH OF SEPARATION (BETWEEN 5 HOURS AND 30 DAYS

		Net Effect of Intervention Option		
	Adjusted	Violent and "established" couples omitted	Violent Couples Omitted	Raw Data
Percent "Reporting" at 60% Cut-off	47.7%	62.0%	63.7%	61.7%
Additive Increase from Baseline	9.8%	17.6%	18.4%	18.7%
Factor of Increase From Baseline	1.26	1.40	1.41	1.44
Significance of Change		.004	.000	.000
Percent "Reporting" at 90% Cut-off	26.2%	30.4%	32.9%	30.6%
Additive Increase from Baseline	3.4%	4.5%	4.5%	3.4%
Factor of Increase From Baseline	1.15	1.17	1.16	1.12
Significance of Change		.227	.134	.151
Differences in Self-Reported Likelihoods				
Mean Difference in Reporting Score from Baseline	12.8	13.3	11.0	12.2
Significance of Difference in Reporting Scores (from paired T-Test)	.000	.000	.000	.000
Standard Deviation of the Differences	24.2	25.1	26.0	25.6
Lower Bound of Confidence Interval for Difference in Scores from Baseline	7.4	7.7	6.7	8.8

Table 10-9
REPORTING LIKELIHOOD WITH CASE WORKER FOLLOW-UP FOR 1 YEAR

		Net Effect of Intervention Option		
	Adjusted	Violent and "established" couples omitted	Violent Couples Omitted	Raw Data
Percent "Reporting" at 60% Cut-off	35.3%	49.4%	50.3%	50.0%
Additive Increase from Baseline	-2.6%	4.9%	5.1%	7.1%
Factor of Increase From Baseline	0.93	1.11	1.11	1.16
Significance of Change		.503	.216	.030
Percent "Reporting" at 90% Cut-off	14.8%	26.6%	31.3%	30.2%
Additive Increase from Baseline	-8.0%	0.7%	2.9%	3.0%
Factor of Increase From Baseline	0.65	1.03	1.10	1.11
Significance of Change		.999	.332	.248
Differences in Self-Reported Likelihoods				
Mean Difference in Reporting Score from Baseline	3.0	6.2	5.1	6.5
Significance of Difference in Reporting Scores (from paired T-Test)	.335	.037	.009	.000
Standard Deviation of the Differences	27.5	22.5	23.2	23.4
Lower Bound of Confidence Interval for Difference in Scores from Baseline (full confidence interval shown for adjusted group since it includes zero)	9.2 to -3.2	0.4	1.3	3.4

As can be seen in Table 10-9, the effects of this intervention on reporting scores are very weak in all categories and nonexistent or reversed in the adjusted category. Also, the changes in reporting decisions were not statistically significant, except in one case. Therefore, the hypothesis that provisions for long-term follow-up would increase victim reporting is rejected.

The next reporting hypothesis was that victims' likelihoods of reporting would be greater when they know they or their partner will be protected in some way from the effects of reporting. This can be broken down into two sub-hypotheses. For the victim, this involves protection from the offender or from certain offender behaviors. For the offender, this involves protection from certain systemic reactions or sanctions.

There were two victim protection options included in this study. The first, mandated separation, had weak effects and was not statistically significant. The second involved giving the offender an order against drinking alcohol for a certain period of time.

The effect of this intervention on reporting was significant and moderate in all but the adjusted group (Table 10-10). For this group, the effect was weaker, even though the frequency with which the partner became drunk was one of the independent predictive variables used in the logistic regression for weighting this group (see Chapter 3).

Table 10-10
REPORTING LIKELIHOOD WITH OFFENDER GIVER AN ORDER AGAINST
DRINKING ALCOHOL FOR A CERTAIN PERIOD OF TIME

| | Net Effect of Intervention Option | | | |
| | | Violent and "established" couples | Violent Couples | Raw |
	Adjusted	omitted	Omitted	Data
Percent "Reporting" at 60% Cut-off	48.8%	66.7%	65.9%	65.2%
Additive Increase from Baseline	10.9%	22.2%	20.6%	22.3%
Factor of Increase From Baseline	1.29	1.50	1.46	1.52
Significance of Change		.007	.000	.000
Percent "Reporting" at 90% Cut-off	24.6%	36.4%	38.0%	38.5%
Additive Increase from Baseline	1.8%	10.4%	9.6%	11.3%
Factor of Increase From Baseline	1.08	1.40	1.34	1.42
Significance of Change		.039	.015	.001
Differences in Self-Reported Likelihoods				
Mean Difference in Reporting Score from Baseline	14.46	16.9	13.9	15.7
Significance of Difference in Reporting Scores (from paired T-Test)	.000	.000	.000	.000
Standard Deviation of the Differences	29.65	29.5	28.9	30.0
Lower Bound of Confidence Interval for Difference in Scores from Baseline	6.75	9.6	8.8	11.5

Thus, one of the victim protection measures failed to meet the acceptance criteria, although it should be noted that this option required victim control and decision making. The other met the criteria for acceptance and had moderate effects, which were weakest in the weighted and adjusted group.

A pair of offender protection measures was tested under the second part of this protection hypothesis. This pair consisted of an offender protection measure and the same measure with a mandatory arrest policy added. The first measure, which would disallow the use of career-affecting sanctions for first time offenders (as long as there was no serious injury involved and the offender successfully completed counseling) has already been discussed briefly above. The complete results for this item are shown in Table 10-11.

Table 10-11
REPORTING LIKELIHOOD WITH NO CAREER AFFECTING SANTIONS USED
AGAINST FIRST TIME OFFENDERS

| | Net Effect of Intervention Option | | | |
	Adjusted	Violent and "established" couples omitted	Violent Couples Omitted	Raw Data
Percent "Reporting" at 60% Cut-off	60.2%	71.3%	73.6%	72.7%
Additive Increase from Baseline	22.3%	26.8%	28.4%	29.7%
Factor of Increase From Baseline	1.59	1.60	1.63	1.69
Significance of Change		.000	.000	.000
Percent "Reporting" at 90% Cut-off	36.2%	36.3%	41.2%	41.5%
Additive Increase from Baseline	13.4%	10.3%	12.8%	14.4%
Factor of Increase From Baseline	1.59	1.40	1.45	1.53
Significance of Change		.064	.001	.000
Differences in Self-Reported Likelihoods				
Mean Difference in Reporting Score from Baseline	19.1	17.5	17.2	19.0
Significance of Difference in Reporting Scores (from paired T-Test)	.000	.000	.000	.000
Standard Deviation of the Differences	35.1	29.2	29.6	30.0
Lower Bound of Confidence Interval for Difference in Scores from Baseline	11.2	10.9	12.4	15.0

As evidenced in the table, this offender protection option shows moderate to strong positive effects across all but the smaller groups.

The next option, discussed below, adds mandatory arrest to the above measure. This option reads, "Likelihood if your partner would be arrested and then released, but that career-affecting actions would not be used (e.g., letters of reprimand, Article 15s)".

Table 10-12
REPORTING LIKELIHOOD WITH MANDATORY ARREST, BUT NO CAREER
AFFECTING ACTIONS FOR FIRST TIME OFENDERS

| | **Net Effect of Intervention Option** | | |
	Adjusted	Violent and "established" couples omitted	Violent Couples Omitted	Raw Data
Percent "Reporting" at 60% Cut-off	37.1%	53.8%	56.9%	51.7%
Additive Increase from Baseline	-0.8%	9.4%	11.7%	8.8%
Factor of Increase From Baseline	0.98	1.21	1.26	1.20
Significance of Change		.210	.029	.057
Percent "Reporting" at 90% Cut-off	23.0%	28.2%	27.8%	25.8%
Additive Increase from Baseline	0.2%	2.3%	-0.6%	-1.3%
Factor of Increase From Baseline	1.01	1.09	0.98	0.95
Significance of Change		.791	.999	.719
Differences in Self-Reported Likelihoods				
Mean Difference in Reporting Score from Baseline	6.8	8.4	6.7	6.9
Significance of Difference in Reporting Scores (from paired T-Test)	.050	.008	.004	.000
Standard Deviation of the Differences	29.3	27.3	26.8	27.9
Lower Bound of Confidence Interval for Difference in Scores from Baseline	0.01	2.2	2.2	3.1

As can be seen in Table 10-12, the addition of a mandatory arrest policy weakened the effects of this intervention substantially, creating only small or nonexistent changes in self-reported likelihood of reporting. Likewise, considering the net impact on the percent of respondents who would report, this arrest plus offender protection intervention provided only very weak increases from the baseline in some groups, and in some groups even caused a decrease in reporting. Only one of the increases was statistically significant. Thus, this intervention fails to meet the acceptance criteria.

Overall, the victim protection option concerning an alcohol restriction for the partner (without a victim choice component) had moderate effects, while the victim-offender separation option (which required victim choice) was not significant. Protecting the offender's career had moderate to strong significant effects, while a separate option, which added mandatory arrest, was not significant.

In the next analysis, a pair of options are examined similar to those just reviewed above. In this case, one is a composite option, while the other adds an arrest component to this composite. After analyzing those two, the focus will turn to arrest and the effect of arrest alone will be extracted from these pairs and analyzed.

The first of this option pair was a composite of offender protection, victim control, educational material, and follow-up options. This option provided for the protection from career affecting actions, the ability to decide on the length of mandated separation, the ability to mandate counseling as a part of treatment, the ability to "suspend" pay and rank forfeitures, the availability of educational material, and case-worker follow-up for one year. The results for this composite mix are shown Table 10-13.

Table 10-13
REPORTING LIKELIHOODS UNDER THE COMPOSITE OPTION

| | **Net Effect of Intervention Option** | | | |
| | | Violent and "established" couples | Violent Couples | Raw |
	Adjusted	omitted	Omitted	Data
Percent "Reporting" at 60% Cut-off	70.7%	79.7%	76.9%	75.1%
Additive Increase from Baseline	32.8%	35.3%	31.6%	32.2%
Factor of Increase From Baseline	1.87	1.79	1.70	1.75
Significance of Change		.000	.000	.000
Percent "Reporting" at 90% Cut-off	43.6%	46.8%	46.9%	47.0%
Additive Increase from Baseline	20.8%	20.9%	18.6%	19.8%
Factor of Increase From Baseline	1.91	1.81	1.65	1.73
Significance of Change		.001	.000	.000
Differences in Self-Reported Likelihoods				
Mean Difference in Reporting Score from Baseline	26.25	23.3	20.3	21.8
Significance of Difference in Reporting Scores (from paired T-Test)	.000	.000	.000	.000
Standard Deviation of the Differences	36.5	31.2	31.2	30.7
Lower Bound of Confidence Interval for Difference in Scores from Baseline	17.9	16.3	15.1	17.7

As indicated in Table 10-13, the composite option had strong and significant effects across all categories, raising individual reporting scores significantly and increasing the reporting percentages by at least a factor of 1.7.

Also, although each of these options had been evaluated separately, this analysis shows that a combination yielded a result more effective than the best of the options separately.

The same composite option, with the addition of a mandatory arrest policy, is evaluated in Tables 10-14 and 10-15.

Table 10-14
REPORTING LIKELIHOODS UNDER THE ARREST + COMPOSITE OPTION
(NET EFFECTS)

| | Net Effect of Intervention Option | | | |
	Adjusted	Violent and "established" couples omitted	Violent Couples Omitted	Raw Data
Percent "Reporting" at 60% Cut-off	51.2%	63.3%	63.0%	60.0%
Additive Increase from Baseline	13.3%	18.8%	17.7%	17.1%
Factor of Increase From Baseline	1.35	1.42	1.39	1.40
Significance of Change		.004	.001	.000
Percent "Reporting" at 90% Cut-off	21.7%	29.1%	33.6%	31.7%
Additive Increase from Baseline	-1.1%	3.2%	5.2%	4.5%
Factor of Increase From Baseline	0.95	1.12	1.18	1.17
Significance of Change		.581	.152	.144

Table 10-15
REPORTING LIKELIHOODS UNDER THE ARREST + COMPOSITE OPTION
(LIKELIHOOD SCORE DIFERENCE)

	Differences in Self-Reported Likelihoods			
Mean Difference in Reporting Score from Baseline	12.7	12.8	10.8	11.5
Significance of Difference in Reporting Scores (from paired T-Test)	.000	.000	.000	.000
Standard Deviation of the Differences	29.7	27.9	26.3	27.0
Lower Bound of Confidence Interval for Difference in Scores from Baseline	5.9	6.5	6.4	7.8

Once arrest is added to this option, its effect on reporting drops drastically. The mean change in reporting scores is cut nearly in half. The effect on total decisions to report under this option is no longer significant for any group using the 90 percent cut-off.

Before moving on to the final reporting hypothesis, the reporting effects of arrest that have been observed will be examined. For this analysis, the two pairs of interventions just discussed will be examined in a different way. By evaluating the differences in each pair, a picture of the effect of arrest on reporting can be gained. The results of this analysis are shown in Table 10-16.

Table 10-16
THE EFFECTS OF ARREST ON REPORTING

| | Net Effect on Percentage of Reporters | | | |
	Adjusted	Violent and "established" couples omitted	Violent Couples Omitted	Raw Data
Pair 1				
Change in Reporting Due to Arrest at 60% Cut-off	-23.1%	-17.5%	-16.7	-21.0%
Factor of Change in Reporting	.62	.75	.77	.71
Significance of Change in Reporting		.004	.000	.000
Change at 90% Cut-off	-13.2%	-8.1%	-13.4%	-15.7%
Factor of Change in Reporting	.64	.78	.67	.62
Significance of Change in Reporting		.180	.001	.000
Pair 2				
Change in Reporting Due to Arrest at 60% Cut-off	-19.5%	-16.4%	-13.9%	-15.1%
Factor of Change in Reporting	.72	.79	.81	.80
Significance of Change in Reporting		.000	.000	.000
Change at 90% Cut-off	-21.9%	-17.7%	-13.3%	-15.3%
Factor of Change in Reporting	.50	.62	.72	.67
Significance of Change in Reporting		.001	.000	.000
	Differences in Self-Reported Likelihoods			
Pair 1				
Mean Difference in Individual Scores Due to Arrest	9.95	7.82	9.72	11.75
Significance of Difference in Reporting Scores (from paired T-Test)	.000	.001	.000	.000
Lower Bound of Confidence Interval for Difference in Scores	5.29	3.10	6.17	8.80
Pair 2				
Mean Difference in Individual Scores Due to Arrest	13.51	10.38	9.32	10.23
Significance of Difference in Reporting Scores (from paired T-Test)	.000	.000	.000	.000
Lower Bound of Confidence Interval for Difference in Scores	9.35	6.35	6.43	7.82

As found in Table 10-16, mandatory arrest had consistent, significant, and strong negative effects on reporting likelihood almost across the board. Arrest seemed to cause a mean drop in likelihood score of around 10 points. It caused a net drop in the theoretical reporting rates of at least 15 percent. These changes in reporting "decisions" were significant in all but one case (the 60 percent cut off in the nonviolent and established small subgroup). The multiplicative factor for the change was about 0.75.

One final reporting hypothesis remains to be tested. This hypothesis is that victim reporting will be greater when the disincentives identified by Caliber Associates are removed. Most of the disincentives mentioned by the Caliber study fell into other categories that have already been tested. However, two related options remain to be tested under this hypothesis.

First, one of the identified disincentives was the loss of privacy. For this reason, an option was tested wherein only the family advocacy case worker and the USAF member's commander would be advised of a reported incident. The results for this option are shown in Table 10-17.

Table 10-17
REPORTING LIKELIHOODS FOR PRIVACY OPTION

| | Net Effect of Intervention Option | | | |
	Adjusted	Violent and "established" couples omitted	Violent Couples Omitted	Raw Data
Percent "Reporting" at 60% Cut-off	52.6%	66.3%	70.5%	70.0%
Additive Increase from Baseline	14.7%	21.8%	25.3%	27.1%
Factor of Increase From Baseline	1.39	1.49	1.56	1.63
Significance of Change		.001	.000	.000
Percent "Reporting" at 90% Cut-off	29.0%	40.0%	43.2%	43.3%
Additive Increase from Baseline	6.2%	14.1%	14.8%	16.2%
Factor of Increase From Baseline	1.27	1.54	1.52	1.59
Significance of Change		.004	.000	.000
Differences in Self-Reported Likelihoods				
Mean Difference in Reporting Score from Baseline	10.31	15.1	15.6	17.0
Significance of Difference in Reporting Scores (from paired T-Test)	.006	.000	.000	.000
Standard Deviation of the Differences	32.09	28.3	28.0	28.3
Lower Bound of Confidence Interval for Difference in Scores from Baseline	3.1	8.7	10.9	13.2

The effect of this privacy option is strong and significant across all categories. It changes the mean reporting score by over 10 points and appears to increase reporting by a factor of 1.5.

The second option in this category addresses the disincentive labeled by Caliber Associates (1996a, 1996b, 1996c) as distrust of the military, as well as also addressing the privacy issue. It involves the ability to report domestic violence to an off-base civilian agency which would handle the entire incident, with the only military involvement in this case being an information-only notification to a case worker at family advocacy for record-keeping and tracking purposes.

Interestingly, this option has no more effect than the previous option, which addressed the privacy issue without addressing the distrust of the military issue. In fact, the strength of this alternative is less than the previous one (Table 10-18).

Table 10-18

REPORTING LIKELIHOOD IF INCIDENT COULD BE REPORTED TO AND
HANDLED BY A CIVILIAN AGENCY

	Net Effect of Intervention Option			
	Adjusted	Violent and "established" couples omitted	Violent Couples Omitted	Raw Data
Percent "Reporting" at 60% Cut-off	64.2%	65.4%	67.6%	65.9%
Additive Increase from Baseline	26.3%	21.0%	22.3%	23.0%
Factor of Increase From Baseline	1.69	1.47	1.49	1.54
Significance of Change		.005	.000	.000
Percent "Reporting" at 90% Cut-off	21.9%	32.1%	37.2%	36.8%
Additive Increase from Baseline	-0.9%	6.2%	8.8%	9.6%
Factor of Increase From Baseline	0.96	1.24	1.31	1.35
Significance of Change		.238	.031	.003
Differences in Self-Reported Likelihoods				
Mean Difference in Reporting Score from Baseline	12.4	14.8	13.4	14.8
Significance of Difference in Reporting Scores (from paired T-Test)	.000	.000	.000	.000
Standard Deviation of the Differences	26.1	32.2	30.0	30.7
Lower Bound of Confidence Interval for Difference in Scores from Baseline	6.5	7.6	8.5	10.7

CONCLUSION

Clearly, the strength of reporting changed significantly from intervention to intervention, in a seemingly rational manner, with the composite creating more change than any one of its members. At a minimum, this seems to suggest valid measurement of a relative strength of effect.

These results showed that required counseling, privacy safeguards, and limitations on sanctions imposed on the offender all affect reporting strongly. Provision of educational material also showed limited promise, but multiple distribution methods will be necessary to get this information out. Restrictions on alcohol usage were also significant. Long-term follow-up was not a strong incentive to report, nor was being able to report to a civilian agency. Surprisingly, victim control over major areas such as arrest and limitation of sanction did not seem to help reporting. Instead, it seemed that in areas such as limitation of sanction, options had a better effect on reporting when they were automatic. Still, victim control should not be ignored; empowerment and bargaining power give the victim a worthwhile end apart from their nonaffect on reporting. The areas over which this control is given, however, must be carefully chosen, for it appears that some options may actually diminish reporting.

The results of this study suggest that several easily implemented measures may hold great promise in decreasing offender recidivism by increasing official reporting and bringing more offenders into the treatment system. The most promising mix seems to be privacy safeguards, mandatory counseling, and some limitations on the sanctions applied to first-time offenders (specifically, career-affecting actions). Also, some provisions for victim control seem to provide promise. Although it would likely face opposition, a provision for alcohol abuse screening for all cases and subsequent restrictions for those found to need it would also help reporting and, as the logistic regression analyses suggest (see Chapter 3), would also affect the likelihood of severe violence. The best strategy is to combine these options in a composite pattern and publicize them through various distribution means. Distribution is critical because reporting behavior cannot be affected by measures that are not known. Thus, informative presentations of the system should be clear and simple.

REFERENCES

Bachman, R., & Saltzman, L. E. (1995). *Violence against women: Estimates from the redesigned survey. Special Report.* NCJ-154348. Available: http://www.ncjrs.org/txfiles/femasci.txt [1996, Oct 24].

Caliber Associates. (1996a). *Abuse Victims Study Final Report.* Unpublished manuscript.

Caliber Associates. (1996b). *The Study of Spousal Abuse in the Armed Forces: Analysis of Spouse Abuse Incidence and Recidivism Rates and Trends.* Unpublished manuscript.

Caliber Associates. (1996c). *Final Report on the Study of Spouse Abuse in the Armed Forces.* Unpublished manuscript.

Edleson, J. L., & Eisikovits, Z. C. (Eds.). (1996). *Future Interventions with Battered Women and Their Families.* London: Sage.

Frisch, L. A. (1992). Research that succeeds, policies that fail. *The Journal of Criminal Law and Criminology, 83*(1), 209-216.

Hilton, Z. (Ed.). (1993). *Legal Responses to Wife Assault: Current Trends and Evaluation.* London: Sage.

Straus, M. A. (1993). Physical assaults by wives: A major social problem. In R. Gelles & D. Loeske (Eds.), *Current Controversies on Family Violence* (pp. 67-87). London: Sage Publications.

West, L. A., Turner, W. M., & Dunwoody, E. (1981). *Wife Abuse in the Armed Forces.* Washington: Center for Women Policy Studies.

Chapter 11

INSTALLATION PREVENTION TEAM TRAINING: PREVENTION AND RISK REDUCTION IN THE U.S. ARMY

MALLARY TYTEL

INTRODUCTION

Readiness, the combination of materiel, logistics, personnel, and training factors that determine a military unit's ability to be committed to combat, is impacted by a host of human-behavior problems. Soldiers' health, welfare, morale, and cohesiveness are among the primary determinants of the success or failure of a mission and can be as critical as that of tactical training and preparations (Holz, Hiller, & McFann, 1994). In support of the combat mission, a commander needs to be able to assess the impact of high-risk behaviors on soldiers' readiness and call upon local subject-matter experts and program managers to institute appropriate interventions consistent with a program for the reduction of spouse and child abuse, assaults, rapes, traffic fatalities, industrial accidents, drug and alcohol offenses, sexually transmitted diseases, and other crimes against persons and property.

People-problems tend to be multi-faceted. A soldier may have an "alcohol problem" in addition to "family problems," "domestic-abuse problems," or "financial problems." On-post human service agencies and staff are separate, organizationally segmented, precisely defined, and often operate knowing only one aspect of a soldier's situation. This narrow focus often forces busy commanders to deal with an array of service providers when sensitive soldier behavioral problems need their attention. In addition, such problems are time consuming. For example, Fort Bragg, NC, personnel collected data and assessed the time spent by the Squad Leader, Platoon Leader, First Sergeant, and Company-level Commander in handling *one* of their soldiers

Note: The views, opinions, and findings contained in this paper are those of the author and should not be construed as official Department of Army positions, policies, or decisions, unless to designated by other official documentation.

involved in a single, high-risk incident. Table 11-1 reflects the combined hours of leadership time expended based upon this assessment.

Table 11-1
COMBINED HOURS OF LEADERSHIP TIME

Type of Incident	COMMAND Hours Involved
Crime (person)	9.4 to 13.4
Drug-related	10 to 11
Alcohol-related	9 to 11
Spouse abuse	3.4
Child abuse	3.4

Source: Fort Bragg, NC, 1995

In seeking to reverse these patterns of behavior, Army prevention education should ideally concentrate upon those areas identified by local installation-program personnel to be most effective in helping commanders maintain readiness. Within the current climate of downsizing and "having to do better with less," limited staffing and a wide range of health-compromising behaviors are both catalysts for a new, systems-based collaborative approach to reversing these behavioral patterns.

INNOVATION DEVELOPMENT

Since 1971, the United States Army Alcohol and Drug Abuse Prevention and Control Program (ADAPCP) has had a principal role in reducing alcohol and other drug abuse in the Army. The ADAPCP functions under the United States Army Center for Substance Abuse Programs (ACSAP), and administers the Army's biochemical testing program and prevention education services in addition to identifying, screening, assessing, and remediating substance abusers.

Within the current political, economic, and social climate, Army stakeholders felt that the time was ripe for implementing a new program in response to the needs of the field. The reduction of forces around the world and at home, coupled with shrinking resources and a changing mission for the twenty-first century, brought increased attention to reports of escalating high-risk behaviors that impact mission readiness and the quality of life on Army installations. The *1995 Department of Defense Survey of Health Related Behaviors Among Military Personnel* (Bray et al.,) was published with two aims:

to continue surveying substance use (sic) among active duty personnel, and to establish baseline data for assessing progress toward *Healthy People 2000* (U.S. Department of Health and Human Services, 1990) and its objectives for active-duty personnel. While progress had been measured, there were still areas of concern. Cigarette smoking remained common, affecting about one in every three military personnel; smokeless tobacco, particularly in men aged twenty-four or younger, affected about one out of five; and the rate of heavy drinking affected slightly more than one in six active-duty personnel. In addition to educational interventions for sexually transmitted diseases, a sizable group of personnel (24%) needed effective mechanisms for managing stress, with 33 percent of surveyed service women reporting high stress levels associated with being a female in the military.

The traditional military values of duty, honor, and integrity were under scrutiny. In the period 1990–1994, more that 19,000 officers left the military with "bad paper" discharges for reasons such as misconduct, family-related problems, drug and alcohol abuse, and financial responsibility; there was also an increase in general officers being removed from promotion lists or edged into early retirement for questionable behavior (Goldman, 1996). Current headlines are full of accusations of sexual harassment and sexual assault, including allegations against the Sergeant Major of the Army, the most senior of the Army's 400,000 enlisted men.

Today's military environment provides a window of opportunity for ACSAP to respond with programmatic and structural shifts in their standard practices in order to meet the challenges of organizational changes and the mission requirements of the Army into the twenty-first century. Important was ACSAP's development of an innovative new process for addressing the identified health-promotion and risk-reduction problems on Army installations. Figure 11-1 illustrates the innovation development process and includes all activities and subsequent outcomes (Rogers, 1995). This innovation *developed a comprehensive installation-wide plan for prevention integrating the specific, structured processes of the Army's Risk Reduction Program, command support, and a collaborative team approach to plan implementation.* A new training program, Installation Prevention Team Training (IPTT), was developed as the diffusion method for communicating this innovation among the members of the U.S. Army system. It encompassed a systems approach, bringing the significant players together from the variety of agencies and organizations on the installation.

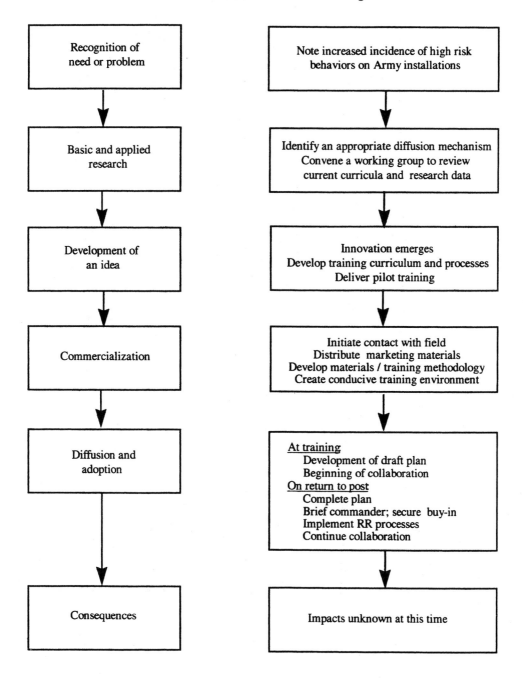

Recognition of need or problem	Note increased incidence of high risk behaviors on Army installations
Basic and applied research	Identify an appropriate diffusion mechanism Convene a working group to review current curricula and research data
Development of an idea	Innovation emerges Develop training curriculum and processes Deliver pilot training
Commercialization	Initiate contact with field Distribute marketing materials Develop materials / training methodology Create conducive training environment
Diffusion and adoption	At training Development of draft plan Beginning of collaboration On return to post Complete plan Brief commander; secure buy-in Implement RR processes Continue collaboration
Consequences	Impacts unknown at this time

Figure 11-1. The innovation development process. Adapted from Rogers (1995), p. 133.

INSTALLATION PREVENTION TEAM TRAINING

The Installation Prevention Team Training (IPTT) program was developed to re-engineer approaches to installation-wide prevention and risk reduction efforts. Through a "fundamental rethinking and redesign of business processes" (Hammer & Champy, 1993, p. 32), an existing Army training course was adapted in order to make the content, materials, and course outcomes relevant to the changing Army organization and mission

Over six months, a multi-discipline, ACSAP-sponsored work group comprised of military and nonmilitary personnel reviewed curricula, the latest research findings, and successful program models from the prevention and health promotion fields. The end result was a team-focused training program based upon the best research, theory, and practices from the civilian sector in prevention, community development, collaboration, strategic planning, and systems thinking.

Training attendees were recruited as installation teams in groups of six to eight members. These individuals were installation program managers who could address and commit resources for installation-wide prevention. They represented a range of post activities and organizations, including Family Advocacy, Safety, Preventive Medicine, Military Police, Health Promotion, Chaplaincy, Drug and Alcohol, and the command group.

Once a team was scheduled for training, an installation point of contact was identified to act as the conduit for receiving and distributing information to the team. All teams then received an information packet and pretraining assignments: (1) Teams were required to come to the training with a community needs assessment; (2) Teams needed to develop and bring with them a common philosophy or understanding about prevention that would be shared with the other teams at the training; (3) Teams needed to bring information about current prevention programs they were involved with on their installation; (4) If the installation as a whole, or individual on-post agencies, had current prevention plans, they were asked to bring them to the training; (5) A team captain was to be designated as the individual responsible for the team at the training site and responsible to the installation commander; and (6) It was strongly recommended that teams meet at least once as a team prior to attending IPTT.

"To strengthen the Installation Prevention Plan through development of an integrated, targeted strategy which supports combat readiness" was the IPTT course purpose. The IPTT curriculum was broken down into competencies of knowledge, skills, and personal mastery, and incorporated the learning disciplines of systems thinking, team learning, shared vision, and mental models (Senge, 1990). The course curriculum is outlined in Figure 11-2.

KNOWLEDGE	SKILLS	PERSONAL MASTERY
History of Prevention	Communication	Value As Team Member
Risk Factors	Conflict Resolution	Increased Awareness of Self
High Risk Behaviors	Development of a Shared	Increased Awareness of Others
Protective Factors	Vision	Fun
Definition of Prevention	Problem Solving	
Public Health Model	Program Planning	
Planning Process	Collaboration	
Systems	Securing Support and Buy-In	
Evaluation	Marketing	
Marketing	Team Building	
Reengineering Approaches		
Risk Reduction Model		
Resources		

Figure 11-2. Training curriculum.

Throughout the training, participant teams worked to develop collaborative strategies to address prevention of high-risk behaviors and learned to apply the Army's Risk Reduction Program (RRP). At the end of the course, teams left with a draft of a comprehensive prevention plan. Within 30 days of returning to their posts, teams were then required to brief their installation commander on the training and present their plans. Installation Prevention Team Training sought to provide commanders, as well as human-service providers, with an opportunity to be proactive in creating an environment in which the well-being of their installation and its members were an integral part of personnel readiness.

Once the program began, IPTT was offered once a month at regional sites, training up to four teams per iteration. From January 1996 through November, 1997, multi-discipline teams from 42 U.S. Army installations around the world attended IPTT. This represented over 70 percent of the total Army community.

During the fall of 1996 and spring of 1997, 90 days after the training commenced, two phases of an outcome-based evaluation of the program were conducted in order to determine the effectiveness of IPTT. Assessment was based upon achievement of four identified key outcomes by the installations:
- Completion of an installation-wide prevention plan
- Adoption of the Army's Risk Reduction Program
- Securing command support and buy-in for installation-wide prevention efforts
- Development on an installation prevention team (IPT) that worked collaboratively to achieve prevention plan goals

A wealth of data was available for examination, specifically the experiences and lessons learned through the development and implementation of a new program in a particular culture. The IPTT training curriculum incorporated prevention and public-health theory and practices which had been developed and tested primarily in civilian communities; the collaboration and team-building curriculum components were consistent with civilian community development processes and theory. The evaluation, therefore, presented an opportunity to examine and extend the applicability of those practices to a different community, especially as they related to the processes and practices of health promotion on Army installations. In addition, this was an opportunity to explore and analyze diffusion theory within the context of the command-driven U.S. Army organization and the implications for future prevention program development and implementation within this particular environment.

IMPLEMENTATION OF THE ARMY'S RISK REDUCTION PROGRAM (RRP)

In November and December 1993, there were a series of violent, high profile incidents in the Fort Campbell, KY, community. The ensuing low morale, extensive negative publicity, and potential for disruption of mission provided a window of opportunity for the Alcohol and Drug Abuse Prevention and Control Program (ADAPCP) office to reorganize in an effort to address these incidents.

The Risk Reduction program began with the consolidation of all available Fort Campbell data on identified high-risk behaviors. These included domestic violence, alcohol and drug offenses, Absences Without Leave (AWOL), crimes against persons and/or property, sexually transmitted diseases, injuries, and financial problems. Based upon incident rates computed for each battalion, the battalions with the highest risk profiles were identified. Data analysis was then conducted by a team of staff members. During analysis, particular consideration was given to the operational tempo and specific events that had occurred in each battalion during the preceding quarter.

Once battalions with the highest number of problem incidents were identified, command consultations were held between commanders and human-service program managers. The data analysis provided the battalion commander with specific information—risk indicators—concerning his/her battalion's incident rate as compared to the post rate, and installation-level analysis in order to track overall results. Selected or indicated intervention activities, education, and command emphasis programs were then initiated in these battalions. The critical feature was that the unit chain of command was actively involved, and they dealt exclusively with the post personnel in those risk areas targeted for reduction. Coordination between installation staff and command was on-going in order to minimize time demands on personnel and maximize efficiency of program and service delivery. Data updates were then conducted on a quarterly basis.

During winter 1994-1995, ACSAP, working with personnel from the field, assumed responsibility for developing and institutionalizing the Risk Reduction Model Army-wide. This entailed a variety of activities: conducting a series of working groups with representatives from ADAPCP programs Army-wide; development of an Outcome Measurements Tool for collecting and organizing existing installation data from a variety of sources already in place; software development for crunching the data; and development of the Unit Risk Inventory (URI), a survey to be used in units, companies, and battalions that would quantify risk as it relates to alcohol, drugs, and other high risk behaviors. Exportation of the Risk Reduction Program (RRP) then began at a select number of Army installations for implementation. Based upon the results reported by Fort Campbell and other implementation pilot sites, RRP is now being promoted for eventual Army-wide adoption.

COLLABORATION

Research in prevention and health promotion has shown that no one system, group, or agency working alone can affect sustainable change (Bernard, 1988; Glanz, Lewis, & Rimer, 1990; Handler et al., 1994; Center for Substance Abuse Prevention, 1995). The very nature of community life prescribes that no major system exists in isolation, that each is inextricably tied to the other systems (Sanders, 1963). Teamwork establishes common ground as the basis for accomplishing mutual goals (Weisbord & Janoff, 1995). Ideally, all institutions and segments of the community should be involved in prevention; collective, empowered partnerships are more effective than individuals or individual agencies working independently (Office of Substance Abuse Prevention, 1989, 1990, 1991).

While the concept of empowerment may not seem applicable within the command-driven Army environment, individuals can become empowered to meet the challenges and issues present in their communities by developing the skills, tools, and the capacity to act effectively. Similar to civilian communities, post networks play an important part in their community, with individuals empowered to respond to a situation when necessary (Covey, 1990). An example of a partnership on an Army installation is the Human Resource Council (HRC). The HRC is a group comprised of installation program managers and command group representatives who gather regularly and whose function and authority vary from installation to installation, ranging from information sharing to policy development and implementation.

Training participants attended IPTT as a team of installation community key players with the power to make decisions and commit resources within their particular programs. While the post commander has the final say on an installation, an effective group, i.e. an installation prevention team, given the authority by the commander, can implement significant changes.

LESSONS LEARNED

Installation Prevention Team Training proved to be an effective mechanism for developing and implementing comprehensive prevention and risk-reduction programs on Army installations in order to prevent and address high-risk behaviors. In revisiting the four key outcomes, the following had been achieved.

Development of an Installation Prevention Plan

This process is based upon identification, a shared vision, a mission and goal, and then objectives, strategies, and action steps to operationalize that goal. Teams well aware of the issues at their post communities articulated the problem areas which provided the focus for planning. Completion of the installation prevention plan was the primary purpose of the training. All the activities and information imparted served to support this, building one piece at a time, until at the end of three days teams left with a working draft of a plan created together. The process paid off. At the time of this writing, a total of 33 teams have completed Installation Prevention Plans incorporating current best-prevention practices. In addition, 27 teams have begun implementing their plans and have identified specific methods for evaluating their efforts.

Implementing the Risk-Reduction Program

Currently, there are 20 installations Army-wide that have implemented the Risk-Reduction Program (RRP), providing service to 50 percent of active-duty soldiers. Battalion commanders strongly support and believe in the program. The process identifies high-risk profile units, communicating with commanders in an effort to coordinate prevention, education, and targeted deterrence-based interventions; it provides a measurement of the impact of these prevention and intervention activities for evaluation and helps to sustain an on-going relationship with commanders in support of mission readiness. In addition, seven other installations suspected they were already doing Risk Reduction on their own, even though it was not the "official" program, and believed that their programs were very successful. The Risk-Reduction Program was developed for soldiers and has been marketed and implemented as such. However, many installations have requested changing some of the risk-reduction processes in order to target and accommodate their civilian populations.

Command Support

All commanders supported their teams participating in the IPTT program. Since returning from the training, 37 teams have briefed their commanders. These briefings included an overview of the IPTT, the focus of the prevention plan, expectations, evaluation strategies, and what was "in it" for the commander and the community. Commanders' reactions have been overwhelmingly positive. When teams have not had an opportunity to brief their commander, it has been because of changes in command or in one instance, "due to the political situation on-post." Specific next steps have been identified by installations, which include implementation of RRP, completing implementation of the prevention plan, working on keeping the team energized, and marketing the program to the installation. Thirty teams report they have a command representative designated as a permanent, active member of their Installation Prevention Teams. Commander feedback on the Risk-Reduction Program was reported as very supportive overall, commanders' finding the process to be an "eye-opener" and relating that it helped them focus on issues in their units. Teams also reported that commanders wanted to be actively involved in the process.

Development of an Installation Prevention Team

The make-up of the installation prevention teams was left to the discretion of the commander. Many participants were self-selected or identified by their position, based upon broad recommendations from headquarters. Within the training process itself, a variety of team-building activities and exercises were embedded to help teams come together around common issues. As exercises shifted in focus from the individual to the team, participants noted with appreciation how partnerships began to be forged. Teams returned to their posts energized and enthusiastic about their plans and ready to begin implementing their prevention programs. All but two teams have continued to meet regularly as a group since returning from the IPTT. The make-up of the installation teams has consistently been one-third military participants, two-thirds civilian participants.

Results in the most successful teams have been attributed to three factors: (1) an on-going commitment to and practice of collaboration among team members since the training; (2) a strong, visible command support and participation in installation prevention efforts; and (3) a competent, focused team leader, who actively took the role of change agent. In the short term, the program has proven to be a success.

For the long term, the best that could be hoped for is the introduction of the innovation within a context that is designed to maximize its diffusion. Analysis of post data since teams attended IPTT and implemented their programs reveal nothing: numbers have gone up and numbers have gone down. It is impossible at this early date to discern verifiable results. This is not atypical in new program implementation. What has been achieved are the desired interim outcomes. Whether this innovation actually becomes diffused throughout the Army and is successful in sustaining long-term positive impacts and change is a question for study of at least 5-10 years duration. It is both unrealistic and naive to declare success or failure of any program with too short a time frame.

As installations begin implementing prevention programs, they have been asked to provide feedback and lessons learned to ACSAP on what does and doesn't work. This information is then analyzed and collated for dissemination back to the field, implementing a prevention field system.

Identification of a problem or need often occurs through a political process that shifts issues to the public's agenda. Installation Prevention Team Training is one response to the fact that the Army exists in a changing set of cultural values in the larger culture. It was not so long ago that spouse abuse, heavy drinking, and other similar behaviors were covered up within the Army culture. We didn't hear about them or see them, but they were there. A shift in how society views these behaviors has influenced the Army to respond to this shift in order to function as part of society. The Army now says that it has to do something about domestic violence, sexual harassment, and adequate daycare facilities just as it once said it needed a medical system.

In addressing high-risk behaviors, there is the temptation to search for the "magic bullet." While there is no cure-all, current research on effective prevention practices suggests three guidelines: selection of appropriate strategies for desired goals, target populations, and conceptual soundness; systems integration, involving the right mix of personnel in both decision making and implementation; and competent program execution, including quality of delivery, timing, intensity, and evaluation. Installations should be challenged to move further away from "same old-same old" with an increased emphasis on leadership. If IPTT has been successful, it is because of the function it serves within the system: it supports mission readiness on the home front, in the workplace, in the barracks, in the training schools, and in the field. It is an instrument of social and cultural change.

REFERENCES

Benard, B. (1988). *Characteristics of Effective Prevention Programs.* Washington, DC: U.S. Department of Health and Human Services.

Bray, R.M., Kroutil, L.A., Wheeless, S.C., Marsden, M.E. Bailey, S.L., Fairbank, J. A., & Harford, T.C. (1995). *1995 Department of Defense Survey of Health of Related Behaviors Among Military Personnel.* Research Triangle Park, NC: Research Triangle Institute.

Center for Substance Abuse Prevention. (1995). *Making Prevention Work.* Washington, DC: U.S. Department of Health and Human Services.

Covey, S.R. (1990). *Principle Centered Leadership.* New York: Fireside.

Glanz, K., Lewis, F., & Rimer, B., Eds. (1990). *Health Behavior and Health Education.* San Francisco: Jossey-Bass.

Goldman, C.L.W.D. (1996). In Pursuit of Character Development: Why the Military is on the Wrong Road. Joint Services Conference on Professional Ethics XVII, Washington, DC.

Hammer, M., & Champy, J. (1993). *Re-engineering the Corporation.* New York: Harper Business.

Handler, A., Schieve, L.A., Ippoliti, P., Gordon, A.K., & Turnick, B.J. (1994). Building Bridges Between Schools of Public Health and Public Health Practice. *Journal of Public Health, 4*(7), 1077-1080.

Chapter 12

EVALUATION OF AN AIR FORCE CHILD PHYSICAL ABUSE PREVENTION PROJECT USING THE RELIABLE CHANGE INDEX

RONALD W. THOMPSON, PENNEY R. RUMA, ALBERT L. BREWSTER, LEASLEY K. BESETSNEY, AND RAYMOND V. BURKE

Child maltreatment is a social problem of staggering proportions. Summary abuse data indicate that there were 1,036,000 confirmed victims of child maltreatment or 16 cases per 1,000 children in the United States in 1994 (Wiese & Daro, 1995). During the same year there were 7.5 cases per 1,000 children in Air Force families (Surgeon General of the Air Force [SGAF], 1996). Even though the rate for Air Force families is only half that in the general population, treatment and prevention of child maltreatment and family violence have been areas of emphasis for the Air Force during the past twenty years. Physical abuse was the most common type of child maltreatment in Air Force families, accounting for 39 percent of the victims in 1992 (Mollerstrom, Patchner, & Milner, 1995). Prevention of child physical abuse in Air Force families is one facet of the USAF Family Advocacy Program's efforts to reduce family violence, and it served as an impetus for implementation of the prevention program evaluated in our study.

Research has clearly indicated that there is no one cause or solution to the problem of child abuse. In the case of physical abuse, however, several studies have indicated that the majority of incidents occur during parents' attempts to discipline their children (Gil, 1970; Kadushin & Martin, 1981). There is also a substantial amount of evidence that abusive parents are more aversive in their interactions with their children (Bousha & Twentyman, 1984; Lorber, Felton, & Reid, 1984). Theoretically, parents who have a learning history which includes family violence and who encounter a build up of life stressors are most likely to develop increasing reliance on coercive disci-

Reprinted from the *Journal of Child and Family Studies, 6,* Thompson, Ronald W., Ruma, Penney R., Brewster, Albert L., Besetsney, Leasley K., & Burke, Raymond V., (1997), with permission from Plenum Publishing.

pline methods which, without intervention, eventually could lead to physical abuse (Wolfe, 1991). This would suggest that prevention efforts should target parent-child interactions generally and child discipline specifically; In keeping with this conclusion, Straus and Smith (1993) emphasized the need to reduce parents' reliance on physical punishment as a critical ingredient in the prevention of physical abuse.

Prevention and treatment studies have found that parent training is a critical service for parents at risk for child abuse, especially if it is provided in the context of other supportive services. A study of Project 12-Ways, for example, noted that of the 15 possible services offered, parent training was the treatment received by an average of 89 percent of families at risk for child abuse in the four years of the study (Lutzker, Wesch, & Rice, 1984). Wasik and Roberts (1994) surveyed 224 home visiting programs for families of abused and neglected children from throughout the country and found that parent training was identified as the most important service offered to maltreating families. Other studies have also indicated the application and effectiveness of parent training for the prevention and treatment of child abuse (Azar, 1989; Dubowitz, 1989).

A number of child abuse prevention programs have been described in the literature. However, there have been limited rigorous and systematic evaluations of these efforts (Daro & McCurdy, 1994), and the majority of studies have focused on early intervention during infancy (Guterman, 1997). We will describe a child physical abuse prevention project which employed parent training with Air Force families. The goal was to prevent the development of coercive parent-child interaction by teaching positive, non-punitive child behavior management skills to Air Force active duty and civilian employee parents and their spouses. The project was a collaborative effort involving the staff from the U.S. Air Force Family Advocacy Program (FAP) and the Boys Town Common Sense Parenting (CSP) program.

METHOD

Air Force Family Advocacy Program

The Air Force developed a Child Advocacy Program and Regulation in April, 1975 as a response to the Child Abuse Prevention and Treatment Act of 1974, Public law 98-457. Department of Defense (DOD) directives were established in 1981 to implement national legislation. These directives mandated the services to develop programs to address child abuse and neglect and spouse abuse. At that time, the primary target of all services was the treatment of perpetrators and victims of domestic violence.

In 1985-86, the Air Force expanded its scope to include focusing on family maltreatment prevention efforts. Outreach workers were hired to provide prevention services. These individuals offer an array of information, education, and support programs at bases worldwide in an effort to reduce domestic violence in the Air Force. Parent training was identified as one of these services that outreach workers could provide to Air Force families.

Boys Town Common Sense Parenting

Father Flanagan's Boys Home (Boys Town) is a child care organization that began as a residential group home program near Omaha, Nebraska. The Boys Town Family Home Program (Coughlin & Shanahan, 1988; Peter, 1986) is based on the Teaching Family Model developed at the University of Kansas (Phillips, Phillips, Fixsen, & Wolf, 1973; Wolf, Phillips, Fixsen, Braukman, Kirigin, Willner, & Shumaker, 1976). Married couples are trained in behavioral principles and serve as primary treatment agents. Because treatment occurs in a family atmosphere, the technology developed for this program has also been adapted to more natural family settings.

Common Sense Parenting (CSP), skill-based parent training program, is one of these adaptations to natural family settings. Previous CSP evaluation studies have indicated positive outcomes with civilian families on child behavior problems, parent attitudes, and satisfaction with family relationships (Thompson, Grow, Ruma, Daly, & Burke, 1993; Thompson, Ruma, Schuchmann, & Burke, 1996).

Prevention Project

The parenting program was offered at Air Force bases worldwide to parents who had not abused their children but who were concerned about child behavior problems. We wanted to influence parent-child interactions before they became destructive by training parents to use specific skills to increase positive interactions and decrease negative, aversion interactions with their children. We also wanted to evaluate the effects of Common Sense Parenting as part of this larger prevention effort.

Research on the impact of child abuse prevention programs has provided limited knowledge for program planners and policy makers in this area. Specifically, studies have not addressed the question of which prevention programs are beneficial with which families, especially for families with children beyond infancy (Daro & McCurdy, 1994). This information is a necessary prerequisite to designing an effective strategy to target prevention programs to the most appropriate groups of families at risk for child maltreatment. Evaluation studies have typically used standardized measures in a pre-post design. This approach, however, presents some methodological problems for evaluating prevention programs. First, statistically significant pre-post differences may not be practically significant, especially with large sample sizes. On the other hand, participants in prevention programs often function in the normal range before intervention and therefore may not make as large gains as participants in treatment studies (Hawley, 1995). Third, pre-post mean comparisons reveal nothing about the variability of outcomes obtained with individual participants and therefore do not indicate which participants are most likely to benefit from the intervention. The current study was designed to address these concerns.

Jacobson and Truax (1991) developed a method to address the limitations of comparing group means by assessing the clinical significance of outcomes in treatment studies. Instead of comparing group means, the procedure involves a determination of whether each participant moves from the clinical to the normal range during treatment and if the participant makes a statistically reliable change (RC). This approach allows the evaluation to examine outcomes for individual participants. As Hawley (1995) pointed out, however, this methodology does not apply as well to prevention studies because many of the participants are not in the clinical range on dependent measures before intervention. Hawley (1995) therefore recommended the reliable change index (RC) portion of the clinical significance methodology for prevention evaluations. Using this approach, researchers can calculate the proportion of participants who make statistically reliable changes on dependent measures. The RC criterion can be used to compare families who significantly improve with those who do not.

We hypothesized that Air Force parents would report significant improvement in child behavior problems and satisfaction with family relationships following parent training as we had found in previous studies with civilian families. We also employed a standardized measure of abuse risk which has been shown to be sensitive to the effects of intervention in previous evaluation studies of abuse prevention and treatment (Milner, 1994). We hypothesized that parents would report significant improvement in abuse risk as well. Finally, we wanted to investigate differences between families who made a significant improvement in abuse risk and those who did not.

Participants

Participants were 379 active duty parents and their spouses who attended CSP classes at 25 Air Force bases in the continental United States (CONUS) and overseas (OCONUS). Parents were most often self-referred, active duty parents who had no prior history of abuse. The most frequently cited reason for enrolling in parent training was parent-child conflict. Parents were asked to identify a "target child." This was defined as the child or adolescent about whose behavior parents were most concerned. Demographic characteristics of participating families are presented in Table 12-1.

Table 12-1
FAMILY DEMOGRAPHICS

Variable	%
Race	
White	73
African American	13
Hispanic	9
Other	5
Family Constellation: 2 Parents	84
Parent Sex: Female	62
Education: Equal to or More Than High School	98
Active Duty	63
Base Location: CONUS	80
Pay Grade: Equal to or Less than E-5	77
Child Gender: Male	58
Mean Parent Age in Years (sd)	33.06
(6.50)	
Mean Child Age in Years (sd)	7.88
(4.16)	

Procedures

Family Advocacy Program staff were taught by experienced parent trainers from Boys Town to deliver the CSP program to USAF families. Staff participated in 40 hours of training in the four basic program components: direct instruction, modeling of parenting skills, role play, and review of in-home skill use.

CSP consists of eight two-hour sessions. Parents received a parenting manual (Burke & Herron, 1992), which provides information and activities to supplement classroom training. Parents are trained to use specific skills to increase positive interaction and decrease the use of negative, aversive methods with their children. They are encouraged to apply the skills each week with their children and report on their progress.

Measures

Using a pre-post evaluation design, parents were asked to complete self-report measures of child behavior problems, satisfaction with family relationships, and child physical abuse potential prior to participation in the program and again at their completion of the program. The length of time between pretest and post test was approximately eight weeks. The same measures were also administered at six months follow-up.

Child Behavior Checklist (CBCL)

The CBCL (Achenbach, 1991a) was used to assess parent perceptions of the behavior problems of the target child. Parents are asked to rate 113 behaviors on a 3-point scale from Not True (0) to Very True (2) of their child. Reliability studies have indicated test-retest reliability coefficients from .89 to .93 for the broadband scores on the CBCL (Achenbach, 1991b). Two broadband problem behavior factors, internalizing (e.g., depression, anxiety) and externalizing (e.g., delinquent behavior, aggression) are included in the overall Total Problem score. On both the broadband factors and the Total Problem score a T-score between 60 and 63 places a child in the borderline clinical range, and a T-score of 64 or greater is considered to be in the clinical range.

Family Satisfaction Scale (FSS)

The FSS (Olson & Wilson, 1982) is a 14-item scale designed to measure overall satisfaction with family relationships. Each item is answered on a 5-point scale from Dissatisfied (1) to Extremely Satisfied (5). Higher scores indicate more family satisfaction. Scores range from 14 to 70. The mean score for parents in the normative sample of 433 parents was 47.00. Olson and Wilson (1982) reported an alpha coefficient of .92 for the total scale and a five-week test-retest reliability coefficient of .75. The scale was originally designed to measure family satisfaction along two separate dimensions, cohesion and adaptability, but factor analytic studies have not supported two separate factors (Olson & Wilson, 1982).

Child Abuse Potential (CAP)

The CAP (Milner, 1986) inventory was used to evaluate parents' potential to engage in physical abuse. It includes 160 items answered by parents in an agree/disagree format. Scores obtained include overall Abuse and Ego

Strength scores. The Abuse Scale can be divided into six factor scores: Distress, Rigidity, Unhappiness, Problems with Child and Self, Problems with Family, and Problems from Others. The inventory also has three validity scales: a lie scale, a random response scale, and an inconsistency scale that produce faking good, faking bad, and random response indicators. The 77-item Abuse Scale score is the one recommended by Milner (1986) for the screening of physical child abusers. A score of 166 or above on the Abuse Scale indicates that the parent has characteristics similar to known, active physical child abusers. Kuder-Richardson internal consistency estimates range from .92 to .95 for the general population, at-risk, neglectful, and physically abusive groups. Test-retest reliability for the Abuse Scale are .91, .90, .83, and .75 for general population subjects across one-day, one-week, one-month, and three-month intervals, respectively. Extensive research on the validity of this instrument has also been reported (Milner, 1986).

RESULTS

Parents' attendance ranged from 4 to 8 sessions. Seventy-two percent of the participants completed six or more parenting sessions. There were no significant differences on demographic variables or pretest outcome measures between parents who completed six or more sessions and those who did not. Pretest data indicated that parents and children were, on the average, in the normal range on all dependent measures.

Pre-post changes on the dependent measures were analyzed using a series of *t*-tests which are presented in Table 12-2. The alpha level was adjusted to p=.01 because of multiple comparisons. Parents reported significant reductions in child behavior problems for both internalizing and externalizing behaviors as well as the total number of reported behavior problems. In addition, there was a significant decrease in parents' risk for child physical abuse and an increase in their satisfaction with family relationships. We again used the adjusted alpha level of p=.01 to test for post to follow-up differences for a small sample of parents (n=35). There were nonsignificant differences from post to follow-up on child behavior problems and satisfaction with family relations. These results indicated that pre-post improvements were maintained from post to follow-up in these areas. A significant decrease in child physical abuse potential from post to follow-up (t=3.94, p<.01) was found, suggesting continued improvement in abuse risk after the program was completed.

Table 12-2
T-TESTS FOR PRE-POST COMPARISONS

	Pre		Post		
Variable	M	SD	M	SD	t
CBCL (n=355)					
External	58.77	10.76	54.97	10.38	8.98*
Internal	55.86	11.14	51.79	11.00	8.63*
Total	58.59	10.90	53.95	10.72	11.51*
FSS (n=379)	45.13	11.00	48.52	48.52	-7.55*
CAP (n=267)					
Abuse Scale	113.28	83.95	92.57	79.10	5.85*

*p < .01

Using the approach of Jacobson and Truax (1991) to ensure that any change found was not due to measurement error, we included the Reliable Change Index (RC) in our analyses of the data. The RC is used to derive the boundaries of a confidence interval around the cutoff point. It is calculated by dividing the difference score (post-test minus pretest) by the standard error of the difference score. To achieve reliable change, a minimum change of 8 T-score points on the CBCL, 7 points on the FSS, and 59 points on the Abuse Scale of the CAP were required. Table 12-3 represents the percentage of parents who made a reliable change (positive or negative) for each of the dependent measures. On average, families scored in the normal range on all measures at pretest which would suggest that large gains would be unlikely. Nevertheless, over 30 percent of the parents reported improvement in the areas of total child behavior problems and satisfaction with family relationships. There was also a relatively high percentage (19%) of parents who reduced their risk for child physical abuse. Much smaller percentages of parents reported deterioration in the areas assessed.

Table 12-3
RELIABLE CHANGE INDEX: IMPROVEMENT AND DETERIORATION EFFECTS

Variable	RCI	RCD
CBCL (n=355)		
External	27.9	5.4
Internal	29.3	8.2
Total	31.3	3.4
FSS (n=379)	30.3	10.3
CAP (n=267)		
Abuse Scale	19.4	5.6

Note. Numbers represent the percentage of parents surpassing 1.96 on Reliable Change Index. RCI = Reliable Change - Improvement; RCD = Reliable Change - Deterioration.

To better understand which families benefited most from CSP in reducing the risk of child physical abuse, we compared families who had made a positive reliable change in child physical abuse risk (RCI) with those who reported deterioration or failed to make a reliable improvement (NRC). We tested for differences on demographic variables and pretest scores for the five dependent measures. Chi-square analyses were used to compare groups on race, parenting status, education level, active duty status, pay grade, base location (CONUS vs. OCONUS), and parent and child gender. No significant differences were found between the two groups for any of these variables. Group comparisons of pretest scores on the Abuse Scale of the CAP inventory, the CBCL Total Problem score, and the FSS are reported in Table 12-4. A significant difference was indicated between groups at pretest for family satisfaction and child abuse potential. Families who made a positive reliable change for abuse risk were at a higher level of risk and reported less satisfaction with family relationships at pretest. There were no differences between parents who improved on abuse risk and those who did not on the number of child behavior problems reported at pretest.

Table 12-4
CHILD PHYSICAL ABUSE RISK: PRETEST COMPARISONS RELIABLE CHANGE–
IMPROVED GROUP VS. NO RELIABLE CHANGE/INCREASE RISK–GROUP

Variables	n	M	SD	n	M	SD	t
CBCL/External	50	59.98	10.52	198	59.24	10.18	-.45
CBCL/Internal	50	56.50	12.67	198	55.83	9.64	-.35
CBCL/Total	50	59.80	10.82	198	58.92	9.82	-.52
FSS	51	40.59	10.67	211	45.45	10.74	2.91*
CAP/Abuse	52	194.21	69.28	215	93.71	75.09	-9.23*

*$p < .01$

DISCUSSION

Our results suggest that the parenting program was a viable child abuse prevention approach for Air Force families. Parents attended because of concerns with child behavior problems. Nearly 75 percent of the parents who enrolled in the program completed at least six of the eight parenting sessions. Parents reported significant improvements in child behavior problems and satisfaction with family relationships, consistent with our previous research with civilian families (Thompson et al., 1993, 1996) and parent training research in general (Graziano & Diament, 1992). In addition, parents reported a significant reduction in their overall potential to engage in physical child abuse. These improvements were maintained at six months follow-up. These findings are consistent with the research which has suggested relationships between child behavior problems, family relationships, and physical abuse potential in both civilian and military families (Kolko, Kazdin, Thomas, & Day, 1993; Mollerstrom et al., 1995).

Because of the limitations of statistical comparisons of pre-post means, the Reliable Change Index (RC) was also used to evaluate effects of the parenting program. Results indicate that substantial percentages of parents reported statistically reliable improvement on dependent measures despite the fact that on average parents and children functioned in the normal range before intervention. Hawley (1995) reported that 0-24 percent of the participants in a marital enrichment study made reliable improvements on different dependent measures using this method, as compared to a range of 19-31 percent in our study. Using the RC, we were also able to determine if parents' ratings deteriorated in the areas assessed during the intervention. In a study of the effectiveness of Marriage Encounter, another example of a prevention program, evaluators found that the participants who made the greatest degree of change were approximately equally divided between those whose scores deteriorated and those who improved (Doherty, Lester, Leigh, 1986). Deleterious effects are more likely with prevention programs that enroll many participants who are functioning in the normal range before intervention than in treatment programs that only enroll participants who deviate significantly from the normal range. In our study 3–10 percent of the participants' ratings deteriorated using the RC criterion, as compared to 0–23 percent in the marital enrichment study reported by Hawley (1995). At a minimum, our results indicate that a much greater proportion of participants reported benefits rather than deterioration after their participation in the program.

Our results also provide some indication of which families are most likely to benefit from a parenting program. First of all, families who made significant reductions in abuse risk were no different on demographic variables than those who did not. Single parenting status, lower income levels, child age, and severity of reported child behavior problems, often cited as risk factors in the child abuse literature, were no different in the group that improved and the one that did not. However, parents who improved scored higher on child abuse potential and reported less satisfaction with their family relationships before their participation. These findings present a mixed picture at best. There is some suggestion that parents at a higher level of risk were more likely to benefit from the prevention program, consistent with the few previous evaluation studies which have addressed this question (Daro & McCurdy, 1994), but our results are not clear on this issue. The fact that parents who benefited differed on only 2 of 16 variables suggests that the two groups were very similar.

Our main hypotheses, that parents would report improvements in child behavior problems, satisfaction with family relationships, and child physical abuse potential were supported by group mean comparisons and more stringent analyses using the RC index. The proportions of parents who improved and deteriorated on dependent measures compared favorably to a marital enrichment study which used the same methodology. Our findings are similar to those reported in a treatment study of an evaluation of parent training with parents of attention deficit hyperactivity disordered children. Anastopoulos, Shelton, DuPaul, and Guevremont (1993) reported RC improvements ranging from 0–32 percent on the dependent measures employed. As indicated by Hawley (1995), however, interpretation of these percentages of improved participants remains difficult because of the limited number of studies that have been reported using the RC index, especially in the prevention literature. Our second objective was to investigate differences between parents who benefitted and those who did not. This information is needed to aid in targeting prevention programs to those who will benefit the most. Our findings on this issue are inconclusive. One possible reason for the absence of significant findings in this area is the fact that we had a very homogenous sample. For example, 73 percent of the participants were Caucasian, 83 percent were married, 98 percent had at least a high school education, and 78 percent were at an E-5 pay grade or below. Perhaps a sample with greater diversity would produce different results.

Our study had some other important limitations as well. First, statistically significant differences between pre and post means, with such a large sample size, may not indicate practical significance. This is especially true because we had no control group, and therefore could not rule out threat to internal validity such as maturation, passage of time, and testing effects. Second, follow-up data were only available for about 10 percent of the participants with pre-post data. The mobility of Air Force families and the geographic size of the study made follow-up data collection extremely difficult. Therefore, a selection bias in the follow-up data cannot be ruled out. Third, we did not directly observe the behavior of either parents or children, so our inferences about benefits are based strictly on parents' perceptions. Fourth, as with most prevention studies, we were unable to follow families long enough to determine if we truly prevented the development of coercive parent-child interaction and child physical abuse.

On the positive side, the proportion of families reporting reduction in child physical abuse potential is encouraging. This result, along with the fact that improved families differed very little from those who didn't improve, suggests that a skills based parenting program would be beneficial for a wide variety of participants in a child abuse prevention program for military families. Evaluative methods that have traditionally been employed in treatment studies may not be the best determinants of efficacy for prevention studies. The Reliable Change Index is one method that provides a relatively simple, straightforward statistic to evaluate whether participants in child abuse prevention programs are making meaningful change. As more and more studies report data using this method, the effectiveness of prevention programs can be better evaluated using criteria generated by the RC index.

REFERENCES

Achenbach, T. M. (1991a). *Child Behavior Checklist.* Burlington, VT: University of Vermont.

Achenbach, T. M. (1991b). *Manual for the Child Checklist/4-18 and 1991 Profile.* Burlington, VT: University of Vermont.

Anastopoulos, A. D., Shelton, T. L., DuPaul, G. J., & Guevremont, D. C. (1993). Parent training for attention-deficit hyperactivity disorder: Its impact on parent functioning. *Journal of Abnormal Child Psychology, 21*, 581-596.

Azar, S. T. (1989). Training parents of abused children. In C. E. Schaefer & J. M. Briesmeister (Eds.), *Handbook of Parent Training* (pp. 424-441). New York: Wiley.

Bousha, D. M., & Twentyman, C. T. (1984). Mother-child interaction style in abuse, neglect, and control: Naturalistic observations in the home. *Journal of Abnormal Psychiatry, 93*, 106-114.

Burke, R. V., & Herron, R. W. (1992). *Common Sense Parenting.* Boys Town, NE: Father Flanagan's Boys' Home.

Coughlin, D., & Shanahan, D. (1988). *Boys Town Family Home Program.* Boys Town, NE: Father Flanagan's Boys' Home.

Daro, D., & McCurdy, K. (1994). Preventing child abuse and neglect: Programmatic interventions. *Child Welfare, 78*, 405-430.

Doherty, W. J., Lester, M. E., & Leigh, G. (1986). Marriage encounter weekends: Couples who win and couples who lose. *Journal of Marital and Family Therapy, 12*, 49-61.

Dubowitz, H. (1989). Prevention of child maltreatment: What is known. *Pediatrics, 83*, 570-577.

Gil, D. (1970). *Violence Against Children: Physical Child Abuse in the United States.* Cambridge, MA: Harvard University Press.

Graziano, A. M., & Diament, D. M. (1992). Parent behavior training: An examination of the paradigm. *Behavior Modification, 16*, 3-38.

Guterman, N. B. (1997). Early prevention of physical child abuse and neglect: Existing evidence and future directions. *Child Maltreatment, 2*, 12-34.

Hawley, D. R. (1995). Assessing change with preventive interventions: The reliable change index. *Family Relations, 44*, 278-284.

Jacobson, N. S., & Truax, P. (1991). Clinical significance: A statistical approach to defining meaningful change in psychotherapy research. *Journal of Consulting and Clinical Psychology, 59*, 12-19.

Kadushin, A., & Martin, J. A. (1981). *Child Abuse: An Interactional Event.* New York: Columbia University Press.

Kolko, D. J., Kazdin, A. E., Thomas, A. M., & Day, B. (1993). Heightened child physical abuse potential: Child, parent, and family dysfunction. *Journal of Interpersonal Violence, 8*, 169-192.

Lorber, R., Felton, D. K., & Reid, J. B. (1984). A social learning approach to the reduction of coercive processes in child abuse families: A molecular analysis. *Advances in Behavior Research and Therapy, 6*, 29-45.

Lutzker, J. R., Wesch, D., & Rice, J. M. (1984). A review of Project 12-Ways: An ecobehavioral approach to the treatment of child abuse and neglect. *Advances in Behavior Research and Therapy, 6*, 63-73.

Milner, J. S. (1986). *The Child Abuse Potential Inventory: Manual.* Webster, NC: Psytec.

Milner, J. S. (1994). Assessing physical child abuse risk: The Child Abuse Potential Inventory. *Child Psychology Review, 14*, 547-583.

Mollerstrom, W. W., Patchner, M. A., & Milner, J. S. (1995). Child Maltreatment: The United States Air Force's Response. *Child Abuse and Neglect, 19*, 325-334.

Olson, D. H., & Wilson, M. (1982). *Family Satisfaction Scale.* St. Paul, MN: University of Minnesota.

Peter, V. J. (1986). *What Makes Boys Town So Special.* Boys Town, NE: Father Flanagan's Boys' Home.

Phillips, E. L., Phillips, E. A., Fixsen, D. L., & Wolf, M.M. (1973). Achievement Place: Behavior shaping works for delinquents. *Psychology Today, 7*, 75-79.

Straus, M. A., & Smith, C. (1993). Family patterns of primary prevention of family violence. *Trends in Health Care, Law and Ethics, 8*(2), 17-25.

Surgeon General of the Air Force. (1996). *Family Advocacy Program Quarterly Report.* Washington, DC: Author.

Thompson, R. W., Grow, C. R., Ruma, P. R., Daly, D. L., & Burke, R. V. (1993). Evaluation of a practical parenting program with middle- and low-income families. *Family Relations, 42*, 21-25.

Thompson, R. W., Ruma, P. R., Schuchmann, L. F., & Burke, R.V. (1996). A cost-effectiveness evaluation of parent training. *Journal of Child and Family Studies, 5*, 415-429.

Wasik, B. H., & Roberts, R. N. (1994). Survey of home visiting programs for abused and neglected children and their families. *Child Abuse and Neglect, 15,* 279-291.

Wiese, D., & Daro, D. (1995). *Current Trends in Child Abuse Reporting and Fatalities: The Results of the 1994 Annual Fifty State Survey.* Chicago: National Committee to Prevent Child Abuse.

Wolf, M. M., Phillips, E. L., Fixsen, D. L., Braukman, C.J., Kirigin, K. A., Willner, A. G., & Shumaker, J. (1976). Achievement Place: The teaching family model. *Child Care Quarterly, 5,* 92-103.

Wolfe, D. A. (1991). *Preventing Physical and Emotional Abuse of Children.* New York: Guilford Press.

A LAST NOTE TO READERS

When I started researching domestic violence in the Navy during the early 1990s, it became clear to me that the information I was seeking–other studies on domestic violence in the military–was very limited. Yes, there were a few. Peter Neidig from Behavioral Science Associates in New York was leading the way in terms of domestic-violence research in the military, but his work, focusing primarily on the Army, left a gap in knowledge about other military branches. There was the work of Murray Straus and his colleagues, which concentrated on domestic violence in the general population, but only a few studies took on the task of examining violence in the military family, most of these studies sporadic and limited in their publication to a few journals.

The intention, therefore, of this book has been to broaden the scope of what is known about domestic violence in the military. We hope that students and professionals alike will find this compilation of research beneficial to their own research needs. Also, as editors, we anticipate that the research documented herein will ignite other studies using the military population. Much still needs to be done; much continues to go unanswered regarding domestic violence in the military.

As just a few examples, future research efforts might focus on obtaining available secondary data from the Family Advocacy Programs of the Air Force, Army, and Navy (Marine Corps data is maintained by the Navy) for analytical purposes; or examine the prevalence of abusive behavior just prior to and immediately following a military member's deployment. Additionally, consideration might be given to replicating Neidig's Army study in the other military branches.

Continued efforts to understand violence in the military community, as well as in the civilian population, may increase the likelihood of practitioners, designing effective treatment and intervention programs. Just as domestic violence was acknowledged as a social problem 25 years ago in the general population, today's military leaders now recognize wife battering and child abuse as problems that erode families and adversely impact mission readiness. Because everyone loses with family violence, the military currently supports ongoing research to combat what was once a hidden and "private" matter. This is an encouraging sign and one which fosters the hope that future military members will be "fit for duty," not only at work but in their homes.

PETER J. MERCIER

GLOSSARY OF MILITARY-RELATED TERMS

Armed Forces: The military forces of a country. Also known as armed services.

Commissioned Officer: Any military officer who holds a commission (been given the authority to carry out a particular task or duty) and ranks as a second lieutenant or higher in the U. S. Army, Air Force, or Marine Corps, or an ensign or above in the U. S. Navy.

Dependent: Although this term literally means subordinate, it refers to the spouse or children of a military member. The spouse and children of the military member rely on that person in terms of obtaining identification cards in order to enter military bases, live in military housing, and shop in military exchanges and commissaries.

Deployment: To station military persons or forces systematically over an area; the movement of forces within an area of military operation; the positioning of forces into a formation for battle; encompasses all activities from origin or home station through destination, specifically including intra-continental United States and international locations. This term refers to military personnel being on a temporary assignment away from their home-base over an extended period of time. For example, Air Force and Army personnel deploy to isolated areas throughout the world, such as the Middle East, for specified periods of time. Navy and Marine Corps personnel deploy on ships to the Persian Gulf, the Mediterranean Sea, and other parts of the world for extended periods. Deployments require family separations.

Family Advocacy Program: A military social service program that focuses on prevention, identification, and treatment of spouse abuse as well as child abuse and neglect. Generally, military family advocacy programs provide families with direct services, and they conduct various prevention, training, and data-collection activities. Those involved in the program include staff of military medical treatment facilities, military lawyers, military police, chaplains, and other installation staff, as well as local civilian child protective services agencies.

Pay Grade: Pertains to the military rank structure, which is divided by enlisted personnel and officers. Newcomers without previous military experience, and without a college education, normally enter the service as recruits in pay grade E-1, the basic pay grade in the armed forces rating structure. The enlisted pay grades range from E-1 though E-9, with increasing responsibility and salary as the pay grade increases. Likewise, the officer pay grade ranges from O-1 (the lowest officer) through O-9 (the most senior officer).

Rank: An official position in the military, such as the rank of sergeant or captain.

Sea Duty: Sea duty refers to Naval personnel, and it is an assignment (generally for three years) to any ship, whether or not it is scheduled for deployment, or to any aircraft squadron, which may or may not be deployable. As an example, an aircraft carrier, any surface ship, or a submarine are all considered sea-duty assignments. Additionally, all aircraft squadrons which deploy with aircraft carriers are considered sea-duty assignments. Sea duty, generally, requires Naval personnel to be away from their families in excess of 150 days per year. Furthermore, certain overseas assignments, whether the Navy member is or is not accompanied by his family, qualify as sea-duty assignments. For example, tours of duty in Iceland, Alaska, and Guantanamo Bay, Cuba, are all considered sea-duty assignments.

Shore Duty: This is all duty performed within the 48 contiguous states, where Navy personnel are assigned to land-based activities and commands. Navy personnel assigned to shore duty are not required to be absent from the corporate limits of the duty station for more than 99 days per year. Certain overseas locations such as London, Tokyo, and Naples, Italy, qualify as shore-duty assignments.

Sponsor: Military member with dependents (spouse and children). Military members are considered sponsors because, due to their affiliation with the armed services, their spouses and children are issued identification cards which will allow them access to military-base facilities and services.

Warrant Officer: An officer in the military, usually a skilled technician, intermediate in rank between a noncommissioned officer and a commissioned officer, having authority by virtue of a warrant (certification).

AUTHOR INDEX

SUBJECT INDEX

A

AAPC (*see* American Association for Protecting Children)

AAS (*see* Abuse Assessment Screen)

Abuse Assessment Screen, 65, 66, 74

Air Force (*see also* Injury rates; Incidence rates), 30–44, 64, 70, 75, 105, 125–140, 141, 155, 157–177, 190–203

Air Force Needs Assessment, 31, 37

American Association for Protecting Children, 125

Armed forces
defined, 206
demographics, 31, 70–72
subpopulation, 3, 63–64, 70, 141

Army (*see also* Spouse abuse), 31, 45, 70, 75, 94, 97, 99, 105, 107–124, 141–153, 178–189

Army Alcohol and Drug Abuse Prevention Control Program, 179, 184–185

Army Center for Substance Abuse Programs, 179, 180, 182, 185, 188

Army Community and Family Support Center, 4

Army Family Demographics System, 142

Army's Risk Reduction Program, 183, 184–185, 186–187

Assault
aggravated, 48–49
physical, 35–36, 157
simple, 48–49

B

BDI (*see* Beck Depression Inventory)

Beck Depression Inventory, 65, 68–69, 73

Boys Town Common Sense Parenting Program, 191, 192, 193–194, 199–201

C

CAP (*see* Child Abuse Potential Inventory)

CBCL (*see* Child Behavior Checklist)

Child abuse (*see also* Child maltreatment), 3, 6–9, 97, 98, 105, 107–124, 125–140, 141–153, 155, 179, 190–191, 196–201, 204
rates in the Air Force, 127–134, 138
rates in the Marine Corps, 20–21

reducing the risk of physical abuse, 196–201

Child Abuse Potential Inventory, 136, 137, 195–196, 197, 198

Child Abuse Prevention and Treatment Act of 1974, 7, 135, 191

Child Behavior Checklist, 195, 197, 198

Child discipline, 190

Child maltreatment (*see also* Child abuse), 105, 107–124, 125–140, 141–153, 190
age of child, 105, 107, 109–123, 143, 144–148, 149–150, 151
child neglect, 109, 111–113, 117–122, 126, 127, 128, 143, 145, 146, 147, 149–150, 151
defined, 126–127
emotional maltreatment, 109, 126, 127, 128, 129, 130, 131, 132, 133, 144, 145, 146, 147–148, 150
physical abuse, 109, 113–116, 120–122, 122, 127, 128, 129, 130, 131, 132, 133, 143–147, 149–150, 190, 196
reducing the risk of, 196–201
sexual abuse, 109, 126, 127, 128, 129, 130, 131, 132, 133, 143, 144, 145, 146, 148, 150, 151–152
sex of child, 105, 107, 109–122, 143, 144–148, 149–150

Child protective service agencies (*see also* Statistics, frequency of child abuse), 125

Commissioned officer, 206

Conflict Tactics Scale, 35–36, 41, 65

Criminal behavior
and combat experience, 84, 85, 86–87, 89, 90–96
and military experience, 89, 92, 94, 96, 98–101

CTS1 (*see* Conflict Tactics Scale)

CTS2 (*see* Revised Conflict Tactics Scale)

Cycle of abuse, 32

D

DAS (*see* Danger Assessment Scale)

Danger Assessment Scale, 65

Defense Manpower Data Center, 33

Department of Defense, 127